MznLnx

Missing Links Exam Preps

Exam Prep for

Basic Marketing

Perreault, McCarthy, & Cannon, 16th Edition

The MznLnx Exam Prep is your link from the texbook and lecture to your exams.
The MznLnx Exam Preps are unauthorized and comprehensive reviews of your textbooks.

MznLnx

Rico
Publications

Exam Prep for Basic Marketing
16th Edition
Perreault, McCarthy, & Cannon

Publisher: Raymond Houge
Assistant Editor: Michael Rouger
Text and Cover Designer: Lisa Buckner
Marketing Manager: Sara Swagger
Project Manager, Editorial Production: Jerry Emerson
Art Director: Vernon Lowerui
Product Manager: Dave Mason
Editorial Assitant: Rachel Guzmanji
Pedagogy: Debra Long
Cover Image: Jim Reed/Getty Images
Text and Cover Printer: City Printing, Inc.
Compositor: Media Mix, Inc.

For more information about our products, contact us at:
Dave.Mason@RicoPublications.com

For permission to use material from this text or product, submit a request online to:
Dave.Mason@RicoPublications.com

Printed in the United States
ISBN:

Contents

Contents (Cont.)

TO THE STUDENT

COMPREHENSIVE

The *MznLnx* Exam Prep series is designed to help you pass your exams. Editors at MznLnx review your textbooks and then prepare these practice exams to help you master the textbook material. Unlike study guides, workbooks, and practice tests provided by the texbook publisher and textbook authors, *MznLnx* gives you ***all*** of the material in each chapter in exam form, not just samples, so you can be sure to nail your exam.

MECHANICAL

The MznLnx Exam Prep series creates exams that will help you learn the subject matter as well as test you on your understanding. Each question is designed to help you master the concept. Just working through the exams, you gain an understanding of the subject--its a simple mechanical process that produces success.

INTEGRATED STUDY GUIDE AND REVIEW

MznLnx is not just a set of exams designed to test you, its also a comprehensive review of the subject content. Each exam question is also a review of the concept, making sure that you will get the answer correct without having to go to other sources of material. You learn as you go! Its the easiest way to pass an exam.

HUMOR

Studying can be tedious and dry. MznLnx's instructional design includes moderate humor within the exam questions on occassion, to break the tedium and revitalize the brain

1. A _________ is a form of qualitative research in which a group of people are asked about their attitude towards a product, service, concept, advertisement, idea, or packaging. Questions are asked in an interactive group setting where participants are free to talk with other group members.

Ernest Dichter originated the idea of having a 'group therapy' for products and this process is what became known as a _________.

a. Cross tabulation
b. Marketing research process
c. Focus group
d. Logit analysis

2. In accounting, _________ has a very specific meaning. It is an outflow of cash or other valuable assets from a person or company to another person or company. This outflow of cash is generally one side of a trade for products or services that have equal or better current or future value to the buyer than to the seller.

a. ADTECH
b. AMAX
c. Expense
d. ACNielsen

3. _________ involves disseminating information about a product, product line, brand, or company. It is one of the four key aspects of the marketing mix. (The other three elements are product marketing, pricing, and distribution). P>_________ is generally sub-divided into two parts:

- Above the line _________: Promotion in the media (e.g. TV, radio, newspapers, Internet and Mobile Phones) in which the advertiser pays an advertising agency to place the ad
- Below the line _________: All other _________. Much of this is intended to be subtle enough for the consumer to be unaware that _________ is taking place. E.g. sponsorship, product placement, endorsements, sales _________, merchandising, direct mail, personal selling, public relations, trade shows

a. Cashmere Agency
b. Promotion
c. Davie Brown Index
d. Bottling lines

4. _________ is defined by the American _________ Association as the activity, set of institutions, and processes for creating, communicating, delivering, and exchanging offerings that have value for customers, clients, partners, and society at large. The term developed from the original meaning which referred literally to going to market, as in shopping, or going to a market to sell goods or services.

_________ practice tends to be seen as a creative industry, which includes advertising, distribution and selling.

a. Marketing myopia
b. Customer acquisition management
c. Product naming
d. Marketing

5. Consumer market research is a form of applied sociology that concentrates on understanding the behaviours, whims and preferences, of consumers in a market-based economy, and aims to understand the effects and comparative success of marketing campaigns. The field of consumer _________ as a statistical science was pioneered by Arthur Nielsen with the founding of the ACNielsen Company in 1923 .

Thus _________ is the systematic and objective identification, collection, analysis, and dissemination of information for the purpose of assisting management in decision making related to the identification and solution of problems and opportunities in marketing.

a. Focus group
b. Marketing research
c. Marketing research process
d. Logit analysis

6. _________ is a set of six steps which defines the tasks to be accomplished in conducting a marketing research study. These include problem definition, developing an approach to problem, research design formulation, field work, data preparation and analysis, and report generation and presentation.

a. Preference-rank translation
b. Market analysis
c. Simple random sampling
d. Marketing research process

7. _________, a business term, is a measure of how products and services supplied by a company meet or surpass customer expectation. It is seen as a key performance indicator within business and is part of the four perspectives of a Balanced Scorecard.

In a competitive marketplace where businesses compete for customers, _________ is seen as a key differentiator and increasingly has become a key element of business strategy.

a. Customer base
b. Supplier diversity
c. Psychological pricing
d. Customer satisfaction

8. A _________ is a written document that details the necessary actions to achieve one or more marketing objectives. It can be for a product or service, a brand, or a product line. _________s cover between one and five years.

a. Marketing strategy
b. Prosumer
c. Disruptive technology
d. Marketing plan

9. _________ is the process of using quantitative methods and qualitative methods to evaluate consumer response to a product idea prior to the introduction of a product to the market. It can also be used to generate communication designed to alter consumer attitudes toward existing products. These methods involve the evaluation by consumers of product concepts having certain rational benefits, such as 'a detergent that removes stains but is gentle on fabrics,' or non-rational benefits, such as 'a shampoo that lets you be yourself.' Such methods are commonly referred to as _________ and have been performed using field surveys, personal interviews and focus groups, in combination with various quantitative methods, to generate and evaluate product concepts.

a. Market analysis
b. Cross tabulation
c. Concept testing
d. Logit analysis

10. In economics, business, retail, and accounting, a _________ is the value of money that has been used up to produce something, and hence is not available for use anymore. In economics, a _________ is an alternative that is given up as a result of a decision. In business, the _________ may be one of acquisition, in which case the amount of money expended to acquire it is counted as _________.

a. Transaction cost
b. Variable cost
c. Fixed costs
d. Cost

11. _________ is a measure of the strength of a brand, product, service relative to competitive offerings. There is often a geographic element to the competitive landscape. In defining _________, you must see to what extent a product, brand, or firm controls a product category in a given geographic area.

a. Productivity
b. Market system
c. Discretionary spending
d. Market dominance

12. _________ in economics and business is the result of an exchange and from that trade we assign a numerical monetary value to a good, service or asset. If I trade 4 apples for an orange, the _________ of an orange is 4 - apples. Inversely, the _________ of an apple is 1/4 oranges.

a. Pricing
b. Contribution margin-based pricing
c. Discounts and allowances
d. Price

13. _________ is a form of communication that typically attempts to persuade potential customers to purchase or to consume more of a particular brand of product or service. 'While now central to the contemporary global economy and the reproduction of global production networks, it is only quite recently that _________ has been more than a marginal influence on patterns of sales and production. The formation of modern _________ was intimately bound up with the emergence of new forms of monopoly capitalism around the end of the 19th and beginning of the 20th century as one element in corporate strategies to create, organize and where possible control markets, especially for mass produced consumer goods.

a. AMAX
b. ACNielsen
c. ADTECH
d. Advertising

14. _________ is a broad label that refers to any individuals or households that use goods and services generated within the economy. The concept of a _________ is used in different contexts, so that the usage and significance of the term may vary.

A _________ is a person who uses any product or service.

a. 6-3-5 Brainwriting
b. Power III
c. 180SearchAssistant
d. Consumer

15. _________ is the study of when, why, how, where and what people do or do not buy products. It blends elements from psychology, sociology,social psychology, anthropology and economics. It attempts to understand the buyer decision making process, both individually and in groups. It studies characteristics of individual consumers such as demographics and behavioural variables in an attempt to understand people's wants. It also tries to assess influences on the consumer from groups such as family, friends, reference groups, and society in general.

a. Communal marketing
b. Multidimensional scaling
c. Consumer confidence
d. Consumer behavior

16. _________, in microeconomics, are the cost advantages that a business obtains due to expansion. They are factors that cause a producer's average cost per unit to fall as output rises. Diseconomies of scale are the opposite.

a. AMAX
b. ACNielsen
c. Economies of scale
d. ADTECH

17. _________ is a concept that denotes the precise probability of specific eventualities. Technically, the notion of _________ is independent from the notion of value and, as such, eventualities may have both beneficial and adverse consequences. However, in general usage the convention is to focus only on potential negative impact to some characteristic of value that may arise from a future event.

a. Power III
b. 180SearchAssistant
c. Risk
d. 6-3-5 Brainwriting

18. _________ is one of the four elements of marketing mix. An organization or set of organizations (go-betweens) involved in the process of making a product or service available for use or consumption by a consumer or business user.

The other three parts of the marketing mix are product, pricing, and promotion.

a. Comparison-Shopping agent
b. Better Living Through Chemistry
c. Japan Advertising Photographers' Association
d. Distribution

19. A _________ is a list of the general tasks and responsibilities of a position. Typically, it also includes to whom the position reports, specifications such as the qualifications needed by the person in the job, salary range for the position, etc. A _________ is usually developed by conducting a job analysis, which includes examining the tasks and sequences of tasks necessary to perform the job.

a. 180SearchAssistant
b. Power III
c. 6-3-5 Brainwriting
d. Job description

20. _________s is the social science that studies the production, distribution, and consumption of goods and services. The term _________s comes from the Ancient Greek οá¼°κονομΐα from οá¼¶κος (oikos, 'house') + νÏŒμος (nomos, 'custom' or 'law'), hence 'rules of the house(hold)'. Current _________ models developed out of the broader field of political economy in the late 19th century, owing to a desire to use an empirical approach more akin to the physical sciences.

a. Industrial organization
b. Economic
c. ADTECH
d. ACNielsen

21. An _________ is the system of production, distribution and consumption of goods and services of an economy. Alternatively, it is the set of of principles and techniques by which problems of economics are addressed, such as the economic problem of scarcity through allocation of finite productive resources. The _________ is composed of people and institutions, including their relationships to productive resources, such as through the convention of property.

a. AMAX
b. ADTECH
c. ACNielsen
d. Economic system

22. _________ refers to the laws and rules defining the ways in which products can be advertised in a particular region. Rules can define a wide number of different aspects, such as placement, timing, and content. In the United States, false advertising and health-related ads are regulated the most.

a. ADTECH
b. AMAX
c. ACNielsen
d. Advertising regulation

23. _________ refers to 'controlling human or societal behaviour by rules or restrictions.' _________ can take many forms: legal restrictions promulgated by a government authority, self-_________, social _________, co-_________ and market _________. One can consider _________ as actions of conduct imposing sanctions (such as a fine.) This action of administrative law, or implementing regulatory law, may be contrasted with statutory or case law.

a. CAN-SPAM
b. Regulation
c. Non-conventional trademark
d. Rule of four

24. A personal and cultural _________ is a relative ethic _________, an assumption upon which implementation can be extrapolated. A _________ system is a set of consistent _________s and measures that is soo not true. A principle _________ is a foundation upon which other _________s and measures of integrity are based.

a. Package-on-Package
b. Perceptual maps
c. Supreme Court of the United States
d. Value

25. In economics, an _________ is any good or commodity, transported from one country to another country in a legitimate fashion, typically for use in trade. _________ goods or services are provided to foreign consumers by domestic producers. _________ is an important part of international trade.

a. ADTECH
b. AMAX
c. ACNielsen
d. Export

26. _________ is an economic model based on price, utility and quantity in a market. It concludes that in a competitive market, price will function to equalize the quantity demanded by consumers, and the quantity supplied by producers, resulting in an economic equilibrium of price and quantity. Similarly, an increase in the number of workers tends to result in lower wages and vice-versa.

a. 6-3-5 Brainwriting
b. Power III
c. 180SearchAssistant
d. Supply and demand

27. _________ is an advertisement in which a particular product specifically mentions a competitor by name for the express purpose of showing why the competitor is inferior to the product naming it.

This should not be confused with parody advertisements, where a fictional product is being advertised for the purpose of poking fun at the particular advertisement, nor should it be confused with the use of a coined brand name for the purpose of comparing the product without actually naming an actual competitor. ('Wikipedia tastes better and is less filling than the Encyclopedia Galactica.')

In the 1980s, during what has been referred to as the cola wars, soft-drink manufacturer Pepsi ran a series of advertisements where people, caught on hidden camera, in a blind taste test, chose Pepsi over rival Coca-Cola.

a. Heavy-up
b. Cost per conversion
c. Comparative advertising
d. GL-70

28. In psychology, philosophy, and the cognitive sciences, _________ is the process of attaining awareness or understanding of sensory information. It is a task far more complex than was imagined in the 1950s and 1960s, when it was predicted that building perceiving machines would take about a decade, a goal which is still very far from fruition. The word _________ comes from the Latin words _________, percepio, meaning 'receiving, collecting, action of taking possession, apprehension with the mind or senses.'

_________ is one of the oldest fields in psychology.

a. Power III
b. 180SearchAssistant
c. Groupthink
d. Perception

29. The _________ is a marketing term and refers to all of the forces outside of marketing that affect marketing management's ability to build and maintain successful relationships with target customers. The _________ consists of both the macroenvironment and the microenvironment.

The microenvironment refers to the forces that are close to the company and affect its ability to serve its customers.

a. Customer franchise
b. Business-to-consumer
c. Market environment
d. Psychographic

30. A _________ dominated business thought from the beginning of capitalism to the mid 1950s, and some argue it still exists in some industries. Business concerned itself primarily with production, manufacturing, and efficiency issues. Say's Law encapsulated this viewpoint, stating: 'Supply creates its own demand'.

a. Production orientation
b. Marketing
c. Blitz QFD
d. Product differentiation

31. The break-even point for a product is the point where total revenue received equals the total costs associated with the sale of the product (TR=TC.) A break-even point is typically calculated in order for businesses to determine if it would be profitable to sell a proposed product, as opposed to attempting to modify an existing product instead so it can be made lucrative. _________ can also be used to analyse the potential profitability of an expenditure in a sales-based business.

In _________, margin of safety is how much output or sales level can fall before a business reaches its break-even point (BEP).

a. Pay Per Sale
b. Contribution margin-based pricing
c. Price skimming
d. Break even analysis

32. A _________ is a process that can allow an organization to concentrate its limited resources on the greatest opportunities to increase sales and achieve a sustainable competitive advantage. A _________ should be centered around the key concept that customer satisfaction is the main goal.

A _________ is most effective when it is an integral component of corporate strategy, defining how the organization will successfully engage customers, prospects, and competitors in the market arena.

a. Marketing strategy
b. Psychographic
c. Cyberdoc
d. Societal marketing

33. _________ refers to the additional value of a commodity over the cost of commodities used to produce it from the previous stage of production. An example is the price of gasoline at the pump over the price of the oil in it. In national accounts used in macroeconomics, it refers to the contribution of the factors of production, i.e., land, labor, and capital goods, to raising the value of a product and corresponds to the incomes received by the owners of these factors. The factors of production provide 'services' which raise the unit price of a product (X) relative to the cost per unit of intermediate goods used up in the production of X. _________ is shared between the factors of production (capital, labor, also human capital), giving rise to issues of distribution.

a. Deregulation
b. Power III
c. Consumer spending
d. Value added

34. _________ in organizations and public policy is both the organizational process of creating and maintaining a plan; and the psychological process of thinking about the activities required to create a desired goal on some scale. As such, it is a fundamental property of intelligent behavior. This thought process is essential to the creation and refinement of a plan, or integration of it with other plans, that is, it combines forecasting of developments with the preparation of scenarios of how to react to them.

a. 180SearchAssistant
b. Power III
c. 6-3-5 Brainwriting
d. Planning

35. A _________ is a plan of action designed to achieve a particular goal.

_________ is different from tactics. In military terms, tactics is concerned with the conduct of an engagement while _________ is concerned with how different engagements are linked.

a. Strategy
b. 180SearchAssistant
c. 6-3-5 Brainwriting
d. Power III

36. _________ is a rivalry between individuals, groups, nations for territory, a niche, or allocation of resources. It arises whenever two or more parties strive for a goal which cannot be shared. _________ occurs naturally between living organisms which co-exist in the same environment.

a. Competition
b. Price competition
c. Non-price competition
d. Price fixing

37. Competitiveness is a comparative concept of the ability and performance of a firm, sub-sector or country to sell and supply goods and/or services in a given market. Although widely used in economics and business management, the usefulness of the concept, particularly in the context of national competitiveness, is vigorously disputed by economists, such as Paul Krugman .

The term may also be applied to markets, where it is used to refer to the extent to which the market structure may be regarded as perfectly _________.

a. Geographical pricing
b. Free trade zone
c. Competitive
d. Customs union

38. _________ is, in very basic words, a position a firm occupies against its competitors.

According to Michael Porter, the three methods for creating a sustainable _________ are through:

1. Cost leadership - Cost advantage occurs when a firm delivers the same services as its competitors but at a lower cost;

2.

a. Competitive advantage
b. 6-3-5 Brainwriting
c. 180SearchAssistant
d. Power III

39. _________ is anything that is intended to save time, energy or frustration. A _________ store at a petrol station, for example, sells items that have nothing to do with gasoline/petrol, but it saves the consumer from having to go to a grocery store. '_________' is a very relative term and its meaning tends to change over time.

a. MaxDiff
b. Demographic profile
c. Convenience
d. Marketing buzz

40. The _________ is a professional association for marketers. As of 2008 it had approximately 40,000 members. There are collegiate chapters on 250 campuses.

a. ACNielsen
b. American Marketing Association
c. AMAX
d. ADTECH

41. _________ is the term given to food that can be prepared and served very quickly. While any meal with low preparation time can be considered to be _________, typically the term refers to food sold in a restaurant or store with low quality preparation and served to the customer in a packaged form for take-out/take-away. The term '_________' was recognized in a dictionary by Merriam-Webster in 1951.

a. 180SearchAssistant
b. Power III
c. 6-3-5 Brainwriting
d. Fast food

42. _________ is the area of applied ethics which deals with the moral principles behind the operation and regulation of marketing. Some areas of _________ overlap with media ethics.

Possible frameworks:

- Value-oriented framework, analyzing ethical problems on the basis of the values which they infringe (e.g. honesty, autonomy, privacy, transparency.) An example of such an approach is the AMA Statement of Ethics.
- Stakeholder-oriented framework, analysing ethical problems on the basis of whom they affect (e.g. consumers, competitors, society as a whole.)
- Process-oriented framework, analysing ethical problems in terms of the categories used by marketing specialists (e.g. research, price, promotion, placement.)

None of these frameworks allows, by itself, a convenient and complete categorization of the great variety of issues in _________.

Contrary to popular impressions, not all marketing is adversarial, and not all marketing is stacked in favour of the marketer.

a. Power III
b. Marketing ethics
c. 6-3-5 Brainwriting
d. 180SearchAssistant

43. _________ is a branch of philosophy which seeks to address questions about morality, such as how a moral outcome can be achieved in a specific situation (applied _________), how moral values should be determined (normative _________), what moral values people actually abide by (descriptive _________), what the fundamental semantic, ontological, and epistemic nature of _________ or morality is (meta-_________), and how moral capacity or moral agency develops and what its nature is (moral psychology.)

Socrates was one of the first Greek philosophers to encourage both scholars and the common citizen to turn their attention from the outside world to the condition of man. In this view, Knowledge having a bearing on human life was placed highest, all other knowledge being secondary.

a. Ethics
b. AMAX
c. ACNielsen
d. ADTECH

44. _________ is the management of the flow of goods, information and other resources, including energy and people, between the point of origin and the point of consumption in order to meet the requirements of consumers (frequently, and originally, military organizations.) _________ involves the integration of information, transportation, inventory, warehousing, material-handling, and packaging. _________ is a channel of the supply chain which adds the value of time and place utility.

a. 180SearchAssistant
b. 6-3-5 Brainwriting
c. Power III
d. Logistics

45. In business and engineering, new _________ is the term used to describe the complete process of bringing a new product or service to market. There are two parallel paths involved in the Nproduct development process: one involves the idea generation, product design, and detail engineering; the other involves market research and marketing analysis. Companies typically see new _________ as the first stage in generating and commercializing new products within the overall strategic process of product life cycle management used to maintain or grow their market share.

a. New product screening
b. Product development
c. New product development
d. Specification tree

46. _________ are a form of online advertising on the World Wide Web intended to attract web traffic or capture email addresses. It works when certain web sites open a new web browser window to display advertisements. The pop-up window containing an advertisement is usually generated by JavaScript, but can be generated by other means as well.

a. Customer intelligence
b. Project Portfolio Management
c. Power III
d. Pop-up ads

1. _________ is defined by the American _________ Association as the activity, set of institutions, and processes for creating, communicating, delivering, and exchanging offerings that have value for customers, clients, partners, and society at large. The term developed from the original meaning which referred literally to going to market, as in shopping, or going to a market to sell goods or services.

_________ practice tends to be seen as a creative industry, which includes advertising, distribution and selling.

a. Customer acquisition management
b. Marketing myopia
c. Product naming
d. Marketing

2. _________ is a fee paid on borrowed assets. It is the price paid for the use of borrowed money , or, money earned by deposited funds . Assets that are sometimes lent with _________ include money, shares, consumer goods through hire purchase, major assets such as aircraft, and even entire factories in finance lease arrangements.

a. ADTECH
b. AMAX
c. Interest
d. ACNielsen

3. _________ in organizations and public policy is both the organizational process of creating and maintaining a plan; and the psychological process of thinking about the activities required to create a desired goal on some scale. As such, it is a fundamental property of intelligent behavior. This thought process is essential to the creation and refinement of a plan, or integration of it with other plans, that is, it combines forecasting of developments with the preparation of scenarios of how to react to them.

a. Planning
b. Power III
c. 180SearchAssistant
d. 6-3-5 Brainwriting

4. _________ is a broad label that refers to any individuals or households that use goods and services generated within the economy. The concept of a _________ is used in different contexts, so that the usage and significance of the term may vary.

A _________ is a person who uses any product or service.

a. Consumer
b. 6-3-5 Brainwriting
c. Power III
d. 180SearchAssistant

5. _________ is a business discipline which is focused on the practical application of marketing techniques and the management of a firm's marketing resources and activities. Marketing managers are often responsible for influencing the level, timing, and composition of customer demand accepted definition of the term. In part, this is because the role of a marketing manager can vary significantly based on a business' size, corporate culture, and industry context.

a. Marketing management
b. Door-to-door
c. Business structure
d. Performance-based advertising

6. The _________ is a marketing term and refers to all of the forces outside of marketing that affect marketing management's ability to build and maintain successful relationships with target customers. The _________ consists of both the macroenvironment and the microenvironment.

The microenvironment refers to the forces that are close to the company and affect its ability to serve its customers.

a. Business-to-consumer
b. Customer franchise
c. Psychographic
d. Market environment

7. The philosophy of _________ holds that the only thing that exists is matter, and is considered a form of physicalism. Fundamentally, all things are composed of material and all phenomena (including consciousness) are the result of material interactions; therefore, matter is the only substance. As a theory, _________ belongs to the class of monist ontology.

a. Power III
b. 180SearchAssistant
c. 6-3-5 Brainwriting
d. Materialism

8. _________ is a business term meaning the market segment to which a particular good or service is marketed. It is mainly defined by age, gender, geography, socio-economic grouping, technographic, or any other combination of demographics. It is generally studied and mapped by an organization through lists and reports containing demographic information that may have an effect on the marketing of key products or services.

a. Distribution
b. Market specialization
c. Category Development Index
d. Brando

9. _________ is a market coverage strategy in which a firm decides to ignore market segment differences and go after the whole market with one offer.it is type of marketing (or attempting to sell through persuasion) of a product to a wide audience. The idea is to broadcast a message that will reach the largest number of people possible. Traditionally _________ has focused on radio, television and newspapers as the medium used to reach this broad audience.

a. Mass marketing
b. Business-to-consumer
c. Marketspace
d. Cyberdoc

10. _________ in marketing and strategic management is an assessment of the strengths and weaknesses of current and potential competitors. This analysis provides both an offensive and defensive strategic context through which to identify opportunities and threats. Competitor profiling coalesces all of the relevant sources of _________ into one framework in the support of efficient and effective strategy formulation, implementation, monitoring and adjustment.

a. 6-3-5 Brainwriting
b. 180SearchAssistant
c. Competitor analysis
d. Power III

11. The _________ is generally accepted as the use and specification of the four p's describing the strategic position of a product in the marketplace. One version of the origins of the _________ starts in 1948 when James Culliton said that a marketing decision should be a result of something similar to a recipe. This version continued in 1953 when Neil Borden, in his American Marketing Association presidential address, took the recipe idea one step further and coined the term 'Marketing-Mix'.

a. Marketing mix
b. 6-3-5 Brainwriting
c. Power III
d. 180SearchAssistant

12. A _________ is a party that mediates between a buyer and a seller. A _________ who also acts as a seller or as a buyer becomes a principal party to the deal. Distinguish agent: one who acts on behalf of a principal.

a. Spokesperson
b. Broker
c. 180SearchAssistant
d. Power III

13. _________ is the provision of service to customers before, during and after a purchase.

According to Turban et al., '_________ is a series of activities designed to enhance the level of customer satisfaction - that is, the feeling that a product or service has met the customer expectation.'

Its importance varies by product, industry and customer.

a. Facing
b. Customer experience
c. COPC Inc.
d. Customer service

14. _________ is a form of communication that typically attempts to persuade potential customers to purchase or to consume more of a particular brand of product or service. 'While now central to the contemporary global economy and the reproduction of global production networks, it is only quite recently that _________ has been more than a marginal influence on patterns of sales and production. The formation of modern _________ was intimately bound up with the emergence of new forms of monopoly capitalism around the end of the 19th and beginning of the 20th century as one element in corporate strategies to create, organize and where possible control markets, especially for mass produced consumer goods.

a. ACNielsen
b. ADTECH
c. Advertising
d. AMAX

15. _________ is an advertisement in which a particular product specifically mentions a competitor by name for the express purpose of showing why the competitor is inferior to the product naming it.

This should not be confused with parody advertisements, where a fictional product is being advertised for the purpose of poking fun at the particular advertisement, nor should it be confused with the use of a coined brand name for the purpose of comparing the product without actually naming an actual competitor. ('Wikipedia tastes better and is less filling than the Encyclopedia Galactica.')

In the 1980s, during what has been referred to as the cola wars, soft-drink manufacturer Pepsi ran a series of advertisements where people, caught on hidden camera, in a blind taste test, chose Pepsi over rival Coca-Cola.

a. Comparative advertising
b. Heavy-up
c. Cost per conversion
d. GL-70

16. A _________ or logistics network is the system of organizations, people, technology, activities, information and resources involved in moving a product or service from supplier to customer. _________ activities transform natural resources, raw materials and components into a finished product that is delivered to the end customer. In sophisticated _________ systems, used products may re-enter the _________ at any point where residual value is recyclable.

a. Purchasing
b. Supply chain
c. Supply chain network
d. Demand chain management

17. In marketing, customer _________, lifetime customer value (LCV), or _________ (LTV) and a new concept of 'customer life cycle management' is the present value of the future cash flows attributed to the customer relationship. Use of customer _________ as a marketing metric tends to place greater emphasis on customer service and long-term customer satisfaction, rather than on maximizing short-term sales.

Customer _________ has intuitive appeal as a marketing concept, because in theory it represents exactly how much each customer is worth in monetary terms, and therefore exactly how much a marketing department should be willing to spend to acquire each customer.

a. Lifetime value
b. Value chain
c. Sweepstakes
d. Brand infiltration

18. _________ involves disseminating information about a product, product line, brand, or company. It is one of the four key aspects of the marketing mix. (The other three elements are product marketing, pricing, and distribution). P>_________ is generally sub-divided into two parts:

- Above the line _________: Promotion in the media (e.g. TV, radio, newspapers, Internet and Mobile Phones) in which the advertiser pays an advertising agency to place the ad
- Below the line _________: All other _________. Much of this is intended to be subtle enough for the consumer to be unaware that _________ is taking place. E.g. sponsorship, product placement, endorsements, sales _________, merchandising, direct mail, personal selling, public relations, trade shows

a. Davie Brown Index
b. Cashmere Agency
c. Bottling lines
d. Promotion

19. _________ is the deliberate attempt to manage the public's perception of a subject. The subjects of _________ include people (for example, politicians and performing artists), goods and services, organizations of all kinds, and works of art or entertainment.

From a marketing perspective, _________ is one component of promotion.

a. Publicity
b. Brando
c. Pearson's chi-square
d. Little value placed on potential benefits

20. _________ is one of the four aspects of promotional mix. (The other three parts of the promotional mix are advertising, personal selling, and publicity/public relations.) Media and non-media marketing communication are employed for a pre-determined, limited time to increase consumer demand, stimulate market demand or improve product availability.

a. Marketing communication
b. Merchandise
c. New Media Strategies
d. Sales promotion

21. A personal and cultural _________ is a relative ethic _________, an assumption upon which implementation can be extrapolated. A _________ system is a set of consistent _________s and measures that is soo not true. A principle _________ is a foundation upon which other _________s and measures of integrity are based.

a. Package-on-Package
b. Perceptual maps
c. Supreme Court of the United States
d. Value

22. A _________ is a written document that details the necessary actions to achieve one or more marketing objectives. It can be for a product or service, a brand, or a product line. _________s cover between one and five years.

a. Disruptive technology
b. Marketing strategy
c. Prosumer
d. Marketing Plan

23. A _________ is a list of the general tasks and responsibilities of a position. Typically, it also includes to whom the position reports, specifications such as the qualifications needed by the person in the job, salary range for the position, etc. A _________ is usually developed by conducting a job analysis, which includes examining the tasks and sequences of tasks necessary to perform the job.

a. Power III
b. 180SearchAssistant
c. 6-3-5 Brainwriting
d. Job description

24.

The net present value (NPV) of all of a company's customers in terms of customer loyalty and indirectly, the revenue that the company can obtain from them.

In deciding the value of a company, it is important to know of how much value its customer base is in terms of future revenues. The greater the _________ , the more future revenue in the lifetime of its clients; this means that a company with a higher _________ can get more money from its customers on average than another company that is identical in all other characteristics.

a. Marginal revenue
b. Total cost
c. Product proliferation
d. Customer equity

25. The break-even point for a product is the point where total revenue received equals the total costs associated with the sale of the product (TR=TC.) A break-even point is typically calculated in order for businesses to determine if it would be profitable to sell a proposed product, as opposed to attempting to modify an existing product instead so it can be made lucrative. _________ can also be used to analyse the potential profitability of an expenditure in a sales-based business.

In _________, margin of safety is how much output or sales level can fall before a business reaches its break-even point (BEP).

a. Price skimming
b. Break even analysis
c. Contribution margin-based pricing
d. Pay Per Sale

26. In economics, business, retail, and accounting, a _________ is the value of money that has been used up to produce something, and hence is not available for use anymore. In economics, a _________ is an alternative that is given up as a result of a decision. In business, the _________ may be one of acquisition, in which case the amount of money expended to acquire it is counted as _________.

a. Variable cost
b. Fixed costs
c. Transaction cost
d. Cost

27. _________ is the activity that the selling organization undertakes to reduce customer account defections. The success of this activity is when the customer account places an additional order before a 12-month period has expired. Note that ideally these orders will need to contribute similar financial amounts to the previous 12 months.

a. First-mover advantage
b. Customer base
c. Customer centricity
d. Customer retention

28. In accounting, _________ has a very specific meaning. It is an outflow of cash or other valuable assets from a person or company to another person or company. This outflow of cash is generally one side of a trade for products or services that have equal or better current or future value to the buyer than to the seller.

a. AMAX
b. ADTECH
c. ACNielsen
d. Expense

29. A _________ is a plan of action designed to achieve a particular goal.

_________ is different from tactics. In military terms, tactics is concerned with the conduct of an engagement while _________ is concerned with how different engagements are linked.

a. 6-3-5 Brainwriting
b. 180SearchAssistant
c. Power III
d. Strategy

30. Competitiveness is a comparative concept of the ability and performance of a firm, sub-sector or country to sell and supply goods and/or services in a given market. Although widely used in economics and business management, the usefulness of the concept, particularly in the context of national competitiveness, is vigorously disputed by economists, such as Paul Krugman .

The term may also be applied to markets, where it is used to refer to the extent to which the market structure may be regarded as perfectly _________.

a. Customs union
b. Geographical pricing
c. Competitive
d. Free trade zone

31. _________ is, in very basic words, a position a firm occupies against its competitors.

According to Michael Porter, the three methods for creating a sustainable _________ are through:

1. Cost leadership - Cost advantage occurs when a firm delivers the same services as its competitors but at a lower cost;

2.

a. Power III
b. 180SearchAssistant
c. 6-3-5 Brainwriting
d. Competitive advantage

32. _________ is one of the four elements of marketing mix. An organization or set of organizations (go-betweens) involved in the process of making a product or service available for use or consumption by a consumer or business user.

The other three parts of the marketing mix are product, pricing, and promotion.

a. Japan Advertising Photographers' Association
b. Comparison-Shopping agent
c. Distribution
d. Better Living Through Chemistry

33. _________ is the study of when, why, how, where and what people do or do not buy products. It blends elements from psychology, sociology,social psychology, anthropology and economics. It attempts to understand the buyer decision making process, both individually and in groups. It studies characteristics of individual consumers such as demographics and behavioural variables in an attempt to understand people's wants. It also tries to assess influences on the consumer from groups such as family, friends, reference groups, and society in general.
a. Multidimensional scaling
b. Consumer confidence
c. Consumer behavior
d. Communal marketing

34. _________ can be defined as the idea generation, concept development, testing and manufacturing or implementation of a physical object or service. _________ers conceptualize and evaluate ideas, making them tangible through products in a more systematic approach. The role of a _________er encompasses many characteristics of the marketing manager, product manager, industrial designer and design engineer.
a. AStore
b. African Americans
c. Albert Einstein
d. Product design

35. _________ consists of the sale of goods or merchandise from a fixed location, such as a department store or kiosk in small or individual lots for direct consumption by the purchaser. _________ may include subordinated services, such as delivery. Purchasers may be individuals or businesses.
a. Warehouse store
b. Charity shop
c. Thrifting
d. Retailing

36. A _________ is an explicit set of requirements to be satisfied by a material, product, or service.

In engineering, manufacturing, and business, it is vital for suppliers, purchasers, and users of materials, products, or services to understand and agree upon all requirements. A _________ is a type of a standard which is often referenced by a contract or procurement document.

a. New product development
b. Product development
c. Product optimization
d. Specification

37. _________ is defined by the Oxford English Dictionary as 'the action or practice of selling among or between established clients, markets, traders, etc.' or 'that of selling an additional product or service to an existing customer'. In practice businesses define _________ in many different ways. Elements that might influence the definition might include: the size of the business, the industry sector it operates within and the financial motivations of those required to define the term.
a. Yield management
b. Freebie marketing
c. Service provider
d. Cross-selling

38. A _________ strategy targets non-buying customers in currently targeted segments. It also targets new customers in new segments. (Winer)

A marketing manager has to think about the following questions before implementing a _________ strategy: Is it profitable? Will it require the introduction of new or modified products? Is the customer and channel well enough researched and understood?

The marketing manager uses these four groups to give more focus to the market segment decision: existing customers, competitor customers, non-buying in current segments, new segments.

a. Kano model
b. Market development
c. Perceptual mapping
d. Commercial planning

39. _________ is one of the four growth strategies of the Product-Market Growth Matrix defined by Ansoff. _________ occurs when a company enters/penetrates a market with current products. The best way to achieve this is by gaining competitors' customers (part of their market share.)

a. Horizontal market
b. Pasar pagi
c. Marketization
d. Market penetration

40. In business and engineering, new _________ is the term used to describe the complete process of bringing a new product or service to market. There are two parallel paths involved in the Nproduct development process: one involves the idea generation, product design, and detail engineering; the other involves market research and marketing analysis. Companies typically see new _________ as the first stage in generating and commercializing new products within the overall strategic process of product life cycle management used to maintain or grow their market share.

a. New product development
b. New product screening
c. Product development
d. Specification tree

41. A _________ is a process that can allow an organization to concentrate its limited resources on the greatest opportunities to increase sales and achieve a sustainable competitive advantage. A _________ should be centered around the key concept that customer satisfaction is the main goal.

A _________ is most effective when it is an integral component of corporate strategy, defining how the organization will successfully engage customers, prospects, and competitors in the market arena.

a. Psychographic
b. Societal marketing
c. Cyberdoc
d. Marketing strategy

42. _________, in microeconomics, are the cost advantages that a business obtains due to expansion. They are factors that cause a producer's average cost per unit to fall as output rises. Diseconomies of scale are the opposite.

a. ACNielsen
b. AMAX
c. ADTECH
d. Economies of scale

43. In economics, _________ describes demand that is not very sensitive to a change in price.

a. ACNielsen
b. AMAX
c. ADTECH
d. Inelastic

44. _________ is a concept that denotes the precise probability of specific eventualities. Technically, the notion of _________ is independent from the notion of value and, as such, eventualities may have both beneficial and adverse consequences. However, in general usage the convention is to focus only on potential negative impact to some characteristic of value that may arise from a future event.

a. 6-3-5 Brainwriting
b. 180SearchAssistant
c. Power III
d. Risk

1. _________ is defined by the American _________ Association as the activity, set of institutions, and processes for creating, communicating, delivering, and exchanging offerings that have value for customers, clients, partners, and society at large. The term developed from the original meaning which referred literally to going to market, as in shopping, or going to a market to sell goods or services.

_________ practice tends to be seen as a creative industry, which includes advertising, distribution and selling.

a. Marketing myopia
b. Product naming
c. Customer acquisition management
d. Marketing

2. _________ is a business discipline which is focused on the practical application of marketing techniques and the management of a firm's marketing resources and activities. Marketing managers are often responsible for influencing the level, timing, and composition of customer demand accepted definition of the term. In part, this is because the role of a marketing manager can vary significantly based on a business' size, corporate culture, and industry context.

a. Business structure
b. Performance-based advertising
c. Door-to-door
d. Marketing management

3. A _________ is a subgroup of people or organizations sharing one or more characteristics that cause them to have similar product and/or service needs. A true _________ meets all of the following criteria: it is distinct from other segments (different segments have different needs), it is homogeneous within the segment (exhibits common needs); it responds similarly to a market stimulus, and it can be reached by a market intervention. The term is also used when consumers with identical product and/or service needs are divided up into groups so they can be charged different amounts.

a. Customer insight
b. Commercial planning
c. Production orientation
d. Market segment

4. _________ is a business term meaning the market segment to which a particular good or service is marketed. It is mainly defined by age, gender, geography, socio-economic grouping, technographic, or any other combination of demographics. It is generally studied and mapped by an organization through lists and reports containing demographic information that may have an effect on the marketing of key products or services.

a. Distribution
b. Market specialization
c. Brando
d. Category Development Index

5. A _________ dominated business thought from the beginning of capitalism to the mid 1950s, and some argue it still exists in some industries. Business concerned itself primarily with production, manufacturing, and efficiency issues. Say's Law encapsulated this viewpoint, stating: 'Supply creates its own demand'.

a. Production orientation
b. Product differentiation
c. Marketing
d. Blitz QFD

6. _________ Management is the succession of strategies used by management as a product goes through its _________. The conditions in which a product is sold changes over time and must be managed as it moves through its succession of stages.

The _________ goes through many phases, involves many professional disciplines, and requires many skills, tools and processes.

a. Chain stores
b. Customer satisfaction
c. Supplier diversity
d. Product life cycle

7. _________ is a broad label that refers to any individuals or households that use goods and services generated within the economy. The concept of a _________ is used in different contexts, so that the usage and significance of the term may vary.

A _________ is a person who uses any product or service.

a. Power III
b. 6-3-5 Brainwriting
c. 180SearchAssistant
d. Consumer

8. _________ is the study of when, why, how, where and what people do or do not buy products. It blends elements from psychology, sociology,social psychology, anthropology and economics. It attempts to understand the buyer decision making process, both individually and in groups. It studies characteristics of individual consumers such as demographics and behavioural variables in an attempt to understand people's wants. It also tries to assess influences on the consumer from groups such as family, friends, reference groups, and society in general.

a. Multidimensional scaling
b. Consumer behavior
c. Consumer confidence
d. Communal marketing

9. _________ is the study of the Earth and its lands, features, inhabitants, and phenomena. A literal translation would be 'to describe or write about the Earth'. The first person to use the word '_________' was Eratosthenes .

a. 180SearchAssistant
b. 6-3-5 Brainwriting
c. Geography
d. Power III

10. The _________ is a marketing term and refers to all of the forces outside of marketing that affect marketing management's ability to build and maintain successful relationships with target customers. The _________ consists of both the macroenvironment and the microenvironment.

The microenvironment refers to the forces that are close to the company and affect its ability to serve its customers.

a. Customer franchise
b. Psychographic
c. Business-to-consumer
d. Market environment

11. The _________ is generally accepted as the use and specification of the four p's describing the strategic position of a product in the marketplace. One version of the origins of the _________ starts in 1948 when James Culliton said that a marketing decision should be a result of something similar to a recipe. This version continued in 1953 when Neil Borden, in his American Marketing Association presidential address, took the recipe idea one step further and coined the term 'Marketing-Mix'.

a. Marketing mix
b. 6-3-5 Brainwriting
c. Power III
d. 180SearchAssistant

12. _________ in organizations and public policy is both the organizational process of creating and maintaining a plan; and the psychological process of thinking about the activities required to create a desired goal on some scale. As such, it is a fundamental property of intelligent behavior. This thought process is essential to the creation and refinement of a plan, or integration of it with other plans, that is, it combines forecasting of developments with the preparation of scenarios of how to react to them.

a. 6-3-5 Brainwriting
b. Power III
c. Planning
d. 180SearchAssistant

13. _________ consists of the sale of goods or merchandise from a fixed location, such as a department store or kiosk in small or individual lots for direct consumption by the purchaser. _________ may include subordinated services, such as delivery. Purchasers may be individuals or businesses.

a. Retailing
b. Charity shop
c. Thrifting
d. Warehouse store

14. _________ is a measure of the strength of a brand, product, service relative to competitive offerings. There is often a geographic element to the competitive landscape. In defining _________, you must see to what extent a product, brand, or firm controls a product category in a given geographic area.

a. Market dominance
b. Productivity
c. Market system
d. Discretionary spending

15. In environmental modeling and especially in hydrology, a _________ model means a model that is acceptably consistent with observed natural processes, i.e. that simulates well, for example, observed river discharge. It is a key concept of the so-called Generalized Likelihood Uncertainty Estimation (GLUE) methodology to quantify how uncertain environmental predictions are.

a. 6-3-5 Brainwriting
b. 180SearchAssistant
c. Power III
d. Behavioral

16. _________ or _________ data refers to selected population characteristics as used in government, marketing or opinion research, or the _________ profiles used in such research. Note the distinction from the term 'demography' Commonly-used _________ include race, age, income, disabilities, mobility (in terms of travel time to work or number of vehicles available), educational attainment, home ownership, employment status, and even location.

a. Albert Einstein
b. African Americans
c. AStore
d. Demographic

17. _________ is a branch of philosophy which seeks to address questions about morality, such as how a moral outcome can be achieved in a specific situation (applied _________), how moral values should be determined (normative _________), what moral values people actually abide by (descriptive _________), what the fundamental semantic, ontological, and epistemic nature of _________ or morality is (meta-_________), and how moral capacity or moral agency develops and what its nature is (moral psychology.)

Socrates was one of the first Greek philosophers to encourage both scholars and the common citizen to turn their attention from the outside world to the condition of man. In this view, Knowledge having a bearing on human life was placed highest, all other knowledge being secondary.

a. AMAX
b. ADTECH
c. Ethics
d. ACNielsen

18. Competitiveness is a comparative concept of the ability and performance of a firm, sub-sector or country to sell and supply goods and/or services in a given market. Although widely used in economics and business management, the usefulness of the concept, particularly in the context of national competitiveness, is vigorously disputed by economists, such as Paul Krugman .

The term may also be applied to markets, where it is used to refer to the extent to which the market structure may be regarded as perfectly _________.

a. Free trade zone
b. Geographical pricing
c. Customs union
d. Competitive

19. _________ is, in very basic words, a position a firm occupies against its competitors.

According to Michael Porter, the three methods for creating a sustainable _________ are through:

1. Cost leadership - Cost advantage occurs when a firm delivers the same services as its competitors but at a lower cost;

2.

a. Power III
b. 180SearchAssistant
c. 6-3-5 Brainwriting
d. Competitive advantage

20. In psychology, philosophy, and the cognitive sciences, _________ is the process of attaining awareness or understanding of sensory information. It is a task far more complex than was imagined in the 1950s and 1960s, when it was predicted that building perceiving machines would take about a decade, a goal which is still very far from fruition. The word _________ comes from the Latin words _________, percepio, meaning 'receiving, collecting, action of taking possession, apprehension with the mind or senses.'

_________ is one of the oldest fields in psychology.

a. Perception
b. 180SearchAssistant
c. Groupthink
d. Power III

21. _________ is the assignment of objects into groups (called clusters) so that objects from the same cluster are more similar to each other than objects from different clusters. Often similarity is assessed according to a distance measure. _________ is a common technique for statistical data analysis, which is used in many fields, including machine learning, data mining, pattern recognition, image analysis and bioinformatics.

a. Clustering
b. Just-In-Case
c. Developed country
d. Comparison-Shopping agent

22. _________ consists of the processes a company uses to track and organize its contacts with its current and prospective customers. _________ software is used to support these processes; information about customers and customer interactions can be entered, stored and accessed by employees in different company departments. Typical _________ goals are to improve services provided to customers, and to use customer contact information for targeted marketing.

a. Customer relationship management
b. Product bundling
c. Demand generation
d. Commercialization

23. A _________ is a structured collection of records or data that is stored in a computer system. The structure is achieved by organizing the data according to a _________ model. The model in most common use today is the relational model.

a. Power III
b. 180SearchAssistant
c. 6-3-5 Brainwriting
d. Database

24. Customer _________ consists of the processes a company uses to track and organize its contacts with its current and prospective customers. CRelationship management software is used to support these processes; information about customers and customer interactions can be entered, stored and accessed by employees in different company departments. Typical CRelationship management goals are to improve services provided to customers, and to use customer contact information for targeted marketing.

a. Marketing
b. Product bundling
c. Relationship management
d. Green marketing

25. _________ is concerned with the provisions and use of accounting information to managers within organizations, to provide them with the basis to make informed business decisions that will allow them to be better equipped in their management and control functions.

In contrast to financial accountancy information, _________ information is:

- usually confidential and used by management, instead of publicly reported;
- forward-looking, instead of historical;
- pragmatically computed using extensive management information systems and internal controls, instead of complying with accounting standards.

This is because of the different emphasis: _________ information is used within an organization, typically for decision-making.

According to the Chartered Institute of Management Accountants (CIManagement accounting), _________ is 'the process of identification, measurement, accumulation, analysis, preparation, interpretation and communication of information used by management to plan, evaluate and control within an entity and to assure appropriate use of and accountability for its Resource (economics)resources. _________ also comprises the preparation of financial reports for non-management groups such as shareholders, creditors, regulatory agencies and tax authorities' (CIManagement accounting Official Terminology.)

a. 6-3-5 Brainwriting
b. Management accounting
c. Power III
d. 180SearchAssistant

26. In marketing, _________ has come to mean the process by which marketers try to create an image or identity in the minds of their target market for its product, brand, or organization. It is the 'relative competitive comparison' their product occupies in a given market as perceived by the target market.

Re-_________ involves changing the identity of a product, relative to the identity of competing products, in the collective minds of the target market.

a. Containerization
b. Moratorium
c. Positioning
d. GE matrix

27. _________ can be defined as the idea generation, concept development, testing and manufacturing or implementation of a physical object or service. _________ers conceptualize and evaluate ideas, making them tangible through products in a more systematic approach. The role of a _________er encompasses many characteristics of the marketing manager, product manager, industrial designer and design engineer.

a. Product design
b. African Americans
c. Albert Einstein
d. AStore

28. In accounting, _________ has a very specific meaning. It is an outflow of cash or other valuable assets from a person or company to another person or company. This outflow of cash is generally one side of a trade for products or services that have equal or better current or future value to the buyer than to the seller.

a. ACNielsen
b. AMAX
c. ADTECH
d. Expense

29. _________ is a graphics technique used by asset marketers that attempts to visually display the perceptions of customers or potential customers. Typically the position of a product, product line, brand, or company is displayed relative to their competition.

Perceptual maps can have any number of dimensions but the most common is two dimensions.

a. Market environment
b. Customer franchise
c. Kano model
d. Perceptual mapping

30. _________ involves disseminating information about a product, product line, brand, or company. It is one of the four key aspects of the marketing mix. (The other three elements are product marketing, pricing, and distribution). P>_________ is generally sub-divided into two parts:

- Above the line _________: Promotion in the media (e.g. TV, radio, newspapers, Internet and Mobile Phones) in which the advertiser pays an advertising agency to place the ad
- Below the line _________: All other _________. Much of this is intended to be subtle enough for the consumer to be unaware that _________ is taking place. E.g. sponsorship, product placement, endorsements, sales _________, merchandising, direct mail, personal selling, public relations, trade shows

a. Promotion
b. Davie Brown Index
c. Cashmere Agency
d. Bottling lines

1. _________ refers to 'controlling human or societal behaviour by rules or restrictions.' _________ can take many forms: legal restrictions promulgated by a government authority, self-_________, social _________, co-_________ and market _________. One can consider _________ as actions of conduct imposing sanctions (such as a fine.) This action of administrative law, or implementing regulatory law, may be contrasted with statutory or case law.

a. Non-conventional trademark
b. Rule of four
c. CAN-SPAM
d. Regulation

2. _________ is defined by the American _________ Association as the activity, set of institutions, and processes for creating, communicating, delivering, and exchanging offerings that have value for customers, clients, partners, and society at large. The term developed from the original meaning which referred literally to going to market, as in shopping, or going to a market to sell goods or services.

_________ practice tends to be seen as a creative industry, which includes advertising, distribution and selling.

a. Customer acquisition management
b. Marketing
c. Marketing myopia
d. Product naming

3. The _________ is the dominant distribution and retail network for North American comic books. It consists of one dominant distributor and the majority of comics specialty stores, as well as other retailers of comic books and related merchandise. The name is no longer a fully accurate description of the model by which it operates, but derives from its original implementation: retailers bypassing existing distributors to make 'direct' purchases from publishers.

a. 180SearchAssistant
b. Direct market
c. 6-3-5 Brainwriting
d. Power III

4. In economics, an externality or spillover of an economic transaction is an impact on a party that is not directly involved in the transaction. In such a case, prices do not reflect the full costs or benefits in production or consumption of a product or service. A positive impact is called an _________ benefit, while a negative impact is called an _________ cost.

a. AMAX
b. ACNielsen
c. External
d. ADTECH

5. The _________ is a marketing term and refers to all of the forces outside of marketing that affect marketing management's ability to build and maintain successful relationships with target customers. The _________ consists of both the macroenvironment and the microenvironment.

The microenvironment refers to the forces that are close to the company and affect its ability to serve its customers.

a. Business-to-consumer
b. Customer franchise
c. Market environment
d. Psychographic

6. _________ in organizations and public policy is both the organizational process of creating and maintaining a plan; and the psychological process of thinking about the activities required to create a desired goal on some scale. As such, it is a fundamental property of intelligent behavior. This thought process is essential to the creation and refinement of a plan, or integration of it with other plans, that is, it combines forecasting of developments with the preparation of scenarios of how to react to them.

a. 6-3-5 Brainwriting
b. 180SearchAssistant
c. Power III
d. Planning

7. _________ consists of the sale of goods or merchandise from a fixed location, such as a department store or kiosk in small or individual lots for direct consumption by the purchaser. _________ may include subordinated services, such as delivery. Purchasers may be individuals or businesses.

a. Retailing
b. Charity shop
c. Warehouse store
d. Thrifting

8. Competitiveness is a comparative concept of the ability and performance of a firm, sub-sector or country to sell and supply goods and/or services in a given market. Although widely used in economics and business management, the usefulness of the concept, particularly in the context of national competitiveness, is vigorously disputed by economists, such as Paul Krugman .

The term may also be applied to markets, where it is used to refer to the extent to which the market structure may be regarded as perfectly _________.

a. Free trade zone
b. Customs union
c. Geographical pricing
d. Competitive

9. _________ is, in very basic words, a position a firm occupies against its competitors.

According to Michael Porter, the three methods for creating a sustainable _________ are through:

1. Cost leadership - Cost advantage occurs when a firm delivers the same services as its competitors but at a lower cost;

2.

a. Power III
b. 180SearchAssistant
c. Competitive advantage
d. 6-3-5 Brainwriting

10. _________ is a measure of the strength of a brand, product, service relative to competitive offerings. There is often a geographic element to the competitive landscape. In defining _________, you must see to what extent a product, brand, or firm controls a product category in a given geographic area.

a. Discretionary spending
b. Productivity
c. Market dominance
d. Market system

11. _________s are used in open sentences. For instance, in the formula x + 1 = 5, x is a _________ which represents an 'unknown' number. _________s are often represented by letters of the Roman alphabet, or those of other alphabets, such as Greek, and use other special symbols.

a. Book of business
b. Quantitative
c. Personalization
d. Variable

12. A _________ is a brief statement of the purpose of a company, organization. It is ideally used to guide the actions of the organization.

_________s often contain the following:

- Purpose of the organization
- The organization's primary stakeholders: clients, stockholders, etc.
- Responsibilities of the organization towards these stockholders
- Products and services offered

Generally shorter _________s are more effective than longer ones.

In developing a _________:

- Encourage input as feasible from employees, volunteers, and other stakeholders
- Publicize it broadly

The _________ can be used to resolve differences between business stakeholders. Stakeholders include: employees including managers and executives, stockholders, board of directors, customers, suppliers, distributors, creditors, governments (local, state, federal, etc.), unions, competitors, NGO's, and the general public.

a. 180SearchAssistant
b. Mission statement
c. Power III
d. 6-3-5 Brainwriting

13. The break-even point for a product is the point where total revenue received equals the total costs associated with the sale of the product (TR=TC.) A break-even point is typically calculated in order for businesses to determine if it would be profitable to sell a proposed product, as opposed to attempting to modify an existing product instead so it can be made lucrative. _________ can also be used to analyse the potential profitability of an expenditure in a sales-based business.

In _________, margin of safety is how much output or sales level can fall before a business reaches its break-even point (BEP).

a. Price skimming
b. Contribution margin-based pricing
c. Pay Per Sale
d. Break even analysis

14. A _________ attribute is one that exists in a range of magnitudes, and can therefore be measured. Measurements of any particular _________ property are expressed as a specific quantity, referred to as a unit, multiplied by a number. Examples of physical quantities are distance, mass, and time.

a. Lifestyle city
b. BeyondROI
c. Quantitative
d. Dolly Dimples

15. Consumer market research is a form of applied sociology that concentrates on understanding the behaviours, whims and preferences, of consumers in a market-based economy, and aims to understand the effects and comparative success of marketing campaigns. The field of consumer _________ as a statistical science was pioneered by Arthur Nielsen with the founding of the ACNielsen Company in 1923 .

Thus _________ is the systematic and objective identification, collection, analysis, and dissemination of information for the purpose of assisting management in decision making related to the identification and solution of problems and opportunities in marketing.

a. Logit analysis
b. Marketing research process
c. Focus group
d. Marketing research

16. Human beings are also considered to be _________ because they have the ability to change raw materials into valuable _________. The term Human _________ can also be defined as the skills, energies, talents, abilities and knowledge that are used for the production of goods or the rendering of services. While taking into account human beings as _________, the following things have to be kept in mind:

- The size of the population
- The capabilities of the individuals in that population

Many _________ cannot be consumed in their original form. They have to be processed in order to change them into more usable commodities.

a. Resources
b. 6-3-5 Brainwriting
c. 180SearchAssistant
d. Power III

17. A _________ is a set of exclusive rights granted by a State to an inventor or his assignee for a limited period of time in exchange for a disclosure of an invention.

The procedure for granting _________s, the requirements placed on the _________ee and the extent of the exclusive rights vary widely between countries according to national laws and international agreements. Typically, however, a _________ application must include one or more claims defining the invention which must be new, inventive, and useful or industrially applicable.

a. Foreign Corrupt Practices Act
b. Patent
c. Product liability
d. Reasonable person standard

18. _________ is a rivalry between individuals, groups, nations for territory, a niche, or allocation of resources. It arises whenever two or more parties strive for a goal which cannot be shared. _________ occurs naturally between living organisms which co-exist in the same environment.

a. Price fixing
b. Price competition
c. Non-price competition
d. Competition

19. A _________ is a plan of action designed to achieve a particular goal.

_________ is different from tactics. In military terms, tactics is concerned with the conduct of an engagement while _________ is concerned with how different engagements are linked.

a. Power III
b. Strategy
c. 6-3-5 Brainwriting
d. 180SearchAssistant

20. _________ in marketing and strategic management is an assessment of the strengths and weaknesses of current and potential competitors. This analysis provides both an offensive and defensive strategic context through which to identify opportunities and threats. Competitor profiling coalesces all of the relevant sources of _________ into one framework in the support of efficient and effective strategy formulation, implementation, monitoring and adjustment.

a. 6-3-5 Brainwriting
b. Competitor analysis
c. Power III
d. 180SearchAssistant

21. _________ is a common market form. Many markets can be considered monopolistically competitive, often including the markets for restaurants, cereal, clothing, shoes and service industries in large cities. Short-run equilibrium of the firm under _________

Monopolistically competitive markets have the following characteristics:

- There are many producers and many consumers in a given market, and no business has total control over the market price.
- Consumers perceive that there are non-price differences among the competitors' products.
- There are few barriers to entry and exit.
- Producers have a degree of control over price.

Long-run equilibrium of the firm under _________

The characteristics of a monopolistically competitive market are almost the same as in perfect competition, with the exception of heterogeneous products, and that _________ involves a great deal of non-price competition (based on subtle product differentiation.) A firm making profits in the short run will break even in the long run because demand will decrease and average total cost will increase.

a. Gross domestic product
b. Macroeconomics
c. Recession
d. Monopolistic competition

22. In economics, a _________ exists when a specific individual or enterprise has sufficient control over a particular product or service to determine significantly the terms on which other individuals shall have access to it. Monopolies are thus characterized by a lack of economic competition for the good or service that they provide and a lack of viable substitute goods. The verb 'monopolize' refers to the process by which a firm gains persistently greater market share than what is expected under perfect competition.

a. Monopoly
b. Power III
c. 6-3-5 Brainwriting
d. 180SearchAssistant

23. _________ is a form of communication that typically attempts to persuade potential customers to purchase or to consume more of a particular brand of product or service. 'While now central to the contemporary global economy and the reproduction of global production networks, it is only quite recently that _________ has been more than a marginal influence on patterns of sales and production. The formation of modern _________ was intimately bound up with the emergence of new forms of monopoly capitalism around the end of the 19th and beginning of the 20th century as one element in corporate strategies to create, organize and where possible control markets, especially for mass produced consumer goods.

a. AMAX
b. Advertising
c. ACNielsen
d. ADTECH

24. _________ refers to the laws and rules defining the ways in which products can be advertised in a particular region. Rules can define a wide number of different aspects, such as placement, timing, and content. In the United States, false advertising and health-related ads are regulated the most.

a. Advertising regulation
b. AMAX
c. ACNielsen
d. ADTECH

25. A craze is a product, idea, cultural movement, or model that gains popularity among a small section of the populace then quickly migrates to the mainstream. Crazes are characterized by their lightning fast adoption and swift departure from public awareness. Crazes and _________s are also characterized by their unusually high interest and sales figures relative to the time they are active in the marketplace, as compared with other similar products, ideas, cultural movements or models.

a. 6-3-5 Brainwriting
b. Fad
c. 180SearchAssistant
d. Power III

26. _________ is a broad label that refers to any individuals or households that use goods and services generated within the economy. The concept of a _________ is used in different contexts, so that the usage and significance of the term may vary.

A _________ is a person who uses any product or service.

a. Power III
b. 6-3-5 Brainwriting
c. 180SearchAssistant
d. Consumer

27. _________s is the social science that studies the production, distribution, and consumption of goods and services. The term _________s comes from the Ancient Greek oá¼°κονομÎ¯α from oá¼¶κος (oikos, 'house') + νÏŒμος (nomos, 'custom' or 'law'), hence 'rules of the house(hold)'. Current _________ models developed out of the broader field of political economy in the late 19th century, owing to a desire to use an empirical approach more akin to the physical sciences.

a. ADTECH
b. ACNielsen
c. Industrial organization
d. Economic

28. In finance, the _________s between two currencies specifies how much one currency is worth in terms of the other. It is the value of a foreign nation's currency in terms of the home nation's currency. For example an _________ of 102 Japanese yen to the United States dollar means that JPY 102 is worth the same as USD 1.

a. ACNielsen
b. ADTECH
c. AMAX
d. Exchange rate

29. In economics, _________ is a rise in the general level of prices of goods and services in an economy over a period of time. The term '_________' once referred to increases in the money supply (monetary _________); however, economic debates about the relationship between money supply and price levels have led to its primary use today in describing price _________. Inflation can also be described as a decline in the real value of money--a loss of purchasing power in the medium of exchange which is also the monetary unit of account.

a. Industrial organization
b. ACNielsen
c. ADTECH
d. Inflation

30. _________ is a fee paid on borrowed assets. It is the price paid for the use of borrowed money , or, money earned by deposited funds . Assets that are sometimes lent with _________ include money, shares, consumer goods through hire purchase, major assets such as aircraft, and even entire factories in finance lease arrangements.

a. Interest
b. AMAX
c. ACNielsen
d. ADTECH

31. _________ refer to a collection of facts usually collected as the result of experience, observation or experiment or a set of premises. This may consist of numbers, words particularly as measurements or observations of a set of variables. _________ are often viewed as a lowest level of abstraction from which information and knowledge are derived.

a. Data
b. Pearson product-moment correlation coefficient
c. Sample size
d. Mean

32. Electronic commerce, commonly known as _________ or eCommerce, consists of the buying and selling of products or services over electronic systems such as the Internet and other computer networks. The amount of trade conducted electronically has grown extraordinarily with wide-spread Internet usage. A wide variety of commerce is conducted in this way, spurring and drawing on innovations in electronic funds transfer, supply chain management, Internet marketing, online transaction processing, electronic data interchange (EDI), inventory management systems, and automated data collection systems.

a. AMAX
b. ADTECH
c. E-commerce
d. ACNielsen

33. The _________ is an independent agency of the United States government, established in 1914 by the _________ Act. Its principal mission is the promotion of 'consumer protection' and the elimination and prevention of what regulators perceive to be harmfully 'anti-competitive' business practices, such as coercive monopoly.

The _________ Act was one of President Wilson's major acts against trusts.

a. 6-3-5 Brainwriting
b. Power III
c. Federal Trade Commission
d. 180SearchAssistant

34. In finance, an _________ is a contract between a buyer and a seller that gives the buyer the right--but not the obligation--to buy or to sell a particular asset (the underlying asset) at a later day at an agreed price. In return for granting the _________, the seller collects a payment (the premium) from the buyer. A call _________ gives the buyer the right to buy the underlying asset; a put _________ gives the buyer of the _________ the right to sell the underlying asset.

a. ADTECH
b. ACNielsen
c. AMAX
d. Option

35. A _________ is an explicit set of requirements to be satisfied by a material, product, or service.

In engineering, manufacturing, and business, it is vital for suppliers, purchasers, and users of materials, products, or services to understand and agree upon all requirements. A _________ is a type of a standard which is often referenced by a contract or procurement document.

a. Product development
b. New product development
c. Product optimization
d. Specification

36. The _________ is the official currency of 16 out of 27 member states of the European Union (EU.) The states, known collectively as the Eurozone are: Austria, Belgium, Cyprus, Finland, France, Germany, Greece, Ireland, Italy, Luxembourg, Malta, the Netherlands, Portugal, Slovakia, Slovenia, and Spain. The currency is also used in a further five European countries, with and without formal agreements and is consequently used daily by some 327 million Europeans.

a. ACNielsen
b. Eurozone
c. ADTECH
d. Euro

37. The _________ is an economic and political union of 27 member states, located primarily in Europe. It was established by the Treaty of Maastricht on 1 November 1993 upon the foundations of the pre-existing European Economic Community. With almost 500 million citizens, the _________ combined generates an estimated 30% share (US$16.8 trillion in 2007) of the nominal gross world product.

a. Eurozone
b. ACNielsen
c. ADTECH
d. European Union

38. The _________ is a trilateral trade bloc in North America created by the governments of the United States, Canada, and Mexico. It superseded the Canada-United States Free Trade Agreement between the US and Canada.

Following diplomatic negotiations dating back to 1990 between the three nations, the leaders met in San Antonio, Texas on December 17, 1992 to sign _________.

a. 6-3-5 Brainwriting
b. 180SearchAssistant
c. North American Free Trade Agreement
d. Power III

39. A _________ is a tax imposed on goods when they are moved across a political boundary. They are usually associated with protectionism, the economic policy of restraining trade between nations. For political reasons, _________s are usually imposed on imported goods, although they may also be imposed on exported goods.

a. Tariff
b. Power III
c. Fiscal policy
d. Monetary policy

40. In 1962, President John F. Kennedy presented a speech to the United States Congress in which he extolled four basic consumer rights, later called The _________.

While later expanded, the original six basic beliefs of consumer protection are the most widely recognized.

In 1985, the concept of consumer rights was endorsed by the United Nations and expanded to included eight basic rights.

a. Power III
b. 180SearchAssistant
c. 6-3-5 Brainwriting
d. Consumer Bill of Rights

41. _________ is a form of government regulation which protects the interests of consumers. For example, a government may require businesses to disclose detailed information about products--particularly in areas where safety or public health is an issue, such as food. _________ is linked to the idea of consumer rights (that consumers have various rights as consumers), and to the formation of consumer organizations which help consumers make better choices in the marketplace.

a. Federal Bureau of Investigation
b. Consumer protection
c. Sound trademark
d. Trademark dilution

42. _________ is the equation of personal happiness with consumption and the purchase of material possessions.

The term is often associated with criticisms of consumption starting with Thorstein Veblen.

Veblen's subject of examination, the newly emergent middle class arising at the turn of the twentieth century, comes to full fruition by the end of the twentieth century through the process of globalization.

In economics, _________ refers to economic policies placing emphasis on consumption.

a. 180SearchAssistant
b. 6-3-5 Brainwriting
c. Power III
d. Consumerism

43. A _________ is a process that can allow an organization to concentrate its limited resources on the greatest opportunities to increase sales and achieve a sustainable competitive advantage. A _________ should be centered around the key concept that customer satisfaction is the main goal.

A _________ is most effective when it is an integral component of corporate strategy, defining how the organization will successfully engage customers, prospects, and competitors in the market arena.

a. Marketing strategy
b. Societal marketing
c. Psychographic
d. Cyberdoc

44. The _________ of 1914 (15 U.S.C Â§Â§ 41-58, as amended) established the Federal Trade Commission (FTC), a bipartisan body of five members appointed by the President of the United States for seven year terms. This Commission was authorized to issue Cease and Desist orders to large corporations to curb unfair trade practices. This Act also gave more flexibility to the US congress for judicial matters.

a. Product liability
b. Gripe site
c. Comparative negligence
d. Federal Trade Commission Act

45. The U.S. _________ is an agency of the United States Department of Health and Human Services and is responsible for regulating and supervising the safety of foods, dietary supplements, drugs, vaccines, biological medical products, blood products, medical devices, radiation-emitting devices, veterinary products, and cosmetics. The FDA also enforces section 361 of the Public Health Service Act and the associated regulations, including sanitation requirements on interstate travel as well as specific rules for control of disease on products ranging from pet turtles to semen donations for assisted reproductive medicine techniques.

The FDA is an agency within the United States Department of Health and Human Services responsible for protecting and promoting the nation's public health.

a. Power III
b. 180SearchAssistant
c. Food and Drug Administration
d. 6-3-5 Brainwriting

46. The _________ of 1936 (or Anti-Price Discrimination Act, 15 U.S.C. Â§ 13) is a United States federal law that prohibits what were considered, at the time of passage, to be anticompetitive practices by producers, specifically price discrimination. It grew out of practices in which chain stores were allowed to purchase goods at lower prices than other retailers.

a. Robinson-Patman Act
b. Trademark infringement
c. Registered trademark symbol
d. Fair Debt Collection Practices Act

47. The United States _________ is an independent agency of the United States government created in 1972 through the Consumer Product Safety Act to protect 'against unreasonable risks of injuries associated with consumer products.' As of 2006 its acting chairman is Nancy Nord, a Republican. The other commissioner is Thomas Hill Moore, a Democrat. Normally the board has three commissioners.

a. 180SearchAssistant
b. 6-3-5 Brainwriting
c. Power III
d. Consumer Product Safety Commission

48. _________ is difficult to define. For example, in 1952, Alfred Kroeber and Clyde Kluckhohn compiled a list of 164 definitions of '_________' in _________: A Critical Review of Concepts and Definitions. However, the word '_________' is most commonly used in three basic senses:

- excellence of taste in the fine arts and humanities
- an integrated pattern of human knowledge, belief, and behavior that depends upon the capacity for symbolic thought and social learning
- the set of shared attitudes, values, goals, and practices that characterizes an institution, organization or group.

When the concept first emerged in eighteenth- and nineteenth-century Europe, it connoted a process of cultivation or improvement, as in agriculture or horticulture. In the nineteenth century, it came to refer first to the betterment or refinement of the individual, especially through education, and then to the fulfillment of national aspirations or ideals.

a. AStore
b. African Americans
c. Albert Einstein
d. Culture

49. _________ is the systematic application of marketing along with other concepts and techniques to achieve specific behavioral goals for a social good. _________ can be applied to promote, for example, merit goods, make the society avoid demerit goods and thus to promote that considers society's well being as a whole. This may include asking people not to smoke in public areas, for example, ask them to use seat belts, prompting to make them follow speed limits.

a. Marketing strategy
b. Psychographic
c. Market development
d. Social Marketing

50. In economics, _________ is the desire to own something and the ability to pay for it. The term _________ signifies the ability or the willingness to buy a particular commodity at a given point of time .

a. Market dominance
b. Market system
c. Discretionary spending
d. Demand

51. _________ is a term in economics, where demand for one good or service occurs as a result of demand for another. This may occur as the former is a part of production of the second. For example, demand for coal leads to _________ for mining, as coal must be mined for coal to be consumed.

a. 6-3-5 Brainwriting
b. 180SearchAssistant
c. Power III
d. Derived demand

52. _________ Management is the succession of strategies used by management as a product goes through its _________. The conditions in which a product is sold changes over time and must be managed as it moves through its succession of stages.

The _________ goes through many phases, involves many professional disciplines, and requires many skills, tools and processes.

a. Customer satisfaction
b. Supplier diversity
c. Product life cycle
d. Chain stores

53. _________ is the process of filtering or screening new product developments before they enter the stage gate process and start to consume significant resources. The Stage-Gate process was created by Dr. Robert Cooper and is a method described by Cooper and Kleinshmidt of a systematic moving of a new product through various stages from the screening process to product launch.

The screening stage is one that permits new product opportunities to be rejected early in the stage gate process.

a. New product screening
b. Specification tree
c. Product development
d. Specification

54. _________ is understood as a business unit within the overall corporate identity which is distinguishable from other business because it serves a defined external market where management can conduct strategic planning in relation to products and markets. When companies become really large, they are best thought of as being composed of a number of businesses (or _________s.)

In the broader domain of strategic management, the phrase '_________' came into use in the 1960s, largely as a result of General Electric's many units.

a. Cost leadership
b. Strategic business unit
c. Corporate strategy
d. Business strategy

55. _________ is exchange of capital, goods, and services across international borders or territories. In most countries, it represents a significant share of gross domestic product (GDP.) While _________ has been present throughout much of history , its economic, social, and political importance has been on the rise in recent centuries.

a. ACNielsen
b. ADTECH
c. Incoterms
d. International trade

1. _________ is a broad label that refers to any individuals or households that use goods and services generated within the economy. The concept of a _________ is used in different contexts, so that the usage and significance of the term may vary.

A _________ is a person who uses any product or service.

a. Consumer
b. 6-3-5 Brainwriting
c. Power III
d. 180SearchAssistant

2. _________ is defined by the American _________ Association as the activity, set of institutions, and processes for creating, communicating, delivering, and exchanging offerings that have value for customers, clients, partners, and society at large. The term developed from the original meaning which referred literally to going to market, as in shopping, or going to a market to sell goods or services.

_________ practice tends to be seen as a creative industry, which includes advertising, distribution and selling.

a. Marketing
b. Marketing myopia
c. Customer acquisition management
d. Product naming

3. The _________ is generally accepted as the use and specification of the four p's describing the strategic position of a product in the marketplace. One version of the origins of the _________ starts in 1948 when James Culliton said that a marketing decision should be a result of something similar to a recipe. This version continued in 1953 when Neil Borden, in his American Marketing Association presidential address, took the recipe idea one step further and coined the term 'Marketing-Mix'.

a. 180SearchAssistant
b. Power III
c. Marketing mix
d. 6-3-5 Brainwriting

4. _________ or _________ data refers to selected population characteristics as used in government, marketing or opinion research, or the _________ profiles used in such research. Note the distinction from the term 'demography' Commonly-used _________ include race, age, income, disabilities, mobility (in terms of travel time to work or number of vehicles available), educational attainment, home ownership, employment status, and even location.

a. African Americans
b. Demographic
c. Albert Einstein
d. AStore

5. In algebra, a _________ is a function depending on n that associates a scalar, det(A), to an n×n square matrix A. The fundamental geometric meaning of a _________ is a scale factor for measure when A is regarded as a linear transformation. _________s are important both in calculus, where they enter the substitution rule for several variables, and in multilinear algebra.

For a fixed nonnegative integer n, there is a unique _________ function for the n×n matrices over any commutative ring R. In particular, this function exists when R is the field of real or complex numbers.

a. Black Friday
b. Motion Picture Association of America's film-rating system
c. Package-on-Package
d. Determinant

6. _________ is the change in population over time, and can be quantified as the change in the number of individuals in a population using 'per unit time' for measurement. The term _________ can technically refer to any species, but almost always refers to humans, and it is often used informally for the more specific demographic term _________ rate , and is often used to refer specifically to the growth of the population of the world.

Simple models of _________ include the Malthusian Growth Model and the logistic model.

a. 6-3-5 Brainwriting
b. 180SearchAssistant
c. Population Growth
d. Power III

7. The _________ or gross domestic income (GDI) is one of the measures of national income and output for a given country's economy. It is the total value of all final goods and services produced in a particular economy; the dollar value of all goods and services produced within a country's borders in a given year. _________ can be defined in three ways, all of which are conceptually identical.

a. Leading indicator
b. Macroeconomics
c. Microeconomics
d. Gross domestic product

8. _________ is the physical growth of urban areas from rural areas as a result of population immigration to an existing urban area. Effects include change in density and administration services. While the exact definition and population size of urbanized areas varies among different countries, _________ is attributed to growth of cities.

a. AMAX
b. ADTECH
c. ACNielsen
d. Urbanization

9. The term _________ is used to describe countries that have a high level of development according to some criteria. Which criteria, and which countries are classified as being developed, is a contentious issue and there is fierce debate about this. Economic criteria have tended to dominate discussions.

a. Completely randomized designs
b. Developed country
c. Brando
d. Bringin' Home the Oil

10. _________s is the social science that studies the production, distribution, and consumption of goods and services. The term _________s comes from the Ancient Greek oá¼°κονομÎ¯α from oá¼¶κος (oikos, 'house') + νÏŒμος (nomos, 'custom' or 'law'), hence 'rules of the house(hold)'. Current _________ models developed out of the broader field of political economy in the late 19th century, owing to a desire to use an empirical approach more akin to the physical sciences.

a. Industrial organization
b. ACNielsen
c. Economic
d. ADTECH

11. _________ is the increase in the amount of the goods and services produced by an economy over time. It is conventionally measured as the percent rate of increase in real gross domestic product, or real GDP. Growth is usually calculated in real terms, i.e. inflation-adjusted terms, in order to net out the effect of inflation on the price of the goods and services produced.

a. Economic growth
b. ADTECH
c. ACNielsen
d. AMAX

12. A _________ is a relatively new executive level position at a corporation, company, organization typically reporting directly to the CEO or board of directors. The _________ is responsible for a brand's image, experience, and promise, and propagating it throughout all aspects of the company. The brand officer oversees marketing, advertising, design, public relations and customer service departments.

a. Power III
b. Financial analyst
c. Chief executive officer
d. Chief brand officer

13. A _________ is a collection of symbols, experiences and associations connected with a product, a service, a person or any other artifact or entity.

_________s have become increasingly important components of culture and the economy, now being described as 'cultural accessories and personal philosophies'.

Some people distinguish the psychological aspect of a _________ from the experiential aspect.

a. Brandable software
b. Brand
c. Store brand
d. Brand equity

14. The United States _________ is the government agency that is responsible for the United States Census. It also gathers other national demographic and economic data.

a. Power III
b. 180SearchAssistant
c. Census Bureau
d. 6-3-5 Brainwriting

15. The _________ is an international financial institution that provides financial and technical assistance to developing countries for development programs (e.g. bridges, roads, schools, etc.) with the stated goal of reducing poverty.

The _________ differs from the _________ Group, in that the _________ comprises only two institutions:

- International Bank for Reconstruction and Development (IBRD)
- International Development Association (IDA)

Whereas the latter incorporates these two in addition to three more:

- International Finance Corporation (IFC)
- Multilateral Investment Guarantee Agency (MIGA)
- International Centre for Settlement of Investment Disputes (ICSID)

John Maynard Keynes (right) represented the UK at the conference, and Harry Dexter White represented the US.

The _________ was created following the ratification of the United Nations Monetary and Financial Conference of the Bretton Woods agreement. The concept was originally conceived in July 1944 at the United Nations Monetary and Financial Conference.

a. 180SearchAssistant
b. Power III
c. World Bank
d. 6-3-5 Brainwriting

16. The _________ is the total number of living humans on Earth at a given time. As of March 2009, the world's population is estimated to be about 6.76 billion. The _________ has been growing continuously since the end of the Black Death around 1400.

a. African Americans
b. AStore
c. Albert Einstein
d. World Population

17. _________ is a form of communication that typically attempts to persuade potential customers to purchase or to consume more of a particular brand of product or service. 'While now central to the contemporary global economy and the reproduction of global production networks, it is only quite recently that _________ has been more than a marginal influence on patterns of sales and production. The formation of modern _________ was intimately bound up with the emergence of new forms of monopoly capitalism around the end of the 19th and beginning of the 20th century as one element in corporate strategies to create, organize and where possible control markets, especially for mass produced consumer goods.

a. AMAX
b. ACNielsen
c. Advertising
d. ADTECH

18. The _________ is a model used to represent the process of explaining the transformation of countries from high birth rates and high death rates to low birth rates and low death rates as part of the economic development of a country from a pre-industrial to an industrialized economy. It is based on an interpretation begun in 1929 by the American demographer Warren Thompson of prior observed changes, or transitions, in birth and death rates in industrialized societies over the past two hundred years.

Most developed countries are beyond stage three of the model; the majority of developing countries are in stage 2 or stage 3.

a. 180SearchAssistant
b. 6-3-5 Brainwriting
c. Power III
d. Demographic transition model

19. In probability theory and statistics, a _________ is described as the number separating the higher half of a sample, a population from the lower half. The _________ of a finite list of numbers can be found by arranging all the observations from lowest value to highest value and picking the middle one. If there is an even number of observations, the _________ is not unique, so one often takes the mean of the two middle values.

a. Linear regression
b. Frequency distribution
c. Statistically significant
d. Median

20. _________ refers to the laws and rules defining the ways in which products can be advertised in a particular region. Rules can define a wide number of different aspects, such as placement, timing, and content. In the United States, false advertising and health-related ads are regulated the most.

a. ADTECH
b. AMAX
c. Advertising regulation
d. ACNielsen

21. In economics, _________ is the desire to own something and the ability to pay for it. The term _________ signifies the ability or the willingness to buy a particular commodity at a given point of time .

.

a. Discretionary spending
b. Demand
c. Market dominance
d. Market system

22. _________ is a term in economics, where demand for one good or service occurs as a result of demand for another. This may occur as the former is a part of production of the second. For example, demand for coal leads to _________ for mining, as coal must be mined for coal to be consumed.

a. 6-3-5 Brainwriting
b. Derived demand
c. Power III
d. 180SearchAssistant

23. In finance, an _________ is a contract between a buyer and a seller that gives the buyer the right--but not the obligation--to buy or to sell a particular asset (the underlying asset) at a later day at an agreed price. In return for granting the _________, the seller collects a payment (the premium) from the buyer. A call _________ gives the buyer the right to buy the underlying asset; a put _________ gives the buyer of the _________ the right to sell the underlying asset.

a. AMAX
b. ACNielsen
c. ADTECH
d. Option

24. _________ refers to 'controlling human or societal behaviour by rules or restrictions.' _________ can take many forms: legal restrictions promulgated by a government authority, self-_________, social _________, co-_________ and market _________. One can consider _________ as actions of conduct imposing sanctions (such as a fine.) This action of administrative law, or implementing regulatory law, may be contrasted with statutory or case law.

a. Rule of four
b. Non-conventional trademark
c. CAN-SPAM
d. Regulation

25. In the United States, the Office of Management and Budget (OMB) has produced a formal definition of metropolitan areas. These are referred to as '_________s' (_________s) and 'Combined Statistical Areas.' An earlier version of the _________ was the 'Standard _________' (SMetropolitan statistical area.) _________s are composed of counties and for some county equivalents.

a. Metropolitan Statistical Area
b. Race and ethnicity in the United States Census
c. 180SearchAssistant
d. Power III

26. _________ is one of the four elements of marketing mix. An organization or set of organizations (go-betweens) involved in the process of making a product or service available for use or consumption by a consumer or business user.

The other three parts of the marketing mix are product, pricing, and promotion.

a. Distribution
b. Better Living Through Chemistry
c. Japan Advertising Photographers' Association
d. Comparison-Shopping agent

27. In economics, _________ is how a nation's total economy is distributed among its population. ._________ has always been a central concern of economic theory and economic policy. Classical economists such as Adam Smith, Thomas Malthus and David Ricardo were mainly concerned with factor _________, that is, the distribution of income between the main factors of production, land, labour and capital.

a. Internality
b. Inflation rate
c. ACNielsen
d. Income distribution

28. _________ is gross income minus income tax on that income.

Discretionary income is income after subtracting taxes and normal expenses (such as rent or mortgage and food) to maintain a certain standard of living. It is the amount of an individual's income available for spending after the essentials (such as food, clothing, and shelter) have been taken care of:

Discretionary income = Gross income - taxes - necessities

Despite the formal definitions above, _________ is commonly used to denote Discretionary income.

a. 180SearchAssistant
b. 6-3-5 Brainwriting
c. Power III
d. Disposable income

29. _________ is income after subtracting taxes and normal expenses (such as rent or mortgage and food) to maintain a certain standard of living. It is the amount of an individual's income available for spending after the essentials (such as food, clothing, and shelter) have been taken care of:

_________ = Gross income - taxes - necessities

Despite the formal definitions above, disposable income is commonly used to denote _________. The meaning should therefore be interpreted from context.

a. 6-3-5 Brainwriting
b. Power III
c. 180SearchAssistant
d. Discretionary income

30. _________ is difficult to define. For example, in 1952, Alfred Kroeber and Clyde Kluckhohn compiled a list of 164 definitions of '_________' in _________: A Critical Review of Concepts and Definitions. However, the word '_________' is most commonly used in three basic senses:

- excellence of taste in the fine arts and humanities
- an integrated pattern of human knowledge, belief, and behavior that depends upon the capacity for symbolic thought and social learning
- the set of shared attitudes, values, goals, and practices that characterizes an institution, organization or group.

When the concept first emerged in eighteenth- and nineteenth-century Europe, it connoted a process of cultivation or improvement, as in agriculture or horticulture. In the nineteenth century, it came to refer first to the betterment or refinement of the individual, especially through education, and then to the fulfillment of national aspirations or ideals.

a. Culture
b. African Americans
c. AStore
d. Albert Einstein

31. _________ is the study of when, why, how, where and what people do or do not buy products. It blends elements from psychology, sociology,social psychology, anthropology and economics. It attempts to understand the buyer decision making process, both individually and in groups. It studies characteristics of individual consumers such as demographics and behavioural variables in an attempt to understand people's wants. It also tries to assess influences on the consumer from groups such as family, friends, reference groups, and society in general.

a. Consumer behavior
b. Multidimensional scaling
c. Consumer confidence
d. Communal marketing

1. In artificial intelligence, an _________ is an autonomous entity which observes and acts upon an environment (i.e. it is an agent) and directs its activity towards achieving goals (i.e. it is rational.) _________s may also learn or use knowledge to achieve their goals. They may be very simple or very complex: a reflex machine such as a thermostat is an _________, as is a human being, as is a community of human beings working together towards a goal.

a. Intelligent agent | b. AMAX
c. ADTECH | d. ACNielsen

2. _________ is defined by the American _________ Association as the activity, set of institutions, and processes for creating, communicating, delivering, and exchanging offerings that have value for customers, clients, partners, and society at large. The term developed from the original meaning which referred literally to going to market, as in shopping, or going to a market to sell goods or services.

_________ practice tends to be seen as a creative industry, which includes advertising, distribution and selling.

a. Marketing | b. Product naming
c. Marketing myopia | d. Customer acquisition management

3. _________ is a form of advertisement, where branded goods or services are placed in a context usually devoid of ads, such as movies, the story line of television shows Broadcasting ' Cable reported, 'Two thirds of advertisers employ 'branded entertainment'--_________--with the vast majority of that (80%) in commercial TV programming.' The story, based on a survey by the Association of National Advertisers, added, 'Reasons for using in-show plugs varied from 'stronger emotional connection' to better dovetailing with relevant content, to targetting a specific group.'

_________ became common in the 1980s, but can be traced back to the nineteenth century in publishing.

a. Power III | b. 6-3-5 Brainwriting
c. 180SearchAssistant | d. Product placement

4. _________ is a broad label that refers to any individuals or households that use goods and services generated within the economy. The concept of a _________ is used in different contexts, so that the usage and significance of the term may vary.

A _________ is a person who uses any product or service.

a. 6-3-5 Brainwriting | b. 180SearchAssistant
c. Consumer | d. Power III

5. _________ is the study of when, why, how, where and what people do or do not buy products. It blends elements from psychology, sociology,social psychology, anthropology and economics. It attempts to understand the buyer decision making process, both individually and in groups. It studies characteristics of individual consumers such as demographics and behavioural variables in an attempt to understand people's wants. It also tries to assess influences on the consumer from groups such as family, friends, reference groups, and society in general.

a. Multidimensional scaling | b. Consumer behavior
c. Communal marketing | d. Consumer confidence

6. _________s is the social science that studies the production, distribution, and consumption of goods and services. The term _________s comes from the Ancient Greek oá¼°κονομÎ¯α from oá¼¶κος (oikos, 'house') + νÏŒμος (nomos, 'custom' or 'law'), hence 'rules of the house(hold)'. Current _________ models developed out of the broader field of political economy in the late 19th century, owing to a desire to use an empirical approach more akin to the physical sciences.

a. ADTECH
b. Industrial organization
c. ACNielsen
d. Economic

7. _________ is difficult to define. For example, in 1952, Alfred Kroeber and Clyde Kluckhohn compiled a list of 164 definitions of '_________' in _________: A Critical Review of Concepts and Definitions. However, the word '_________' is most commonly used in three basic senses:

- excellence of taste in the fine arts and humanities
- an integrated pattern of human knowledge, belief, and behavior that depends upon the capacity for symbolic thought and social learning
- the set of shared attitudes, values, goals, and practices that characterizes an institution, organization or group.

When the concept first emerged in eighteenth- and nineteenth-century Europe, it connoted a process of cultivation or improvement, as in agriculture or horticulture. In the nineteenth century, it came to refer first to the betterment or refinement of the individual, especially through education, and then to the fulfillment of national aspirations or ideals.

a. Culture
b. Albert Einstein
c. African Americans
d. AStore

8. A _________ is a plan of action designed to achieve a particular goal.

_________ is different from tactics. In military terms, tactics is concerned with the conduct of an engagement while _________ is concerned with how different engagements are linked.

a. Strategy
b. Power III
c. 6-3-5 Brainwriting
d. 180SearchAssistant

9. _________ in organizations and public policy is both the organizational process of creating and maintaining a plan; and the psychological process of thinking about the activities required to create a desired goal on some scale. As such, it is a fundamental property of intelligent behavior. This thought process is essential to the creation and refinement of a plan, or integration of it with other plans, that is, it combines forecasting of developments with the preparation of scenarios of how to react to them.

a. 180SearchAssistant
b. Power III
c. 6-3-5 Brainwriting
d. Planning

10. In operant conditioning, _________ occurs when an event following a response causes an increase in the probability of that response occurring in the future. Response strength can be assessed by measures such as the frequency with which the response is made (for example, a pigeon may peck a key more times in the session), or the speed with which it is made (for example, a rat may run a maze faster.) The environment change contingent upon the response is called a reinforcer.

a. Completely randomized designs
b. Relationship Management Application
c. Reinforcement
d. Generic brands

11. A _________ is a collection of symbols, experiences and associations connected with a product, a service, a person or any other artifact or entity.

_________s have become increasingly important components of culture and the economy, now being described as 'cultural accessories and personal philosophies'.

Some people distinguish the psychological aspect of a _________ from the experiential aspect.

a. Brandable software
b. Store brand
c. Brand
d. Brand equity

12. _________ was originally coined by Austrian psychologist Alfred Adler in 1929. The current broader sense of the word dates from 1961.

In sociology, a _________ is the way a person lives.

a. Power III
b. Lifestyle
c. 6-3-5 Brainwriting
d. 180SearchAssistant

13. In the field of marketing, demographics, opinion research, and social research in general, _________ variables are any attributes relating to personality, values, attitudes, interests, or lifestyles. They are also called IAO variables . They can be contrasted with demographic variables (such as age and gender), behavioral variables (such as usage rate or loyalty), and bizographic variables (such as industry, seniority and functional area.)

a. Business-to-business
b. Lifetime value
c. Psychographic
d. Marketing myopia

14. The _________ is generally accepted as the use and specification of the four p's describing the strategic position of a product in the marketplace. One version of the origins of the _________ starts in 1948 when James Culliton said that a marketing decision should be a result of something similar to a recipe. This version continued in 1953 when Neil Borden, in his American Marketing Association presidential address, took the recipe idea one step further and coined the term 'Marketing-Mix'.

a. Power III
b. 180SearchAssistant
c. Marketing mix
d. 6-3-5 Brainwriting

15. _________ is a form of communication that typically attempts to persuade potential customers to purchase or to consume more of a particular brand of product or service. 'While now central to the contemporary global economy and the reproduction of global production networks, it is only quite recently that _________ has been more than a marginal influence on patterns of sales and production. The formation of modern _________ was intimately bound up with the emergence of new forms of monopoly capitalism around the end of the 19th and beginning of the 20th century as one element in corporate strategies to create, organize and where possible control markets, especially for mass produced consumer goods.

a. Advertising
b. ACNielsen
c. AMAX
d. ADTECH

16. _________ is the study of the Earth and its lands, features, inhabitants, and phenomena. A literal translation would be 'to describe or write about the Earth'. The first person to use the word '_________' was Eratosthenes .

a. Power III
b. 180SearchAssistant
c. 6-3-5 Brainwriting
d. Geography

17. _________ involves disseminating information about a product, product line, brand, or company. It is one of the four key aspects of the marketing mix. (The other three elements are product marketing, pricing, and distribution). P>_________ is generally sub-divided into two parts:

- Above the line _________: Promotion in the media (e.g. TV, radio, newspapers, Internet and Mobile Phones) in which the advertiser pays an advertising agency to place the ad
- Below the line _________: All other _________. Much of this is intended to be subtle enough for the consumer to be unaware that _________ is taking place. E.g. sponsorship, product placement, endorsements, sales _________, merchandising, direct mail, personal selling, public relations, trade shows

a. Bottling lines
b. Cashmere Agency
c. Davie Brown Index
d. Promotion

18. _________ is a concept that arose out of the theory of two-step flow of communication propounded by Paul Lazarsfeld and Elihu Katz. This theory is one of several models that try to explain the diffusion of innovations, ideas, or commercial products.

The opinion leader is the agent who is an active media user and who interprets the meaning of media messages or content for lower-end media users.

a. Elasticity
b. Intellectual property
c. ACNielsen
d. Opinion leadership

19. A _________ is a sociological concept referring to a group to which an individual or another group is compared.

_________s are used in order to evaluate and determine the nature of a given individual or other group's characteristics and sociological attributes. It is the group to which the individual relates or aspires relate himself or self psychologically.

a. Power III
b. Mociology
c. Reference group
d. Minority

20. _________ refers to the laws and rules defining the ways in which products can be advertised in a particular region. Rules can define a wide number of different aspects, such as placement, timing, and content. In the United States, false advertising and health-related ads are regulated the most.

a. ADTECH
b. Advertising regulation
c. AMAX
d. ACNielsen

21. _________ is one of the four elements of marketing mix. An organization or set of organizations (go-betweens) involved in the process of making a product or service available for use or consumption by a consumer or business user.

The other three parts of the marketing mix are product, pricing, and promotion.

a. Comparison-Shopping agent
b. Better Living Through Chemistry
c. Japan Advertising Photographers' Association
d. Distribution

22. _________ refers to 'controlling human or societal behaviour by rules or restrictions.' _________ can take many forms: legal restrictions promulgated by a government authority, self-_________, social _________, co-_________ and market _________. One can consider _________ as actions of conduct imposing sanctions (such as a fine.) This action of administrative law, or implementing regulatory law, may be contrasted with statutory or case law.

a. Non-conventional trademark
b. CAN-SPAM
c. Rule of four
d. Regulation

23. _________ refers to a business or organization attempting to acquire goods or services to accomplish the goals of the enterprise. Though there are several organizations that attempt to set standards in the _________ process, processes can vary greatly between organizations. Typically the word '_________' is not used interchangeably with the word 'procurement', since procurement typically includes Expediting, Supplier Quality, and Traffic and Logistics (T'L) in addition to _________.

a. Purchasing
b. Supply chain
c. Supply network
d. Drop shipping

24. In economics, an externality or spillover of an economic transaction is an impact on a party that is not directly involved in the transaction. In such a case, prices do not reflect the full costs or benefits in production or consumption of a product or service. A positive impact is called an _________ benefit, while a negative impact is called an _________ cost.

a. ACNielsen
b. ADTECH
c. AMAX
d. External

25. The _________ is a marketing term and refers to all of the forces outside of marketing that affect marketing management's ability to build and maintain successful relationships with target customers. The _________ consists of both the macroenvironment and the microenvironment.

The microenvironment refers to the forces that are close to the company and affect its ability to serve its customers.

a. Psychographic
b. Customer franchise
c. Business-to-consumer
d. Market environment

26. A _________ or logistics network is the system of organizations, people, technology, activities, information and resources involved in moving a product or service from supplier to customer. _________ activities transform natural resources, raw materials and components into a finished product that is delivered to the end customer. In sophisticated _________ systems, used products may re-enter the _________ at any point where residual value is recyclable.

a. Supply chain
b. Purchasing
c. Supply chain network
d. Demand chain management

27. _________ is systematic determination of merit, worth, and significance of something or someone using criteria against a set of standards. _________ often is used to characterize and appraise subjects of interest in a wide range of human enterprises, including the arts, criminal justice, foundations and non-profit organizations, government, health care, and other human services.

Depending on the topic of interest, there are professional groups which look to the quality and rigor of the _________ process.

a. ADTECH
b. AMAX
c. ACNielsen
d. Evaluation

28. _________ is a fee paid on borrowed assets. It is the price paid for the use of borrowed money , or, money earned by deposited funds . Assets that are sometimes lent with _________ include money, shares, consumer goods through hire purchase, major assets such as aircraft, and even entire factories in finance lease arrangements.

a. ADTECH
b. AMAX
c. Interest
d. ACNielsen

1. _________ is an advertisement in which a particular product specifically mentions a competitor by name for the express purpose of showing why the competitor is inferior to the product naming it.

This should not be confused with parody advertisements, where a fictional product is being advertised for the purpose of poking fun at the particular advertisement, nor should it be confused with the use of a coined brand name for the purpose of comparing the product without actually naming an actual competitor. ('Wikipedia tastes better and is less filling than the Encyclopedia Galactica.')

In the 1980s, during what has been referred to as the cola wars, soft-drink manufacturer Pepsi ran a series of advertisements where people, caught on hidden camera, in a blind taste test, chose Pepsi over rival Coca-Cola.

a. GL-70
b. Heavy-up
c. Cost per conversion
d. Comparative advertising

2. _________ is one of the four elements of marketing mix. An organization or set of organizations (go-betweens) involved in the process of making a product or service available for use or consumption by a consumer or business user.

The other three parts of the marketing mix are product, pricing, and promotion.

a. Distribution
b. Japan Advertising Photographers' Association
c. Better Living Through Chemistry
d. Comparison-Shopping agent

3. _________ is a term commonly used to describe commerce transactions between businesses like the one between a manufacturer and a wholesaler or a wholesaler and a retailer i.e both the buyer and the seller are business entity.This is unlike business-to-consumers (B2C) which involve a business entity and end consumer, or business-to-government (B2G) which involve a business entity and government.

The volume of B2B transactions is much higher than the volume of B2C transactions. The primary reason for this is that in a typical supply chain there will be many B2B transactions involving subcomponent or raw materials, and only one B2C transaction, specifically sale of the finished product to the end customer.

a. Customer relationship management
b. Business-to-business
c. Social marketing
d. Disruptive technology

4. _________ is a form of communication that typically attempts to persuade potential customers to purchase or to consume more of a particular brand of product or service. 'While now central to the contemporary global economy and the reproduction of global production networks, it is only quite recently that _________ has been more than a marginal influence on patterns of sales and production. The formation of modern _________ was intimately bound up with the emergence of new forms of monopoly capitalism around the end of the 19th and beginning of the 20th century as one element in corporate strategies to create, organize and where possible control markets, especially for mass produced consumer goods.

a. ADTECH
b. ACNielsen
c. AMAX
d. Advertising

5. _________ is a broad label that refers to any individuals or households that use goods and services generated within the economy. The concept of a _________ is used in different contexts, so that the usage and significance of the term may vary.

A _________ is a person who uses any product or service.

a. Consumer
b. 180SearchAssistant
c. 6-3-5 Brainwriting
d. Power III

6. _________ is the study of when, why, how, where and what people do or do not buy products. It blends elements from psychology, sociology,social psychology, anthropology and economics. It attempts to understand the buyer decision making process, both individually and in groups. It studies characteristics of individual consumers such as demographics and behavioural variables in an attempt to understand people's wants. It also tries to assess influences on the consumer from groups such as family, friends, reference groups, and society in general.

a. Consumer behavior
b. Communal marketing
c. Consumer confidence
d. Multidimensional scaling

7. _________ is a value showing the reliability of a person to others because of his/her integrity, truthfulness, and trustfulness, traits that can encourage someone to depend on him/her.

The wider use of this noun is in Systems engineering.

_________ as applied to a computer system is defined by the IFIP 10.4 Working Group on Dependable Computing and Fault Tolerance as:

> '[..] the trustworthiness of a computing system which allows reliance to be justifiably placed on the service it delivers [..]'

an alternative and broader definition is provided by IEC IEV 191-02-03:

> '_________ the collective term used to describe the availability performance and its influencing factors : reliability performance, maintainability performance and maintenance support performance'

This concept can be further extended to encompass mechanisms to increase and maintain the _________ of a system .

a. Power III
b. 6-3-5 Brainwriting
c. 180SearchAssistant
d. Dependability

8. _________ refers to the laws and rules defining the ways in which products can be advertised in a particular region. Rules can define a wide number of different aspects, such as placement, timing, and content. In the United States, false advertising and health-related ads are regulated the most.

a. ACNielsen
b. ADTECH
c. AMAX
d. Advertising regulation

9. _________ refers to 'controlling human or societal behaviour by rules or restrictions.' _________ can take many forms: legal restrictions promulgated by a government authority, self-_________, social _________, co-_________ and market _________. One can consider _________ as actions of conduct imposing sanctions (such as a fine.) This action of administrative law, or implementing regulatory law, may be contrasted with statutory or case law.

a. Rule of four
b. CAN-SPAM
c. Regulation
d. Non-conventional trademark

10. _________ can be regarded as an outcome of mental processes (cognitive process) leading to the selection of a course of action among several alternatives. Every _________ process produces a final choice. The output can be an action or an opinion of choice.

a. Decision making
b. 6-3-5 Brainwriting
c. Power III
d. 180SearchAssistant

11. _________ refers to a business or organization attempting to acquire goods or services to accomplish the goals of the enterprise. Though there are several organizations that attempt to set standards in the _________ process, processes can vary greatly between organizations. Typically the word '_________' is not used interchangeably with the word 'procurement', since procurement typically includes Expediting, Supplier Quality, and Traffic and Logistics (T'L) in addition to _________.

a. Purchasing
b. Drop shipping
c. Supply network
d. Supply chain

12. A _________ is an explicit set of requirements to be satisfied by a material, product, or service.

In engineering, manufacturing, and business, it is vital for suppliers, purchasers, and users of materials, products, or services to understand and agree upon all requirements. A _________ is a type of a standard which is often referenced by a contract or procurement document.

a. Product optimization
b. Specification
c. Product development
d. New product development

13. _________ refers to the confirmation of certain characteristics of an object, person, or organization. This confirmation is often, but not always, provided by some form of external review, education, or assessment. One of the most common types of _________ in modern society is professional _________, where a person is certified as being able to competently complete a job or task, usually by the passing of an examination.

a. 6-3-5 Brainwriting
b. Certification
c. Power III
d. 180SearchAssistant

14. A _________, in marketing, procurement, and organizational studies, is a group of employees, family members, or members of any type of organization responsible for purchasing an item for the organization. In a business setting, major purchases typically require input from various parts of the organization, including finance, accounting, purchasing, information technology management, and senior management. Highly technical purchases, such as information systems or production equipment, also require the expertise of technical specialists.

a. Marketing myopia
b. Commercialization
c. Packshot
d. Buying center

15. _________ is a fee paid on borrowed assets. It is the price paid for the use of borrowed money , or, money earned by deposited funds . Assets that are sometimes lent with _________ include money, shares, consumer goods through hire purchase, major assets such as aircraft, and even entire factories in finance lease arrangements.

a. ADTECH
b. AMAX
c. Interest
d. ACNielsen

16. In business and engineering, new _________ is the term used to describe the complete process of bringing a new product or service to market. There are two parallel paths involved in the Nproduct development process: one involves the idea generation, product design, and detail engineering; the other involves market research and marketing analysis. Companies typically see new _________ as the first stage in generating and commercializing new products within the overall strategic process of product life cycle management used to maintain or grow their market share.

a. Specification tree
b. New product development
c. Product development
d. New product screening

17. A personal and cultural _________ is a relative ethic _________, an assumption upon which implementation can be extrapolated. A _________ system is a set of consistent _________s and measures that is soo not true. A principle _________ is a foundation upon which other _________s and measures of integrity are based.

a. Supreme Court of the United States
b. Perceptual maps
c. Value
d. Package-on-Package

18. _________ refer to a collection of facts usually collected as the result of experience, observation or experiment or a set of premises. This may consist of numbers, words particularly as measurements or observations of a set of variables. _________ are often viewed as a lowest level of abstraction from which information and knowledge are derived.

a. Pearson product-moment correlation coefficient
b. Data
c. Sample size
d. Mean

19. A _________ is defined by the International Co-operative Alliance's Statement on the Co-operative Identity as an autonomous association of persons united voluntarily to meet their common economic, social, and cultural needs and aspirations through a jointly-owned and democratically-controlled enterprise. It is a business organization owned and operated by a group of individuals for their mutual benefit. A _________ may also be defined as a business owned and controlled equally by the people who use its services or who work at it.

a. Power III
b. 180SearchAssistant
c. 6-3-5 Brainwriting
d. Cooperative

20. _________ is an inventory strategy implemented to improve the return on investment of a business by reducing in-process inventory and its associated carrying costs. In order to achieve JIT the process must have signals of what is going on elsewhere within the process. This means that the process is often driven by a series of signals, which can be Kanban , that tell production processes when to make the next part.

a. Personalization
b. Promotion
c. Just-in-time
d. Clutter

21. In economics, business, retail, and accounting, a _________ is the value of money that has been used up to produce something, and hence is not available for use anymore. In economics, a _________ is an alternative that is given up as a result of a decision. In business, the _________ may be one of acquisition, in which case the amount of money expended to acquire it is counted as _________.

a. Transaction cost
b. Fixed costs
c. Cost
d. Variable cost

22. _________ in organizations and public policy is both the organizational process of creating and maintaining a plan; and the psychological process of thinking about the activities required to create a desired goal on some scale. As such, it is a fundamental property of intelligent behavior. This thought process is essential to the creation and refinement of a plan, or integration of it with other plans, that is, it combines forecasting of developments with the preparation of scenarios of how to react to them.

a. Planning
b. 6-3-5 Brainwriting
c. Power III
d. 180SearchAssistant

23. _________ is defined by the American _________ Association as the activity, set of institutions, and processes for creating, communicating, delivering, and exchanging offerings that have value for customers, clients, partners, and society at large. The term developed from the original meaning which referred literally to going to market, as in shopping, or going to a market to sell goods or services.

_________ practice tends to be seen as a creative industry, which includes advertising, distribution and selling.

a. Marketing myopia
b. Product naming
c. Customer acquisition management
d. Marketing

24. Customer _________ consists of the processes a company uses to track and organize its contacts with its current and prospective customers. CRelationship management software is used to support these processes; information about customers and customer interactions can be entered, stored and accessed by employees in different company departments. Typical CRelationship management goals are to improve services provided to customers, and to use customer contact information for targeted marketing.

a. Relationship management
b. Marketing
c. Green marketing
d. Product bundling

25. A _________ is a plan of action designed to achieve a particular goal.

_________ is different from tactics. In military terms, tactics is concerned with the conduct of an engagement while _________ is concerned with how different engagements are linked.

a. 6-3-5 Brainwriting
b. Power III
c. 180SearchAssistant
d. Strategy

26. Electronic commerce, commonly known as _________ or eCommerce, consists of the buying and selling of products or services over electronic systems such as the Internet and other computer networks. The amount of trade conducted electronically has grown extraordinarily with wide-spread Internet usage. A wide variety of commerce is conducted in this way, spurring and drawing on innovations in electronic funds transfer, supply chain management, Internet marketing, online transaction processing, electronic data interchange (EDI), inventory management systems, and automated data collection systems.

a. AMAX
b. E-commerce
c. ACNielsen
d. ADTECH

27. A _________ is the space, actual or metaphorical, in which a market operates. The term is also used in a trademark law context to denote the actual consumer environment, ie. the 'real world' in which products and services are provided and consumed.

a. 180SearchAssistant
b. Power III
c. 6-3-5 Brainwriting
d. Marketplace

28. _________ is a recursive process where two or more people or organizations work together toward an intersection of common goals -- for example, an intellectual endeavor that is creative in nature--by sharing knowledge, learning and building consensus. _________ does not require leadership and can sometimes bring better results through decentralization and egalitarianism. In particular, teams that work collaboratively can obtain greater resources, recognition and reward when facing competition for finite resources._________ is also present in opposing goals exhibiting the notion of adversarial _________, though this notion is atypical of the annotation that people have given towards their understanding of _________.

a. Collaboration
b. 180SearchAssistant
c. Power III
d. 6-3-5 Brainwriting

29. Competitiveness is a comparative concept of the ability and performance of a firm, sub-sector or country to sell and supply goods and/or services in a given market. Although widely used in economics and business management, the usefulness of the concept, particularly in the context of national competitiveness, is vigorously disputed by economists, such as Paul Krugman .

The term may also be applied to markets, where it is used to refer to the extent to which the market structure may be regarded as perfectly _________.

a. Customs union
b. Free trade zone
c. Geographical pricing
d. Competitive

30. A _________ is a tool used in industrial business-to-business procurement. It is a type of auction in which the role of the buyer and seller are reversed, with the primary objective to drive purchase prices downward. In an ordinary auction, buyers compete to obtain a good or service.

a. Fulfillment house
b. Vendor Managed Inventory
c. Materials management
d. Reverse auction

31. A _________ is a type of wholesale merchant business that buys goods and bulk products from importers, other wholesalers and then sells to retailers. _________s can deal in any commodity destined for the retail market. Typical categories are food, lumber, hardware, fuel, and textiles.

a. Chief privacy officer
b. Refusal to deal
c. Jobbing house
d. Tacit collusion

32. _________ is the study of the Earth and its lands, features, inhabitants, and phenomena. A literal translation would be 'to describe or write about the Earth'. The first person to use the word '_________' was Eratosthenes .

a. 6-3-5 Brainwriting
b. 180SearchAssistant
c. Power III
d. Geography

33. An _________ is the manufacturing of a good or service within a category. Although _________ is a broad term for any kind of economic production, in economics and urban planning _________ is a synonym for the secondary sector, which is a type of economic activity involved in the manufacturing of raw materials into goods and products.

There are four key industrial economic sectors: the primary sector, largely raw material extraction industries such as mining and farming; the secondary sector, involving refining, construction, and manufacturing; the tertiary sector, which deals with services (such as law and medicine) and distribution of manufactured goods; and the quaternary sector, a relatively new type of knowledge _________ focusing on technological research, design and development such as computer programming, and biochemistry.

a. ACNielsen
b. AMAX
c. Industry
d. ADTECH

34. The _________ or _________ is used by business and government to classify and measure economic activity in Canada, Mexico and the United States. It has largely replaced the older Standard Industrial Classification system; however, certain government departments and agencies, such as the U.S. Securities and Exchange Commission (SEC), still use the SIC codes.

The _________ numbering system is a six-digit code.

a. North American Industry Classification System
b. 6-3-5 Brainwriting
c. 180SearchAssistant
d. Power III

35. _________ is a measure of the strength of a brand, product, service relative to competitive offerings. There is often a geographic element to the competitive landscape. In defining _________, you must see to what extent a product, brand, or firm controls a product category in a given geographic area.

a. Market dominance
b. Market system
c. Productivity
d. Discretionary spending

36. Wholesaling, historically called jobbing, is the sale of goods or merchandise to retailers, to industrial, commercial, institutional or to other wholesalers and related subordinated services.

According to the United Nations Statistics Division, '_________' is the resale (sale without transformation) of new and used goods to retailers, to industrial, commercial, institutional or professional users or involves acting as an agent or broker in buying merchandise for such persons or companies. Wholesalers frequently physically assemble, sort and grade goods in large lots, break bulk, repack and redistribute in smaller lots.

a. Supply network
b. Wholesale
c. Purchasing
d. Supply chain network

37. _________ is the realization of an application idea, model, design, specification, standard, algorithm an _________ is a realization of a technical specification or algorithm as a program, software component, or other computer system. Many _________s may exist for a given specification or standard.

a. ADTECH
b. ACNielsen
c. AMAX
d. Implementation

38. The _________ is an independent agency of the United States government, established in 1914 by the _________ Act. Its principal mission is the promotion of 'consumer protection' and the elimination and prevention of what regulators perceive to be harmfully 'anti-competitive' business practices, such as coercive monopoly.

The _________ Act was one of President Wilson's major acts against trusts.

a. Power III
b. 180SearchAssistant
c. 6-3-5 Brainwriting
d. Federal Trade Commission

39. A _________ is a list of the general tasks and responsibilities of a position. Typically, it also includes to whom the position reports, specifications such as the qualifications needed by the person in the job, salary range for the position, etc. A _________ is usually developed by conducting a job analysis, which includes examining the tasks and sequences of tasks necessary to perform the job.

a. 6-3-5 Brainwriting
b. 180SearchAssistant
c. Job description
d. Power III

40. The _________ of 1977 (15 U.S.C. Â§Â§ 78dd-1, et seq.) is a United States federal law known primarily for two of its main provisions, one that addresses accounting transparency requirements under the Securities Exchange Act of 1934 and another concerning bribery of foreign officials.

a. Trademark dilution
b. Copyright
c. Foreign Corrupt Practices Act
d. Tenth Amendment

41. A _________ is a business that is independently owned and operated, with a small number of employees and relatively low volume of sales. The legal definition of 'small' often varies by country and industry, but is generally under 100 employees in the United States and under 50 employees in the European Union. In comparison, the definition of mid-sized business by the number of employees is generally under 500 in the U.S. and 250 for the European Union.

a. Product support
b. Time to market
c. Customer centricity
d. Small Business

42. The _________ is a United States government agency that provides support to small businesses.

The mission of the _________ is 'to maintain and strengthen the nation's economy by enabling the establishment and viability of small businesses and by assisting in the economic recovery of communities after disasters.'

The _________ makes loans directly to businesses and acts as a guarantor on bank loans. In some circumstances it also makes loans to victims of natural disasters, works to get government procurement contracts for small businesses, and assists businesses with management, technical and training issues.

a. 6-3-5 Brainwriting
b. 180SearchAssistant
c. Power III
d. Small Business Administration

43. A supply chain is the system of organizations, people, technology, activities, information and resources involved in moving a product or service from _________ to customer. Supply chain activities transform natural resources, raw materials and components into a finished product that is delivered to the end customer. In sophisticated supply chain systems, used products may re-enter the supply chain at any point where residual value is recyclable.

a. Bringin' Home the Oil
b. Rebate
c. Supplier
d. Product line extension

1. _________ is defined by the American _________ Association as the activity, set of institutions, and processes for creating, communicating, delivering, and exchanging offerings that have value for customers, clients, partners, and society at large. The term developed from the original meaning which referred literally to going to market, as in shopping, or going to a market to sell goods or services.

_________ practice tends to be seen as a creative industry, which includes advertising, distribution and selling.

a. Marketing myopia
b. Customer acquisition management
c. Marketing
d. Product naming

2. _________ is the process of using quantitative methods and qualitative methods to evaluate consumer response to a product idea prior to the introduction of a product to the market. It can also be used to generate communication designed to alter consumer attitudes toward existing products. These methods involve the evaluation by consumers of product concepts having certain rational benefits, such as 'a detergent that removes stains but is gentle on fabrics,' or non-rational benefits, such as 'a shampoo that lets you be yourself.' Such methods are commonly referred to as _________ and have been performed using field surveys, personal interviews and focus groups, in combination with various quantitative methods, to generate and evaluate product concepts.

a. Logit analysis
b. Market analysis
c. Cross tabulation
d. Concept testing

3. A _________ is a list of the general tasks and responsibilities of a position. Typically, it also includes to whom the position reports, specifications such as the qualifications needed by the person in the job, salary range for the position, etc. A _________ is usually developed by conducting a job analysis, which includes examining the tasks and sequences of tasks necessary to perform the job.

a. 6-3-5 Brainwriting
b. 180SearchAssistant
c. Job description
d. Power III

4. _________ refer to a collection of facts usually collected as the result of experience, observation or experiment or a set of premises. This may consist of numbers, words particularly as measurements or observations of a set of variables. _________ are often viewed as a lowest level of abstraction from which information and knowledge are derived.

a. Sample size
b. Data
c. Pearson product-moment correlation coefficient
d. Mean

5. _________ constitute a class of computer-based information systems including knowledge-based systems that support decision-making activities.

_________ are a specific class of computerized information system that supports business and organizational decision-making activities. A properly-designed _________ is an interactive software-based system intended to help decision makers compile useful information from raw data, documents, personal knowledge, and/or business models to identify and solve problems and make decisions.

a. Power III
b. 180SearchAssistant
c. 6-3-5 Brainwriting
d. Decision support systems

6. A _________ is a commercial building for storage of goods. _________s are used by manufacturers, importers, exporters, wholesalers, transport businesses, customs, etc. They are usually large plain buildings in industrial areas of cities and towns.

a. 180SearchAssistant
b. 6-3-5 Brainwriting
c. Power III
d. Warehouse

7. _________, in strategic management and marketing, is the percentage or proportion of the total available market or market segment that is being serviced by a company. It can be expressed as a company's sales revenue (from that market) divided by the total sales revenue available in that market. It can also be expressed as a company's unit sales volume (in a market) divided by the total volume of units sold in that market.

a. Demand generation
b. Customer relationship management
c. Cyberdoc
d. Market share

8. Consumer market research is a form of applied sociology that concentrates on understanding the behaviours, whims and preferences, of consumers in a market-based economy, and aims to understand the effects and comparative success of marketing campaigns. The field of consumer _________ as a statistical science was pioneered by Arthur Nielsen with the founding of the ACNielsen Company in 1923 .

Thus _________ is the systematic and objective identification, collection, analysis, and dissemination of information for the purpose of assisting management in decision making related to the identification and solution of problems and opportunities in marketing.

a. Focus group
b. Marketing research process
c. Logit analysis
d. Marketing research

9. _________ is a set of six steps which defines the tasks to be accomplished in conducting a marketing research study. These include problem definition, developing an approach to problem, research design formulation, field work, data preparation and analysis, and report generation and presentation.

a. Marketing research process
b. Market analysis
c. Preference-rank translation
d. Simple random sampling

10. _________ often refers to either primary or secondary research. Secondary research involves a company using information compiled from various sources, which is about a new or existing product. The advantages of secondary research are that it is relatively cheap and easily accessible.

a. Questionnaire
b. Market research
c. Mystery shoppers
d. Mystery shopping

11. _________ is a marketing term, and involves evaluating the situation and trends in a particular company's market. _________ is often called the 'three c's', which refers to the three major elements that must be studied:

- Customers
- Costs
- Competition

The number of 'c's' is sometimes extended to four, five, or even six, with 'Collaboration', 'Company', and 'Competitive advantage'.

- Marketing mix
- SWOT analysis

.

a. Power III
b. 180SearchAssistant
c. 6-3-5 Brainwriting
d. Situation analysis

12. Electronic commerce, commonly known as _________ or eCommerce, consists of the buying and selling of products or services over electronic systems such as the Internet and other computer networks. The amount of trade conducted electronically has grown extraordinarily with wide-spread Internet usage. A wide variety of commerce is conducted in this way, spurring and drawing on innovations in electronic funds transfer, supply chain management, Internet marketing, online transaction processing, electronic data interchange (EDI), inventory management systems, and automated data collection systems.

a. AMAX
b. ACNielsen
c. ADTECH
d. E-commerce

13. Combining Existing _________ Sources with New Primary Data Sources

Imagine that we could get hold of a good collection of surveys taken in earlier years, such as detailed studies about changes going on in this phase and hopefully additional studies in the years to come. Analyzing this data base over time could give us a good picture of what changes actually have taken place in the orientation of the population and of the extent to which new technical concepts did have an impact on subgroups of the population. Furthermore, data archives can help to prepare studies on change over time by monitoring what questions have been asked in earlier years and alerting principal investigators to important questions which should be repeated in planned research projects.

a. 6-3-5 Brainwriting
b. 180SearchAssistant
c. Secondary data
d. Power III

14. _________ is a term commonly used to describe commerce transactions between businesses like the one between a manufacturer and a wholesaler or a wholesaler and a retailer i.e both the buyer and the seller are business entity.This is unlike business-to-consumers (B2C) which involve a business entity and end consumer, or business-to-government (B2G) which involve a business entity and government.

The volume of B2B transactions is much higher than the volume of B2C transactions. The primary reason for this is that in a typical supply chain there will be many B2B transactions involving subcomponent or raw materials, and only one B2C transaction, specifically sale of the finished product to the end customer.

a. Social marketing
b. Customer relationship management
c. Disruptive technology
d. Business-to-business

15. A _________ is a form of qualitative research in which a group of people are asked about their attitude towards a product, service, concept, advertisement, idea, or packaging. Questions are asked in an interactive group setting where participants are free to talk with other group members.

Ernest Dichter originated the idea of having a 'group therapy' for products and this process is what became known as a _________.

a. Marketing research process
b. Focus group
c. Cross tabulation
d. Logit analysis

16. Human beings are also considered to be _________ because they have the ability to change raw materials into valuable _________. The term Human _________ can also be defined as the skills, energies, talents, abilities and knowledge that are used for the production of goods or the rendering of services. While taking into account human beings as _________, the following things have to be kept in mind:

- The size of the population
- The capabilities of the individuals in that population

Many _________ cannot be consumed in their original form. They have to be processed in order to change them into more usable commodities.

a. 180SearchAssistant
b. 6-3-5 Brainwriting
c. Resources
d. Power III

17. A _________ is a type of website, usually maintained by an individual with regular entries of commentary, descriptions of events, or other material such as graphics or video. Entries are commonly displayed in reverse-chronological order. '_________' can also be used as a verb, meaning to maintain or add content to a _________.

a. 180SearchAssistant
b. Power III
c. 6-3-5 Brainwriting
d. Blog

18. _________ is a form of communication that typically attempts to persuade potential customers to purchase or to consume more of a particular brand of product or service. 'While now central to the contemporary global economy and the reproduction of global production networks, it is only quite recently that _________ has been more than a marginal influence on patterns of sales and production. The formation of modern _________ was intimately bound up with the emergence of new forms of monopoly capitalism around the end of the 19th and beginning of the 20th century as one element in corporate strategies to create, organize and where possible control markets, especially for mass produced consumer goods.

a. ADTECH
b. ACNielsen
c. AMAX
d. Advertising

19. _________ refers to the laws and rules defining the ways in which products can be advertised in a particular region. Rules can define a wide number of different aspects, such as placement, timing, and content. In the United States, false advertising and health-related ads are regulated the most.

a. Advertising regulation
b. AMAX
c. ACNielsen
d. ADTECH

20. _________ is a fee paid on borrowed assets. It is the price paid for the use of borrowed money , or, money earned by deposited funds . Assets that are sometimes lent with _________ include money, shares, consumer goods through hire purchase, major assets such as aircraft, and even entire factories in finance lease arrangements.

a. Interest
b. ADTECH
c. AMAX
d. ACNielsen

21. _________ in organizations and public policy is both the organizational process of creating and maintaining a plan; and the psychological process of thinking about the activities required to create a desired goal on some scale. As such, it is a fundamental property of intelligent behavior. This thought process is essential to the creation and refinement of a plan, or integration of it with other plans, that is, it combines forecasting of developments with the preparation of scenarios of how to react to them.

a. Power III
b. Planning
c. 180SearchAssistant
d. 6-3-5 Brainwriting

22. _________ refers to 'controlling human or societal behaviour by rules or restrictions.' _________ can take many forms: legal restrictions promulgated by a government authority, self-_________, social _________, co-_________ and market _________. One can consider _________ as actions of conduct imposing sanctions (such as a fine.) This action of administrative law, or implementing regulatory law, may be contrasted with statutory or case law.

a. Rule of four
b. Regulation
c. Non-conventional trademark
d. CAN-SPAM

23. _________ is a magazine, delivering news, analysis and data on marketing and media. The magazine was started as a broadsheet newspaper in Chicago in 1930. Today, its content appears in a print weekly distributed around the world and on many electronic platforms, including: AdAge.com, daily e-mail newsletters called Ad Age Daily, Ad Age's Mediaworks and Ad Age Digital; weekly newsletters such as Madison ' Vine (about branded entertainment) and Ad Age China; podcasts called Why It Matters and various videos.

a. Ethical Consumer
b. Outsert
c. Advertising Age
d. Adweek

24. _________ are retail outlets, usually corporate owned businesses, that share brands and central management, often with standardized business methods and practices, and these may include stores, restaurants, and some service-oriented businesses.

The displacement of independent businesses by chains has generated controversy in many countries, and has sparked increased collaboration among independent businesses and communities to prevent chain proliferation. Such efforts occur within national trade groups such as the American Booksellers Association, as well as community-based coalitions such as Independent Business Alliances.

a. Customer base
b. Product life cycle management
c. Supplier diversity
d. Chain stores

25. The United States _________ is the Cabinet department of the United States government concerned with promoting economic growth. It was originally created as the United States _________ and Labor on February 14, 1903. It was subsequently renamed to the _________ on March 4, 1913, and its bureaus and agencies specializing in labor were transferred to the new Department of Labor.

a. 180SearchAssistant
b. Power III
c. Department of Commerce
d. 6-3-5 Brainwriting

26. _________s is the social science that studies the production, distribution, and consumption of goods and services. The term _________s comes from the Ancient Greek οá¼°κονομÎ¯α from οá¼¶κος (oikos, 'house') + νÏŒμος (nomos, 'custom' or 'law'), hence 'rules of the house(hold)'. Current _________ models developed out of the broader field of political economy in the late 19th century, owing to a desire to use an empirical approach more akin to the physical sciences.

a. ADTECH
b. Industrial organization
c. ACNielsen
d. Economic

27. The Oxford University Press defines _________ as 'marketing on a worldwide scale reconciling or taking commercial advantage of global operational differences, similarities and opportunities in order to meet global objectives.' Oxford University Press' Glossary of Marketing Terms.

Here are three reasons for the shift from domestic to _________ as given by the authors of the textbook, _________ Management--3rd Edition by Masaaki Kotabe and Kristiaan Helsen, 2004.

One of the product categories in which global competition has been easy to track is in U.S. automotive sales.

a. Global Marketing
b. Digital marketing
c. Guerrilla Marketing
d. Diversity marketing

28. _________ is a mathematical science pertaining to the collection, analysis, interpretation or explanation, and presentation of data. It also provides tools for prediction and forecasting based on data. It is applicable to a wide variety of academic disciplines, from the natural and social sciences to the humanities, government and business.

a. Type I error
b. Null hypothesis
c. Median
d. Statistics

29. The _________ is an international organization whose stated aims are to facilitate cooperation in international law, international security, economic development, social progress, human rights and achieving world peace. The _________ was founded in 1945 after World War II to replace the League of Nations, to stop wars between countries and to provide a platform for dialogue.

There are currently 192 member states, including nearly every recognized independent state in the world.

a. AMAX
b. ADTECH
c. ACNielsen
d. United Nations

30. _________ is the practice of individuals including commercial businesses, governments and institutions, facilitating the sale of their products or services to other companies or organizations that in turn resell them, use them as components in products or services they offer _________ is also called business-to-_________ for short. (Note that while marketing to government entities shares some of the same dynamics of organizational marketing, B2G Marketing is meaningfully different.)

a. Law of disruption
b. Mass marketing
c. Disruptive technology
d. Business marketing

31. The _________ business model is one in which participants bid for products and services over the Internet. The functionality of buying and selling in an auction format is made possible through auction software which regulates the various processes involved.

Several types of _________s are possible.

a. ADTECH
b. AMAX
c. ACNielsen
d. Online auction

32. An _________ is one type of focus group, and is a sub-set of online research methods.

A moderator invites prescreened, qualified respondents who represent the target of interest to log on to conferencing software at a pre-arranged time and to take part in an _________. Some researchers will offer incentives for participating but this raises a number of ethical questions.

a. Automated surveys
b. Online focus group
c. Intangibility
d. Engagement

33. _________ is a term for unprocessed data, it is also known as primary data. It is a relative term _________ can be input to a computer program or used in manual analysis procedures such as gathering statistics from a survey.

a. Product manager
b. Shoppers Food ' Pharmacy
c. Chief marketing officer
d. Raw data

34. A _________ attribute is one that exists in a range of magnitudes, and can therefore be measured. Measurements of any particular _________ property are expressed as a specific quantity, referred to as a unit, multiplied by a number. Examples of physical quantities are distance, mass, and time.

a. Dolly Dimples
b. Lifestyle city
c. BeyondROI
d. Quantitative

35. A _________ is a research instrument consisting of a series of questions and other prompts for the purpose of gathering information from respondents. Although they are often designed for statistical analysis of the responses, this is not always the case. The _________ was invented by Sir Francis Galton.

a. Mystery shopping
b. Mystery shoppers
c. Market research
d. Questionnaire

36. _________ a research method involving the use of questionnaires and/or statistical surveys to gather data about people and their thoughts and behaviours.

a. Control chart
b. Z-test
c. T-test
d. Survey research

37. An _________ is a special-purpose computer system designed to perform one or a few dedicated functions, often with real-time computing constraints. It is usually embedded as part of a complete device including hardware and mechanical parts. In contrast, a general-purpose computer, such as a personal computer, can do many different tasks depending on programming.

a. ADTECH
b. AMAX
c. ACNielsen
d. Embedded system

38. _________ in survey research refers to the ratio of number of people who answered the survey divided by the number of people in the sample. It is usually expressed in the form of a percentage.

Example: if 1,000 surveys were sent by mail, and 257 were successfully completed and returned, then the _________ would be 25.7 %.

a. Reference value
b. Sentence completion tests
c. Response rate
d. Power III

39. _________ is either an activity of a living being (such as a human), consisting of receiving knowledge of the outside world through the senses, or the recording of data using scientific instruments. The term may also refer to any datum collected during this activity.

The scientific method requires _________s of nature to formulate and test hypotheses.

a. ADTECH
b. ACNielsen
c. AMAX
d. Observation

40. _________ are used to collect quantitative information about items in a population. Surveys of human populations and institutions are common in political polling and government, health, social science and marketing research. A survey may focus on opinions or factual information depending on its purpose, and many surveys involve administering questions to individuals.

a. Statistical surveys
b. Convergent
c. BeyondROI
d. Gross Margin Return on Inventory Investment

41. A _________ is an optical machine-readable representation of data. Originally, _________s represented data in the widths (lines) and the spacings of parallel lines and may be referred to as linear or 1D (1 dimensional) barcodes or symbologies. But they also come in patterns of squares, dots, hexagons and other geometric patterns within images termed 2D (2 dimensional) matrix codes or symbologies.

a. Bar code
b. 180SearchAssistant
c. Power III
d. 6-3-5 Brainwriting

42. _________ is a broad label that refers to any individuals or households that use goods and services generated within the economy. The concept of a _________ is used in different contexts, so that the usage and significance of the term may vary.

A _________ is a person who uses any product or service.

a. Power III
b. 6-3-5 Brainwriting
c. Consumer
d. 180SearchAssistant

43. A _________ is a tool used to measure the viewing habits of TV and cable audiences.

The _________ is a 'box', about the size of a paperback book. The box is hooked up to each television set and is accompanied by a remote control unit.

a. Power III
b. 180SearchAssistant
c. 6-3-5 Brainwriting
d. People Meter

44. _________ involves disseminating information about a product, product line, brand, or company. It is one of the four key aspects of the marketing mix. (The other three elements are product marketing, pricing, and distribution). P>_________ is generally sub-divided into two parts:

- Above the line _________: Promotion in the media (e.g. TV, radio, newspapers, Internet and Mobile Phones) in which the advertiser pays an advertising agency to place the ad
- Below the line _________: All other _________. Much of this is intended to be subtle enough for the consumer to be unaware that _________ is taking place. E.g. sponsorship, product placement, endorsements, sales _________, merchandising, direct mail, personal selling, public relations, trade shows

a. Bottling lines
b. Cashmere Agency
c. Davie Brown Index
d. Promotion

45. An _________ or ad agency is a service business dedicated to creating, planning and handling advertising (and sometimes other forms of promotion) for its clients. An ad agency is independent from the client and provides an outside point of view to the effort of selling the client's products or services. An agency can also handle overall marketing and branding strategies and sales promotions for its clients.

a. Advertising research
b. Onsert
c. Openad
d. Advertising agency

46. A _________ is a relatively new executive level position at a corporation, company, organization typically reporting directly to the CEO or board of directors. The _________ is responsible for a brand's image, experience, and promise, and propagating it throughout all aspects of the company. The brand officer oversees marketing, advertising, design, public relations and customer service departments.

a. Financial analyst
b. Chief executive officer
c. Power III
d. Chief brand officer

47. _________ consists of the processes a company uses to track and organize its contacts with its current and prospective customers. _________ software is used to support these processes; information about customers and customer interactions can be entered, stored and accessed by employees in different company departments. Typical _________ goals are to improve services provided to customers, and to use customer contact information for targeted marketing.

a. Demand generation
b. Product bundling
c. Commercialization
d. Customer relationship management

48. Customer _________ consists of the processes a company uses to track and organize its contacts with its current and prospective customers. CRelationship management software is used to support these processes; information about customers and customer interactions can be entered, stored and accessed by employees in different company departments. Typical CRelationship management goals are to improve services provided to customers, and to use customer contact information for targeted marketing.

a. Marketing
b. Relationship management
c. Product bundling
d. Green marketing

49. In statistics, a _________ is an interval estimate of a population parameter. Instead of estimating the parameter by a single value, an interval likely to include the parameter is given. Thus, _________s are used to indicate the reliability of an estimate.

a. T-test
b. Linear regression
c. Sample mean
d. Confidence interval

50. The _________ is an independent agency of the United States government, established in 1914 by the _________ Act. Its principal mission is the promotion of 'consumer protection' and the elimination and prevention of what regulators perceive to be harmfully 'anti-competitive' business practices, such as coercive monopoly.

The _________ Act was one of President Wilson's major acts against trusts.

a. Power III
b. 180SearchAssistant
c. Federal Trade Commission
d. 6-3-5 Brainwriting

51. A _________ is an explicit set of requirements to be satisfied by a material, product, or service.

In engineering, manufacturing, and business, it is vital for suppliers, purchasers, and users of materials, products, or services to understand and agree upon all requirements. A _________ is a type of a standard which is often referenced by a contract or procurement document.

a. Product development
b. Product optimization
c. New product development
d. Specification

52. An _________ is the manufacturing of a good or service within a category. Although _________ is a broad term for any kind of economic production, in economics and urban planning _________ is a synonym for the secondary sector, which is a type of economic activity involved in the manufacturing of raw materials into goods and products.

There are four key industrial economic sectors: the primary sector, largely raw material extraction industries such as mining and farming; the secondary sector, involving refining, construction, and manufacturing; the tertiary sector, which deals with services (such as law and medicine) and distribution of manufactured goods; and the quaternary sector, a relatively new type of knowledge _________ focusing on technological research, design and development such as computer programming, and biochemistry.

a. ACNielsen
b. ADTECH
c. AMAX
d. Industry

53. The general definition of an _________ is an evaluation of a person, organization, system, process, project or product. _________s are performed to ascertain the validity and reliability of information; also to provide an assessment of a system's internal control. The goal of an _________ is to express an opinion on the person/organization/system (etc) in question, under evaluation based on work done on a test basis.

a. AMAX
b. ADTECH
c. ACNielsen
d. Audit

1. _________ is an advertisement in which a particular product specifically mentions a competitor by name for the express purpose of showing why the competitor is inferior to the product naming it.

This should not be confused with parody advertisements, where a fictional product is being advertised for the purpose of poking fun at the particular advertisement, nor should it be confused with the use of a coined brand name for the purpose of comparing the product without actually naming an actual competitor. ('Wikipedia tastes better and is less filling than the Encyclopedia Galactica.')

In the 1980s, during what has been referred to as the cola wars, soft-drink manufacturer Pepsi ran a series of advertisements where people, caught on hidden camera, in a blind taste test, chose Pepsi over rival Coca-Cola.

a. GL-70
b. Cost per conversion
c. Heavy-up
d. Comparative advertising

2. A _________ is a collection of symbols, experiences and associations connected with a product, a service, a person or any other artifact or entity.

_________s have become increasingly important components of culture and the economy, now being described as 'cultural accessories and personal philosophies'.

Some people distinguish the psychological aspect of a _________ from the experiential aspect.

a. Brand
b. Brandable software
c. Store brand
d. Brand equity

3. _________ is a form of communication that typically attempts to persuade potential customers to purchase or to consume more of a particular brand of product or service. 'While now central to the contemporary global economy and the reproduction of global production networks, it is only quite recently that _________ has been more than a marginal influence on patterns of sales and production. The formation of modern _________ was intimately bound up with the emergence of new forms of monopoly capitalism around the end of the 19th and beginning of the 20th century as one element in corporate strategies to create, organize and where possible control markets, especially for mass produced consumer goods.

a. ACNielsen
b. ADTECH
c. AMAX
d. Advertising

4. _________, in microeconomics, are the cost advantages that a business obtains due to expansion. They are factors that cause a producer's average cost per unit to fall as output rises. Diseconomies of scale are the opposite.

a. ACNielsen
b. AMAX
c. Economies of scale
d. ADTECH

5. There are many important decisions about product and service development and marketing. In the process of product development and marketing we should focus on strategic decisions about product attributes, product branding, product packaging, product labeling and product support services. But product strategy also calls for building a _________.

a. Pinstorm
b. Macromarketing
c. Technology acceptance model
d. Product line

6. _________ is anything that is intended to save time, energy or frustration. A _________ store at a petrol station, for example, sells items that have nothing to do with gasoline/petrol, but it saves the consumer from having to go to a grocery store. '_________' is a very relative term and its meaning tends to change over time.

a. MaxDiff
b. Marketing buzz
c. Convenience
d. Demographic profile

7. An _________ is an unplanned or otherwise spontaneous purchase. One who tends to make such purchases is referred to as an impulse purchaser or impulse buyer.

Marketers and retailers tend to exploit these impulses which are tied to the basic want for instant gratification.

a. ACNielsen
b. ADTECH
c. AMAX
d. Impulse purchase

8. _________ is the examining of goods or services from retailers with the intent to purchase at that time. _________ is an activity of selection and/or purchase. In some contexts it is considered a leisure activity as well as an economic one.

a. Khodebshchik
b. Hawkers
c. Discount store
d. Shopping

9. _________ is defined by the American _________ Association as the activity, set of institutions, and processes for creating, communicating, delivering, and exchanging offerings that have value for customers, clients, partners, and society at large. The term developed from the original meaning which referred literally to going to market, as in shopping, or going to a market to sell goods or services.

_________ practice tends to be seen as a creative industry, which includes advertising, distribution and selling.

a. Marketing myopia
b. Customer acquisition management
c. Product naming
d. Marketing

10. A _________ is a relatively new executive level position at a corporation, company, organization typically reporting directly to the CEO or board of directors. The _________ is responsible for a brand's image, experience, and promise, and propagating it throughout all aspects of the company. The brand officer oversees marketing, advertising, design, public relations and customer service departments.

a. Chief executive officer
b. Financial analyst
c. Power III
d. Chief brand officer

11. In economics, _________ is the desire to own something and the ability to pay for it. The term _________ signifies the ability or the willingness to buy a particular commodity at a given point of time .

.

a. Market system
b. Demand
c. Market dominance
d. Discretionary spending

12. _________ is a term in economics, where demand for one good or service occurs as a result of demand for another. This may occur as the former is a part of production of the second. For example, demand for coal leads to _________ for mining, as coal must be mined for coal to be consumed.

a. Derived demand
b. 6-3-5 Brainwriting
c. Power III
d. 180SearchAssistant

13. _________ is one of the four Ps of the marketing mix. The other three aspects are product, promotion, and place. It is also a key variable in microeconomic price allocation theory.

a. Competitor indexing
b. Relationship based pricing
c. Price
d. Pricing

14. _________ is a broad label that refers to any individuals or households that use goods and services generated within the economy. The concept of a _________ is used in different contexts, so that the usage and significance of the term may vary.

A _________ is a person who uses any product or service.

a. 180SearchAssistant
b. 6-3-5 Brainwriting
c. Power III
d. Consumer

15. _________ is the study of when, why, how, where and what people do or do not buy products. It blends elements from psychology, sociology,social psychology, anthropology and economics. It attempts to understand the buyer decision making process, both individually and in groups. It studies characteristics of individual consumers such as demographics and behavioural variables in an attempt to understand people's wants. It also tries to assess influences on the consumer from groups such as family, friends, reference groups, and society in general.

a. Consumer behavior
b. Consumer confidence
c. Communal marketing
d. Multidimensional scaling

16. In economics, the _________ can be defined as the graph depicting the relationship between the price of a certain commodity, and the amount of it that consumers are willing and able to purchase at that given price. It is a graphic representation of a demand schedule The _________ for all consumers together follows from the _________ of every individual consumer: the individual demands at each price are added together.

_________s are used to estimate behaviors in competitive markets, and are often combined with supply curves to estimate the equilibrium price (the price at which sellers together are willing to sell the same amount as buyers together are willing to buy, also known as market clearing price) and the equilibrium quantity (the amount of that good or service that will be produced and bought without surplus/excess supply or shortage/excess demand) of that market.

a. Power III
b. 6-3-5 Brainwriting
c. 180SearchAssistant
d. Demand curve

17. In economics, _________ is the ratio of the percent change in one variable to the percent change in another variable. It is a tool for measuring the responsiveness of a function to changes in parameters in a relative way. Commonly analyzed are _________ of substitution, price and wealth.

a. Opinion leadership
b. Intellectual property
c. Elasticity
d. ACNielsen

18. Price _________ is defined as the measure of responsiveness in the quantity demanded for a commodity as a result of change in price of the same commodity. It is a measure of how consumers react to a change in price. In other words, it is percentage change in quantity demanded as per the percentage change in price of the same commodity.
    a. AMAX
    b. ACNielsen
    c. Elasticity of demand
    d. ADTECH

19. In accounting, _________ has a very specific meaning. It is an outflow of cash or other valuable assets from a person or company to another person or company. This outflow of cash is generally one side of a trade for products or services that have equal or better current or future value to the buyer than to the seller.
    a. AMAX
    b. Expense
    c. ACNielsen
    d. ADTECH

20. A _________ is something that is acted upon or used by or by human labour or industry, for use as a building material to create some product or structure. Often the term is used to denote material that came from nature and is in an unprocessed or minimally processed state. Iron ore, logs, and crude oil, would be examples.
    a. Power III
    b. 6-3-5 Brainwriting
    c. 180SearchAssistant
    d. Raw material

21. _________ are infrequent, technical, or unique functions performed by independent contractors or consultants whose occupation is the rendering of such services. Examples of _________ contracts include: accountants, actuaries, appraisers, archaeologists, architects, attorneys, brokerage firms, business consultants, business development managers, copywriters, engineers, law firms, physicians, public relations professionals, recruiters, researchers, real estate brokers, translators, software engineers and web designers. While not limited to licentiates (individuals holding professional licenses), the services are considered 'professional' and the contract may run to partnerships, firms, or corporations as well as to individuals.
    a. Spokesperson
    b. Professional services
    c. 180SearchAssistant
    d. Power III

22. In some countries, notably the United States, a trademark used to identify a service rather than a product is called a _________ or servicemark. When a _________ is federally registered, the standard registration symbol Â® or 'Reg U.S. Pat ' TM Off' may be used (the same symbol is used to mark registered trademarks.) Before it is registered, it is common practice (but has no legal standing) to use the _________ symbol â„ (a superscript '_________'.)
    a. Trespass to land
    b. Screener
    c. Trademark classification
    d. Service mark

23. A _________ or trade mark, identified by the symbols â„¢ (not yet registered) and Â® (registered) business organization or other legal entity to identify that the products and/or services to consumers with which the _________ appears originate from a unique source of origin, and to distinguish its products or services from those of other entities. A _________ is a type of intellectual property, and typically a name, word, phrase, logo, symbol, design, image, or a combination of these elements. There is also a range of non-conventional _________s comprising marks which do not fall into these standard categories.
    a. Power III
    b. Risk management
    c. 180SearchAssistant
    d. Trademark

24. _________ in organizations and public policy is both the organizational process of creating and maintaining a plan; and the psychological process of thinking about the activities required to create a desired goal on some scale. As such, it is a fundamental property of intelligent behavior. This thought process is essential to the creation and refinement of a plan, or integration of it with other plans, that is, it combines forecasting of developments with the preparation of scenarios of how to react to them.

a. Planning
b. 180SearchAssistant
c. Power III
d. 6-3-5 Brainwriting

25. _________ is marketing based on relationship and value. It may be used to market a service or a product.

Marketing a service-base business is different from marketing a goods-base business.

a. Power III
b. 6-3-5 Brainwriting
c. 180SearchAssistant
d. Services Marketing

26. A _________ is a plan of action designed to achieve a particular goal.

_________ is different from tactics. In military terms, tactics is concerned with the conduct of an engagement while _________ is concerned with how different engagements are linked.

a. 6-3-5 Brainwriting
b. 180SearchAssistant
c. Power III
d. Strategy

27. _________ refers to the marketing effects or outcomes that accrue to a product with its brand name compared with those that would accrue if the same product did not have the brand name . And, at the root of these marketing effects is consumers' knowledge. In other words, consumers' knowledge about a brand makes manufacturers/advertisers respond differently or adopt appropriately adapt measures for the marketing of the brand .

a. Brand aversion
b. Brand image
c. Product extension
d. Brand equity

28. _________ is difficult to define. For example, in 1952, Alfred Kroeber and Clyde Kluckhohn compiled a list of 164 definitions of '_________' in _________: A Critical Review of Concepts and Definitions. However, the word '_________' is most commonly used in three basic senses:

- excellence of taste in the fine arts and humanities
- an integrated pattern of human knowledge, belief, and behavior that depends upon the capacity for symbolic thought and social learning
- the set of shared attitudes, values, goals, and practices that characterizes an institution, organization or group.

When the concept first emerged in eighteenth- and nineteenth-century Europe, it connoted a process of cultivation or improvement, as in agriculture or horticulture. In the nineteenth century, it came to refer first to the betterment or refinement of the individual, especially through education, and then to the fulfillment of national aspirations or ideals.

a. African Americans
b. Albert Einstein
c. AStore
d. Culture

29. _________ can be defined as the idea generation, concept development, testing and manufacturing or implementation of a physical object or service. _________ers conceptualize and evaluate ideas, making them tangible through products in a more systematic approach. The role of a _________er encompasses many characteristics of the marketing manager, product manager, industrial designer and design engineer.

a. African Americans
b. Albert Einstein
c. AStore
d. Product design

30. The United States _________ is the government agency that is responsible for the United States Census. It also gathers other national demographic and economic data.

a. 6-3-5 Brainwriting
b. Power III
c. 180SearchAssistant
d. Census Bureau

31. A _________ product is an imitation which infringes upon a production monopoly held by either a state or corporation. Goods are produced with the intent to bypass this monopoly and thus take advantage of the established worth of the previous product. The word _________ frequently describes both the forgeries of currency and documents, as well as the imitations of clothing, software, pharmaceuticals, watches, electronics, and company logos and brands.

a. Power III
b. 180SearchAssistant
c. Counterfeit
d. 6-3-5 Brainwriting

32. An _________ or ad agency is a service business dedicated to creating, planning and handling advertising (and sometimes other forms of promotion) for its clients. An ad agency is independent from the client and provides an outside point of view to the effort of selling the client's products or services. An agency can also handle overall marketing and branding strategies and sales promotions for its clients.

a. Openad
b. Advertising research
c. Onsert
d. Advertising agency

33. Consumer market research is a form of applied sociology that concentrates on understanding the behaviours, whims and preferences, of consumers in a market-based economy, and aims to understand the effects and comparative success of marketing campaigns. The field of consumer _________ as a statistical science was pioneered by Arthur Nielsen with the founding of the ACNielsen Company in 1923 .

Thus _________ is the systematic and objective identification, collection, analysis, and dissemination of information for the purpose of assisting management in decision making related to the identification and solution of problems and opportunities in marketing.

a. Marketing research
b. Marketing research process
c. Logit analysis
d. Focus group

34. A _________ is a type of wholesale merchant business that buys goods and bulk products from importers, other wholesalers and then sells to retailers. _________s can deal in any commodity destined for the retail market. Typical categories are food, lumber, hardware, fuel, and textiles.

a. Refusal to deal
b. Tacit collusion
c. Chief privacy officer
d. Jobbing house

35. The brand name of a product that is distributed nationally under a brand name owned by the producer or distributor, as opposed to local brands (products distributed only in some areas of the country), and private label brands (products that carry the brand of the retailer rather than the producer.)

_________s must compete with local and private brands._________s are produced by ,widely distuted by, and carry the name of the manufacturer.

- Local brands may appeal to those consumers who favor small, local producers over large national or global producers, and may be willing to pay a premium to 'buy local'

- The private label producer can offer lower prices because they avoid the cost of marketing and advertising to create and protect the brand. In North America, large retailers such as Loblaws, Walgreen and Wal-Mart all offer private label products.

a. National brand
b. Specialty catalogs
c. Market intelligence
d. Line extension

36. _________ is when a large distribution channel member (usually a retailer), buys from a manufacturer in bulk and puts its own name on the product. This strategy is only practical when the retailer does very high levels of volume. The advantages to the retailer are:

- more freedom and flexibility in pricing
- more control over product attributes and quality
- higher margins (or lower selling price)
- eliminates much of the manufacturer's promotional costs

The advantages to the manufacturer are:

- reduced promotional costs
- stability of sales volume (at least while the contract is operative)

- Kumar, Nirmalya; Steenkamp, Jan-Benedict E.M., Private Label Strategy - How to Meet the Store Brand Challenge. Harvard Business Press 2007

- private label
- brand management
- brand
- product management
- marketing

.

a. Promotion
b. Rural market
c. Customization
d. Private branding

37. _________ is one of the four elements of marketing mix. An organization or set of organizations (go-betweens) involved in the process of making a product or service available for use or consumption by a consumer or business user.

The other three parts of the marketing mix are product, pricing, and promotion.

a. Comparison-Shopping agent
b. Japan Advertising Photographers' Association
c. Better Living Through Chemistry
d. Distribution

38. The U.S. _________ is an agency of the United States Department of Health and Human Services and is responsible for regulating and supervising the safety of foods, dietary supplements, drugs, vaccines, biological medical products, blood products, medical devices, radiation-emitting devices, veterinary products, and cosmetics. The FDA also enforces section 361 of the Public Health Service Act and the associated regulations, including sanitation requirements on interstate travel as well as specific rules for control of disease on products ranging from pet turtles to semen donations for assisted reproductive medicine techniques.

The FDA is an agency within the United States Department of Health and Human Services responsible for protecting and promoting the nation's public health.

a. 180SearchAssistant
b. Power III
c. 6-3-5 Brainwriting
d. Food and Drug Administration

39. The _________ is an independent agency of the United States government, established in 1914 by the _________ Act. Its principal mission is the promotion of 'consumer protection' and the elimination and prevention of what regulators perceive to be harmfully 'anti-competitive' business practices, such as coercive monopoly.

The _________ Act was one of President Wilson's major acts against trusts.

a. Federal Trade Commission
b. 6-3-5 Brainwriting
c. 180SearchAssistant
d. Power III

40. An _________ is quite usually a standard guarantee from the seller of a product that specifies the extent to which the quality or performance of the product is assured and states the conditions under which the product can be returned, replaced, or repaired. It is often given in the form of a specific, written 'Warranty' document. However, a warranty may also arise by operation of law based upon the seller's description of the goods, and perhaps their source and quality, and any material deviation from that specification would violate the guarantee.

a. Express warranty
b. Energy Star
c. Imperial Group v. Philip Morris
d. Office for Harmonization in the Internal Market

41. A _________ is an explicit set of requirements to be satisfied by a material, product, or service.

In engineering, manufacturing, and business, it is vital for suppliers, purchasers, and users of materials, products, or services to understand and agree upon all requirements. A _________ is a type of a standard which is often referenced by a contract or procurement document.

a. New product development
b. Product optimization
c. Product development
d. Specification

1. _________ is the realization of an application idea, model, design, specification, standard, algorithm an _________ is a realization of a technical specification or algorithm as a program, software component, or other computer system. Many _________s may exist for a given specification or standard.

a. AMAX
b. ADTECH
c. ACNielsen
d. Implementation

2. In business and engineering, _________ is the term used to describe the complete process of bringing a new product or service to market. There are two parallel paths involved in the _________ process: one involves the idea generation, product design, and detail engineering; the other involves market research and marketing analysis. Companies typically see _________ as the first stage in generating and commercializing new products within the overall strategic process of product life cycle management used to maintain or grow their market share.

a. Specification
b. New product development
c. Product development
d. Product optimization

3. In business and engineering, new _________ is the term used to describe the complete process of bringing a new product or service to market. There are two parallel paths involved in the Nproduct development process: one involves the idea generation, product design, and detail engineering; the other involves market research and marketing analysis. Companies typically see new _________ as the first stage in generating and commercializing new products within the overall strategic process of product life cycle management used to maintain or grow their market share.

a. New product screening
b. Product development
c. Specification tree
d. New product development

4. _________ is a form of communication that typically attempts to persuade potential customers to purchase or to consume more of a particular brand of product or service. 'While now central to the contemporary global economy and the reproduction of global production networks, it is only quite recently that _________ has been more than a marginal influence on patterns of sales and production. The formation of modern _________ was intimately bound up with the emergence of new forms of monopoly capitalism around the end of the 19th and beginning of the 20th century as one element in corporate strategies to create, organize and where possible control markets, especially for mass produced consumer goods.

a. ACNielsen
b. Advertising
c. AMAX
d. ADTECH

5. The break-even point for a product is the point where total revenue received equals the total costs associated with the sale of the product (TR=TC.) A break-even point is typically calculated in order for businesses to determine if it would be profitable to sell a proposed product, as opposed to attempting to modify an existing product instead so it can be made lucrative. _________ can also be used to analyse the potential profitability of an expenditure in a sales-based business.

In _________, margin of safety is how much output or sales level can fall before a business reaches its break-even point (BEP).

a. Price skimming
b. Break even analysis
c. Contribution margin-based pricing
d. Pay Per Sale

6. An _________ or ad agency is a service business dedicated to creating, planning and handling advertising (and sometimes other forms of promotion) for its clients. An ad agency is independent from the client and provides an outside point of view to the effort of selling the client's products or services. An agency can also handle overall marketing and branding strategies and sales promotions for its clients.

a. Advertising research
b. Openad
c. Onsert
d. Advertising agency

7. A _________ is a relatively new executive level position at a corporation, company, organization typically reporting directly to the CEO or board of directors. The _________ is responsible for a brand's image, experience, and promise, and propagating it throughout all aspects of the company. The brand officer oversees marketing, advertising, design, public relations and customer service departments.

a. Financial analyst
b. Chief executive officer
c. Power III
d. Chief brand officer

8. _________ is defined by the American _________ Association as the activity, set of institutions, and processes for creating, communicating, delivering, and exchanging offerings that have value for customers, clients, partners, and society at large. The term developed from the original meaning which referred literally to going to market, as in shopping, or going to a market to sell goods or services.

_________ practice tends to be seen as a creative industry, which includes advertising, distribution and selling.

a. Marketing myopia
b. Marketing
c. Product naming
d. Customer acquisition management

9. _________ Management is the succession of strategies used by management as a product goes through its _________. The conditions in which a product is sold changes over time and must be managed as it moves through its succession of stages.

The _________ goes through many phases, involves many professional disciplines, and requires many skills, tools and processes.

a. Supplier diversity
b. Customer satisfaction
c. Chain stores
d. Product life cycle

10. A _________ is a collection of symbols, experiences and associations connected with a product, a service, a person or any other artifact or entity.

_________s have become increasingly important components of culture and the economy, now being described as 'cultural accessories and personal philosophies'.

Some people distinguish the psychological aspect of a _________ from the experiential aspect.

a. Brandable software
b. Brand
c. Store brand
d. Brand equity

11. Competitiveness is a comparative concept of the ability and performance of a firm, sub-sector or country to sell and supply goods and/or services in a given market. Although widely used in economics and business management, the usefulness of the concept, particularly in the context of national competitiveness, is vigorously disputed by economists, such as Paul Krugman .

The term may also be applied to markets, where it is used to refer to the extent to which the market structure may be regarded as perfectly _________.

a. Customs union
b. Geographical pricing
c. Free trade zone
d. Competitive

12. A _________ is a plan of action designed to achieve a particular goal.

_________ is different from tactics. In military terms, tactics is concerned with the conduct of an engagement while _________ is concerned with how different engagements are linked.

a. Power III
b. 6-3-5 Brainwriting
c. Strategy
d. 180SearchAssistant

13. _________ involves disseminating information about a product, product line, brand, or company. It is one of the four key aspects of the marketing mix. (The other three elements are product marketing, pricing, and distribution). P>_________ is generally sub-divided into two parts:

- Above the line _________: Promotion in the media (e.g. TV, radio, newspapers, Internet and Mobile Phones) in which the advertiser pays an advertising agency to place the ad
- Below the line _________: All other _________. Much of this is intended to be subtle enough for the consumer to be unaware that _________ is taking place. E.g. sponsorship, product placement, endorsements, sales _________, merchandising, direct mail, personal selling, public relations, trade shows

a. Davie Brown Index
b. Cashmere Agency
c. Promotion
d. Bottling lines

14. In grammar, the _________ is the form of an adjective or adverb which denotes the degree or grade by which a person, thing and is used in this context with a subordinating conjunction, such as than, as...as, etc.

The structure of a _________ in English consists normally of the positive form of the adjective or adverb, plus the suffix -er e.g. 'he is taller than his father is', or 'the village is less picturesque than the town nearby'.

a. Power III
b. Comparative
c. 6-3-5 Brainwriting
d. 180SearchAssistant

15. A _________ product is an imitation which infringes upon a production monopoly held by either a state or corporation. Goods are produced with the intent to bypass this monopoly and thus take advantage of the established worth of the previous product. The word _________ frequently describes both the forgeries of currency and documents, as well as the imitations of clothing, software, pharmaceuticals, watches, electronics, and company logos and brands.

a. 6-3-5 Brainwriting
b. Counterfeit
c. Power III
d. 180SearchAssistant

16. A _________ is a set of exclusive rights granted by a State to an inventor or his assignee for a limited period of time in exchange for a disclosure of an invention.

The procedure for granting _________s, the requirements placed on the _________ee and the extent of the exclusive rights vary widely between countries according to national laws and international agreements. Typically, however, a _________ application must include one or more claims defining the invention which must be new, inventive, and useful or industrially applicable.

a. Foreign Corrupt Practices Act
b. Patent
c. Reasonable person standard
d. Product liability

17. Consumer market research is a form of applied sociology that concentrates on understanding the behaviours, whims and preferences, of consumers in a market-based economy, and aims to understand the effects and comparative success of marketing campaigns. The field of consumer _________ as a statistical science was pioneered by Arthur Nielsen with the founding of the ACNielsen Company in 1923 .

Thus _________ is the systematic and objective identification, collection, analysis, and dissemination of information for the purpose of assisting management in decision making related to the identification and solution of problems and opportunities in marketing.

a. Logit analysis
b. Focus group
c. Marketing research process
d. Marketing research

18. In economics, _________ is the desire to own something and the ability to pay for it. The term _________ signifies the ability or the willingness to buy a particular commodity at a given point of time .

.

a. Discretionary spending
b. Demand
c. Market system
d. Market dominance

19. A craze is a product, idea, cultural movement, or model that gains popularity among a small section of the populace then quickly migrates to the mainstream. Crazes are characterized by their lightning fast adoption and swift departure from public awareness. Crazes and _________s are also characterized by their unusually high interest and sales figures relative to the time they are active in the marketplace, as compared with other similar products, ideas, cultural movements or models.

a. 6-3-5 Brainwriting
b. 180SearchAssistant
c. Power III
d. Fad

20. The _________ is a marketing term and refers to all of the forces outside of marketing that affect marketing management's ability to build and maintain successful relationships with target customers. The _________ consists of both the macroenvironment and the microenvironment.

The microenvironment refers to the forces that are close to the company and affect its ability to serve its customers.

a. Psychographic
b. Business-to-consumer
c. Customer franchise
d. Market environment

21. _________ in organizations and public policy is both the organizational process of creating and maintaining a plan; and the psychological process of thinking about the activities required to create a desired goal on some scale. As such, it is a fundamental property of intelligent behavior. This thought process is essential to the creation and refinement of a plan, or integration of it with other plans, that is, it combines forecasting of developments with the preparation of scenarios of how to react to them.

a. Planning
b. 180SearchAssistant
c. 6-3-5 Brainwriting
d. Power III

22. _________ is one of the four Ps of the marketing mix. The other three aspects are product, promotion, and place. It is also a key variable in microeconomic price allocation theory.

a. Pricing
b. Competitor indexing
c. Relationship based pricing
d. Price

23. _________ consists of the sale of goods or merchandise from a fixed location, such as a department store or kiosk in small or individual lots for direct consumption by the purchaser. _________ may include subordinated services, such as delivery. Purchasers may be individuals or businesses.

a. Charity shop
b. Thrifting
c. Warehouse store
d. Retailing

24. _________ is, in very basic words, a position a firm occupies against its competitors.

According to Michael Porter, the three methods for creating a sustainable _________ are through:

1. Cost leadership - Cost advantage occurs when a firm delivers the same services as its competitors but at a lower cost;

2.

a. Power III
b. 180SearchAssistant
c. 6-3-5 Brainwriting
d. Competitive advantage

25. The _________ is an independent agency of the United States government, established in 1914 by the _________ Act. Its principal mission is the promotion of 'consumer protection' and the elimination and prevention of what regulators perceive to be harmfully 'anti-competitive' business practices, such as coercive monopoly.

The _________ Act was one of President Wilson's major acts against trusts.

a. 6-3-5 Brainwriting
b. Federal Trade Commission
c. Power III
d. 180SearchAssistant

26. A _________ is an explicit set of requirements to be satisfied by a material, product, or service.

In engineering, manufacturing, and business, it is vital for suppliers, purchasers, and users of materials, products, or services to understand and agree upon all requirements. A _________ is a type of a standard which is often referenced by a contract or procurement document.

a. New product development
b. Product optimization
c. Product development
d. Specification

27. _________ is subcontracting a process, such as product design or manufacturing, to a third-party company. The decision to outsource is often made in the interest of lowering cost or making better use of time and energy costs, redirecting or conserving energy directed at the competencies of a particular business, or to make more efficient use of land, labor, capital, (information) technology and resources. _________ became part of the business lexicon during the 1980s.

a. In-house
b. Outsourcing
c. ACNielsen
d. Intangible assets

28. _________ is the process of a product becoming obsolete and/or non-functional after a certain period or amount of use in a way that is planned or designed by the manufacturer. _________ has potential benefits for a producer because the product fails and the consumer is under pressure to purchase again, whether from the same manufacturer (a replacement part or a newer model), or from a competitor which might also rely on _________. The purpose of _________ is to hide the real cost per use from the consumer, and charge a higher price than they would otherwise be willing to pay (or would be unwilling to spend all at once.)

a. 6-3-5 Brainwriting
b. Planned obsolescence
c. Power III
d. 180SearchAssistant

29. _________ in marketing and strategic management is an assessment of the strengths and weaknesses of current and potential competitors. This analysis provides both an offensive and defensive strategic context through which to identify opportunities and threats. Competitor profiling coalesces all of the relevant sources of _________ into one framework in the support of efficient and effective strategy formulation, implementation, monitoring and adjustment.

a. 180SearchAssistant
b. 6-3-5 Brainwriting
c. Power III
d. Competitor analysis

30. _________ is a broad label that refers to any individuals or households that use goods and services generated within the economy. The concept of a _________ is used in different contexts, so that the usage and significance of the term may vary.

A _________ is a person who uses any product or service.

a. Consumer
b. Power III
c. 6-3-5 Brainwriting
d. 180SearchAssistant

31. _________ is the study of when, why, how, where and what people do or do not buy products. It blends elements from psychology, sociology,social psychology, anthropology and economics. It attempts to understand the buyer decision making process, both individually and in groups. It studies characteristics of individual consumers such as demographics and behavioural variables in an attempt to understand people's wants. It also tries to assess influences on the consumer from groups such as family, friends, reference groups, and society in general.

a. Communal marketing
b. Multidimensional scaling
c. Consumer confidence
d. Consumer behavior

32. The _________ was enacted in 1972 by the United States Congress. It established the United States Consumer Product Safety Commission as an independent agency of the United States federal government and defined its basic authority. The act gives CPSC the power to develop safety standards and pursue recalls for products that present unreasonable or substantial risks of injury or death to consumers.

a. 180SearchAssistant
b. Power III
c. 6-3-5 Brainwriting
d. Consumer Product Safety Act

33. The United States _________ is an independent agency of the United States government created in 1972 through the Consumer Product Safety Act to protect 'against unreasonable risks of injuries associated with consumer products.' As of 2006 its acting chairman is Nancy Nord, a Republican. The other commissioner is Thomas Hill Moore, a Democrat. Normally the board has three commissioners.

a. 180SearchAssistant
b. 6-3-5 Brainwriting
c. Consumer Product Safety Commission
d. Power III

34. _________ is the process of using quantitative methods and qualitative methods to evaluate consumer response to a product idea prior to the introduction of a product to the market. It can also be used to generate communication designed to alter consumer attitudes toward existing products. These methods involve the evaluation by consumers of product concepts having certain rational benefits, such as 'a detergent that removes stains but is gentle on fabrics,' or non-rational benefits, such as 'a shampoo that lets you be yourself.' Such methods are commonly referred to as _________ and have been performed using field surveys, personal interviews and focus groups, in combination with various quantitative methods, to generate and evaluate product concepts.

a. Cross tabulation
b. Market analysis
c. Logit analysis
d. Concept testing

35. _________ is systematic determination of merit, worth, and significance of something or someone using criteria against a set of standards. _________ often is used to characterize and appraise subjects of interest in a wide range of human enterprises, including the arts, criminal justice, foundations and non-profit organizations, government, health care, and other human services.

Depending on the topic of interest, there are professional groups which look to the quality and rigor of the _________ process.

a. AMAX
b. ACNielsen
c. ADTECH
d. Evaluation

36. A _________ is a form of qualitative research in which a group of people are asked about their attitude towards a product, service, concept, advertisement, idea, or packaging. Questions are asked in an interactive group setting where participants are free to talk with other group members.

Ernest Dichter originated the idea of having a 'group therapy' for products and this process is what became known as a _________.

a. Marketing research process
b. Focus group
c. Logit analysis
d. Cross tabulation

37. _________ is the area of law in which manufacturers, distributors, suppliers, retailers, and others who make products available to the public are held responsible for the injuries those products cause.

In the United States, the claims most commonly associated with _________ are negligence, strict liability, breach of warranty, and various consumer protection claims. The majority of _________ laws are determined at the state level and vary widely from state to state.

a. Product liability
b. Mediation
c. Registered trademark symbol
d. Trespass to land

38. _________ is the process of filtering or screening new product developments before they enter the stage gate process and start to consume significant resources. The Stage-Gate process was created by Dr. Robert Cooper and is a method described by Cooper and Kleinshmidt of a systematic moving of a new product through various stages from the screening process to product launch.

The screening stage is one that permits new product opportunities to be rejected early in the stage gate process.

a. Product development
b. Specification tree
c. New product screening
d. Specification

39. A _________ is the distribution (whether public or private) of an initial or upgraded version of a computer software product. The software engineers and company doing the work decide on how to distribute the program or system, or changes to that program or system. Software patches are one method of distributing the changes, as are downloads and compact discs.

a. Power III
b. 6-3-5 Brainwriting
c. 180SearchAssistant
d. Software release

40. _________ is the process or cycle of introducing a new product into the market. The actual launch of a new product is the final stage of new product development, and the one where the most money will have to be spent for advertising, sales promotion, and other marketing efforts. In the case of a new consumer packaged good, costs will be at least $ 10 million, but can reach up to $ 200 million.

a. Confusion marketing
b. Customer Interaction Tracker
c. Sweepstakes
d. Commercialization

41. A _________ researches, selects, develops, and places a company's products.

A _________ considers numerous factors such as target demographic, the products offered by the competition, and how well the product fits in with the company's business model. Generally, a _________ manages one or more tangible products.

a. Promotional mix
b. Pick and pack
c. Power III
d. Product manager

42. The phrase _________, according to the Organization for Economic Co-operation and Development, refers to 'creative work undertaken on a systematic basis in order to increase the stock of knowledge, including knowledge of man, culture and society, and the use of this stock of knowledge to devise new applications [sic]' Though it is questionable that an organization is needed for this definition, as it is quite obvious that _________ refers to the _________ of something.

New product design and development is more often than not a crucial factor in the survival of a company. In an industry that is fast changing, firms must continually revise their design and range of products.

a. Research and development

b. 6-3-5 Brainwriting

c. Power III

d. 180SearchAssistant

1. _________ is defined by the American _________ Association as the activity, set of institutions, and processes for creating, communicating, delivering, and exchanging offerings that have value for customers, clients, partners, and society at large. The term developed from the original meaning which referred literally to going to market, as in shopping, or going to a market to sell goods or services.

_________ practice tends to be seen as a creative industry, which includes advertising, distribution and selling.

a. Marketing myopia
b. Customer acquisition management
c. Product naming
d. Marketing

2. A _________ is a party that mediates between a buyer and a seller. A _________ who also acts as a seller or as a buyer becomes a principal party to the deal. Distinguish agent: one who acts on behalf of a principal.

a. Power III
b. 180SearchAssistant
c. Spokesperson
d. Broker

3. In economics, business, retail, and accounting, a _________ is the value of money that has been used up to produce something, and hence is not available for use anymore. In economics, a _________ is an alternative that is given up as a result of a decision. In business, the _________ may be one of acquisition, in which case the amount of money expended to acquire it is counted as _________.

a. Variable cost
b. Fixed costs
c. Transaction cost
d. Cost

4. A _________ or logistics network is the system of organizations, people, technology, activities, information and resources involved in moving a product or service from supplier to customer. _________ activities transform natural resources, raw materials and components into a finished product that is delivered to the end customer. In sophisticated _________ systems, used products may re-enter the _________ at any point where residual value is recyclable.

a. Supply chain
b. Purchasing
c. Demand chain management
d. Supply chain network

5. _________ generally refers to a list of all planned expenses and revenues. It is a plan for saving and spending. A _________ is an important concept in microeconomics, which uses a _________ line to illustrate the trade-offs between two or more goods.

a. Power III
b. 6-3-5 Brainwriting
c. Budget
d. 180SearchAssistant

6. _________ is one of the four elements of marketing mix. An organization or set of organizations (go-betweens) involved in the process of making a product or service available for use or consumption by a consumer or business user.

The other three parts of the marketing mix are product, pricing, and promotion.

a. Japan Advertising Photographers' Association
b. Comparison-Shopping agent
c. Better Living Through Chemistry
d. Distribution

7. The _________ is the dominant distribution and retail network for North American comic books. It consists of one dominant distributor and the majority of comics specialty stores, as well as other retailers of comic books and related merchandise. The name is no longer a fully accurate description of the model by which it operates, but derives from its original implementation: retailers bypassing existing distributors to make 'direct' purchases from publishers.

a. 180SearchAssistant
b. Direct market
c. Power III
d. 6-3-5 Brainwriting

8. The _________ is a marketing term and refers to all of the forces outside of marketing that affect marketing management's ability to build and maintain successful relationships with target customers. The _________ consists of both the macroenvironment and the microenvironment.

The microenvironment refers to the forces that are close to the company and affect its ability to serve its customers.

a. Market environment
b. Business-to-consumer
c. Psychographic
d. Customer franchise

9. _________ is a mathematical science pertaining to the collection, analysis, interpretation or explanation, and presentation of data. It also provides tools for prediction and forecasting based on data. It is applicable to a wide variety of academic disciplines, from the natural and social sciences to the humanities, government and business.
a. Median
b. Type I error
c. Null hypothesis
d. Statistics

10. _________ are infrequent, technical, or unique functions performed by independent contractors or consultants whose occupation is the rendering of such services. Examples of _________ contracts include: accountants, actuaries, appraisers, archaeologists, architects, attorneys, brokerage firms, business consultants, business development managers, copywriters, engineers, law firms, physicians, public relations professionals, recruiters, researchers, real estate brokers, translators, software engineers and web designers. While not limited to licentiates (individuals holding professional licenses), the services are considered 'professional' and the contract may run to partnerships, firms, or corporations as well as to individuals.
a. Power III
b. Spokesperson
c. 180SearchAssistant
d. Professional services

11. _________ refers to a business or organization attempting to acquire goods or services to accomplish the goals of the enterprise. Though there are several organizations that attempt to set standards in the _________ process, processes can vary greatly between organizations. Typically the word '_________' is not used interchangeably with the word 'procurement', since procurement typically includes Expediting, Supplier Quality, and Traffic and Logistics (T'L) in addition to _________.
a. Drop shipping
b. Supply chain
c. Supply network
d. Purchasing

12. A _________ is a list of the general tasks and responsibilities of a position. Typically, it also includes to whom the position reports, specifications such as the qualifications needed by the person in the job, salary range for the position, etc. A _________ is usually developed by conducting a job analysis, which includes examining the tasks and sequences of tasks necessary to perform the job.
a. Power III
b. 180SearchAssistant
c. Job description
d. 6-3-5 Brainwriting

13. _________ is an advertisement in which a particular product specifically mentions a competitor by name for the express purpose of showing why the competitor is inferior to the product naming it.

This should not be confused with parody advertisements, where a fictional product is being advertised for the purpose of poking fun at the particular advertisement, nor should it be confused with the use of a coined brand name for the purpose of comparing the product without actually naming an actual competitor. ('Wikipedia tastes better and is less filling than the Encyclopedia Galactica.')

In the 1980s, during what has been referred to as the cola wars, soft-drink manufacturer Pepsi ran a series of advertisements where people, caught on hidden camera, in a blind taste test, chose Pepsi over rival Coca-Cola.

a. Heavy-up
b. GL-70
c. Cost per conversion
d. Comparative advertising

14. The _________, a unit of the United States Department of Labor, is the principal fact-finding agency for the U.S. government in the broad field of labor economics and statistics. The BLS is an independent national statistical agency that collects, processes, analyzes, and disseminates essential statistical data to the American public, the U.S. Congress, other Federal agencies, State and local governments, business, and labor representatives. The BLS also serves as a statistical resource to the Department of Labor.

a. Gross national product
b. Consumer Expenditure Survey
c. Power III
d. Bureau of Labor Statistics

15. _________ Management is the succession of strategies used by management as a product goes through its _________. The conditions in which a product is sold changes over time and must be managed as it moves through its succession of stages.

The _________ goes through many phases, involves many professional disciplines, and requires many skills, tools and processes.

a. Supplier diversity
b. Product life cycle
c. Chain stores
d. Customer satisfaction

16. In microeconomics and management, the term _________ describes a style of management control. Vertically integrated companies are united through a hierarchy with a common owner. Usually each member of the hierarchy produces a different product or (market-specific) service, and the products combine to satisfy a common need.

a. Mass customization
b. Power III
c. Vertical integration
d. Flanking marketing warfare strategies

17. The break-even point for a product is the point where total revenue received equals the total costs associated with the sale of the product (TR=TC.) A break-even point is typically calculated in order for businesses to determine if it would be profitable to sell a proposed product, as opposed to attempting to modify an existing product instead so it can be made lucrative. _________ can also be used to analyse the potential profitability of an expenditure in a sales-based business.

In _________, margin of safety is how much output or sales level can fall before a business reaches its break-even point (BEP).

a. Price skimming
b. Break even analysis
c. Pay Per Sale
d. Contribution margin-based pricing

18. In calculus, a function f defined on a subset of the real numbers with real values is called _________, if for all x and y such that $x \leq y$ one has $f(x) \leq f(y)$, so f preserves the order. In layman's terms, the sign of the slope is always positive (the curve tending upwards) or zero (i.e., non-decreasing, or asymptotic, or depicted as a horizontal, flat line) Likewise, a function is called monotonically decreasing (non-increasing) if, whenever $x \leq y$, then $f(x) \geq f(y)$, so it reverses the order.

a. Power III
b. 180SearchAssistant
c. 6-3-5 Brainwriting
d. Monotonic

19. _________ is a branch of philosophy which seeks to address questions about morality, such as how a moral outcome can be achieved in a specific situation (applied _________), how moral values should be determined (normative _________), what moral values people actually abide by (descriptive _________), what the fundamental semantic, ontological, and epistemic nature of _________ or morality is (meta-_________), and how moral capacity or moral agency develops and what its nature is (moral psychology.)

Socrates was one of the first Greek philosophers to encourage both scholars and the common citizen to turn their attention from the outside world to the condition of man. In this view, Knowledge having a bearing on human life was placed highest, all other knowledge being secondary.

a. ADTECH
b. AMAX
c. Ethics
d. ACNielsen

20. _________ is the term given to food that can be prepared and served very quickly. While any meal with low preparation time can be considered to be _________, typically the term refers to food sold in a restaurant or store with low quality preparation and served to the customer in a packaged form for take-out/take-away. The term '_________' was recognized in a dictionary by Merriam-Webster in 1951.

a. Fast food
b. Power III
c. 180SearchAssistant
d. 6-3-5 Brainwriting

21. _________ is a form of communication that typically attempts to persuade potential customers to purchase or to consume more of a particular brand of product or service. 'While now central to the contemporary global economy and the reproduction of global production networks, it is only quite recently that _________ has been more than a marginal influence on patterns of sales and production. The formation of modern _________ was intimately bound up with the emergence of new forms of monopoly capitalism around the end of the 19th and beginning of the 20th century as one element in corporate strategies to create, organize and where possible control markets, especially for mass produced consumer goods.

a. ADTECH
b. ACNielsen
c. AMAX
d. Advertising

1. _________ is a broad label that refers to any individuals or households that use goods and services generated within the economy. The concept of a _________ is used in different contexts, so that the usage and significance of the term may vary.

A _________ is a person who uses any product or service.

a. 6-3-5 Brainwriting
b. Consumer
c. Power III
d. 180SearchAssistant

2. _________ is one of the four elements of marketing mix. An organization or set of organizations (go-betweens) involved in the process of making a product or service available for use or consumption by a consumer or business user.

The other three parts of the marketing mix are product, pricing, and promotion.

a. Better Living Through Chemistry
b. Comparison-Shopping agent
c. Japan Advertising Photographers' Association
d. Distribution

3. _________ is the management of the flow of goods, information and other resources, including energy and people, between the point of origin and the point of consumption in order to meet the requirements of consumers (frequently, and originally, military organizations.) _________ involves the integration of information, transportation, inventory, warehousing, material-handling, and packaging. _________ is a channel of the supply chain which adds the value of time and place utility.

a. Power III
b. 180SearchAssistant
c. 6-3-5 Brainwriting
d. Logistics

4. _________ is the realization of an application idea, model, design, specification, standard, algorithm an _________ is a realization of a technical specification or algorithm as a program, software component, or other computer system. Many _________s may exist for a given specification or standard.

a. Implementation
b. AMAX
c. ACNielsen
d. ADTECH

5. _________ is the provision of service to customers before, during and after a purchase.

According to Turban et al., '_________ is a series of activities designed to enhance the level of customer satisfaction - that is, the feeling that a product or service has met the customer expectation.'

Its importance varies by product, industry and customer.

a. Customer experience
b. COPC Inc.
c. Facing
d. Customer service

6. _________ is an advertisement in which a particular product specifically mentions a competitor by name for the express purpose of showing why the competitor is inferior to the product naming it.

This should not be confused with parody advertisements, where a fictional product is being advertised for the purpose of poking fun at the particular advertisement, nor should it be confused with the use of a coined brand name for the purpose of comparing the product without actually naming an actual competitor. ('Wikipedia tastes better and is less filling than the Encyclopedia Galactica.')

In the 1980s, during what has been referred to as the cola wars, soft-drink manufacturer Pepsi ran a series of advertisements where people, caught on hidden camera, in a blind taste test, chose Pepsi over rival Coca-Cola.

a. Heavy-up
b. Cost per conversion
c. Comparative advertising
d. GL-70

7. In economics, business, retail, and accounting, a _________ is the value of money that has been used up to produce something, and hence is not available for use anymore. In economics, a _________ is an alternative that is given up as a result of a decision. In business, the _________ may be one of acquisition, in which case the amount of money expended to acquire it is counted as _________.

a. Transaction cost
b. Fixed costs
c. Variable cost
d. Cost

8. In economics, and cost accounting, _________ describes the total economic cost of production and is made up of variable costs, which vary according to the quantity of a good produced and include inputs such as labor and raw materials, plus fixed costs, which are independent of the quantity of a good produced and include inputs (capital) that cannot be varied in the short term, such as buildings and machinery. _________ in economics includes the total opportunity cost of each factor of production in addition to fixed and variable costs.

The rate at which _________ changes as the amount produced changes is called marginal cost.

a. Product proliferation
b. Household production function
c. Hoarding
d. Total cost

9. A _________ is a plan of action designed to achieve a particular goal.

_________ is different from tactics. In military terms, tactics is concerned with the conduct of an engagement while _________ is concerned with how different engagements are linked.

a. 180SearchAssistant
b. 6-3-5 Brainwriting
c. Power III
d. Strategy

10. _________ is subcontracting a process, such as product design or manufacturing, to a third-party company. The decision to outsource is often made in the interest of lowering cost or making better use of time and energy costs, redirecting or conserving energy directed at the competencies of a particular business, or to make more efficient use of land, labor, capital, (information) technology and resources. _________ became part of the business lexicon during the 1980s.

a. In-house
b. ACNielsen
c. Outsourcing
d. Intangible assets

11. _________ is the process of a product becoming obsolete and/or non-functional after a certain period or amount of use in a way that is planned or designed by the manufacturer. _________ has potential benefits for a producer because the product fails and the consumer is under pressure to purchase again, whether from the same manufacturer (a replacement part or a newer model), or from a competitor which might also rely on _________. The purpose of _________ is to hide the real cost per use from the consumer, and charge a higher price than they would otherwise be willing to pay (or would be unwilling to spend all at once.)

a. Power III
b. 180SearchAssistant
c. Planned obsolescence
d. 6-3-5 Brainwriting

12. _________ is a form of communication that typically attempts to persuade potential customers to purchase or to consume more of a particular brand of product or service. 'While now central to the contemporary global economy and the reproduction of global production networks, it is only quite recently that _________ has been more than a marginal influence on patterns of sales and production. The formation of modern _________ was intimately bound up with the emergence of new forms of monopoly capitalism around the end of the 19th and beginning of the 20th century as one element in corporate strategies to create, organize and where possible control markets, especially for mass produced consumer goods.

a. AMAX
b. ADTECH
c. ACNielsen
d. Advertising

13. _________ is an inventory strategy implemented to improve the return on investment of a business by reducing in-process inventory and its associated carrying costs. In order to achieve JIT the process must have signals of what is going on elsewhere within the process. This means that the process is often driven by a series of signals, which can be Kanban , that tell production processes when to make the next part.

a. Personalization
b. Promotion
c. Just-in-time
d. Clutter

14. _________ is defined by the American _________ Association as the activity, set of institutions, and processes for creating, communicating, delivering, and exchanging offerings that have value for customers, clients, partners, and society at large. The term developed from the original meaning which referred literally to going to market, as in shopping, or going to a market to sell goods or services.

_________ practice tends to be seen as a creative industry, which includes advertising, distribution and selling.

a. Marketing myopia
b. Product naming
c. Customer acquisition management
d. Marketing

15. A _________ or logistics network is the system of organizations, people, technology, activities, information and resources involved in moving a product or service from supplier to customer. _________ activities transform natural resources, raw materials and components into a finished product that is delivered to the end customer. In sophisticated _________ systems, used products may re-enter the _________ at any point where residual value is recyclable.

a. Supply chain network
b. Demand chain management
c. Purchasing
d. Supply Chain

16. _________ in organizations and public policy is both the organizational process of creating and maintaining a plan; and the psychological process of thinking about the activities required to create a desired goal on some scale. As such, it is a fundamental property of intelligent behavior. This thought process is essential to the creation and refinement of a plan, or integration of it with other plans, that is, it combines forecasting of developments with the preparation of scenarios of how to react to them.

a. 180SearchAssistant
b. Power III
c. 6-3-5 Brainwriting
d. Planning

17. _________ are infrequent, technical, or unique functions performed by independent contractors or consultants whose occupation is the rendering of such services. Examples of _________ contracts include: accountants, actuaries, appraisers, archaeologists, architects, attorneys, brokerage firms, business consultants, business development managers, copywriters, engineers, law firms, physicians, public relations professionals, recruiters, researchers, real estate brokers, translators, software engineers and web designers. While not limited to licentiates (individuals holding professional licenses), the services are considered 'professional' and the contract may run to partnerships, firms, or corporations as well as to individuals.

a. 180SearchAssistant
b. Professional services
c. Spokesperson
d. Power III

18. _________ is marketing based on relationship and value. It may be used to market a service or a product.

Marketing a service-base business is different from marketing a goods-base business.

a. Services Marketing
b. 6-3-5 Brainwriting
c. 180SearchAssistant
d. Power III

19. _________ refers to the structured transmission of data between organizations by electronic means. It is used to transfer electronic documents from one computer system to another (ie) from one trading partner to another trading partner. It is more than mere E-mail; for instance, organizations might replace bills of lading and even checks with appropriate _________ messages.

a. AMAX
b. ACNielsen
c. ADTECH
d. Electronic data interchange

20. _________ refer to a collection of facts usually collected as the result of experience, observation or experiment or a set of premises. This may consist of numbers, words particularly as measurements or observations of a set of variables. _________ are often viewed as a lowest level of abstraction from which information and knowledge are derived.

a. Mean
b. Pearson product-moment correlation coefficient
c. Data
d. Sample size

21. In finance, an _________ is a contract between a buyer and a seller that gives the buyer the right--but not the obligation--to buy or to sell a particular asset (the underlying asset) at a later day at an agreed price. In return for granting the _________, the seller collects a payment (the premium) from the buyer. A call _________ gives the buyer the right to buy the underlying asset; a put _________ gives the buyer of the _________ the right to sell the underlying asset.

a. ACNielsen
b. AMAX
c. ADTECH
d. Option

22. _________ is a mathematical science pertaining to the collection, analysis, interpretation or explanation, and presentation of data. It also provides tools for prediction and forecasting based on data. It is applicable to a wide variety of academic disciplines, from the natural and social sciences to the humanities, government and business.

a. Median
b. Null hypothesis
c. Statistics
d. Type I error

23. A personal and cultural _________ is a relative ethic _________, an assumption upon which implementation can be extrapolated. A _________ system is a set of consistent _________s and measures that is soo not true. A principle _________ is a foundation upon which other _________s and measures of integrity are based.

a. Supreme Court of the United States
b. Perceptual maps
c. Package-on-Package
d. Value

24. _________ is a system of intermodal freight transport using standard intermodal containers that are standardised by the International Organization for Standardization (ISO.) These can be loaded and sealed intact onto container ships, railroad cars, planes, and trucks.

a. Containerization
b. Scientific controls
c. BeyondROI
d. Rebate

25. In economics, _________ is a rise in the general level of prices of goods and services in an economy over a period of time. The term '_________' once referred to increases in the money supply (monetary _________); however, economic debates about the relationship between money supply and price levels have led to its primary use today in describing price _________. Inflation can also be described as a decline in the real value of money--a loss of purchasing power in the medium of exchange which is also the monetary unit of account.

a. ADTECH
b. Industrial organization
c. Inflation
d. ACNielsen

26. _________ consists of the sale of goods or merchandise from a fixed location, such as a department store or kiosk in small or individual lots for direct consumption by the purchaser. _________ may include subordinated services, such as delivery. Purchasers may be individuals or businesses.

a. Warehouse store
b. Thrifting
c. Charity shop
d. Retailing

27. _________, in microeconomics, are the cost advantages that a business obtains due to expansion. They are factors that cause a producer's average cost per unit to fall as output rises. Diseconomies of scale are the opposite.

a. ADTECH
b. ACNielsen
c. AMAX
d. Economies of scale

28. A _________ is a type of business entity in which partners (owners) share with each other the profits or losses of the business undertaking in which all have invested. _________s are often favored over corporations for taxation purposes, as the _________ structure does not generally incur a tax on profits before it is distributed to the partners (i.e. there is no dividend tax levied.) However, depending on the _________ structure and the jurisdiction in which it operates, owners of a _________ may be exposed to greater personal liability than they would as shareholders of a corporation.

a. Brand piracy
b. Partnership
c. Competition law
d. Fair Debt Collection Practices Act

29. _________ is a list for goods and materials held available in stock by a business. It is also used for a list of the contents of a household and for a list for testamentary purposes of the possessions of someone who has died. In accounting _________ is considered an asset.

a. Ending Inventory
b. ACNielsen
c. ADTECH
d. Inventory

30. _________ is the use of an object (typically referred to as an RFID tag) applied to or incorporated into a product, animal, or person for the purpose of identification and tracking using radio waves. Some tags can be read from several meters away and beyond the line of sight of the reader.

Most RFID tags contain at least two parts.

a. 180SearchAssistant
b. Radio-frequency identification
c. Power III
d. 6-3-5 Brainwriting

31. A _________ is a commercial building for storage of goods. _________s are used by manufacturers, importers, exporters, wholesalers, transport businesses, customs, etc. They are usually large plain buildings in industrial areas of cities and towns.

a. 180SearchAssistant
b. Power III
c. 6-3-5 Brainwriting
d. Warehouse

32. A _________ for a set of products is a warehouse or other specialized building, often with refrigeration or air conditioning, which is stocked with products (goods) to be re-distributed to retailers, wholesalers or directly to consumers. A _________ is a principle part, the 'order processing' element, of the entire 'order fulfillment' process. _________s are usually thought of as being 'demand driven'.

a. 6-3-5 Brainwriting
b. 180SearchAssistant
c. Power III
d. Distribution center

1. _________ consists of the sale of goods or merchandise from a fixed location, such as a department store or kiosk in small or individual lots for direct consumption by the purchaser. _________ may include subordinated services, such as delivery. Purchasers may be individuals or businesses.

a. Charity shop
b. Thrifting
c. Retailing
d. Warehouse store

2. _________ is a broad label that refers to any individuals or households that use goods and services generated within the economy. The concept of a _________ is used in different contexts, so that the usage and significance of the term may vary.

A _________ is a person who uses any product or service.

a. Power III
b. 6-3-5 Brainwriting
c. Consumer
d. 180SearchAssistant

3. _________ is the study of when, why, how, where and what people do or do not buy products. It blends elements from psychology, sociology,social psychology, anthropology and economics. It attempts to understand the buyer decision making process, both individually and in groups. It studies characteristics of individual consumers such as demographics and behavioural variables in an attempt to understand people's wants. It also tries to assess influences on the consumer from groups such as family, friends, reference groups, and society in general.

a. Consumer confidence
b. Multidimensional scaling
c. Communal marketing
d. Consumer behavior

4. _________ is defined by the American _________ Association as the activity, set of institutions, and processes for creating, communicating, delivering, and exchanging offerings that have value for customers, clients, partners, and society at large. The term developed from the original meaning which referred literally to going to market, as in shopping, or going to a market to sell goods or services.

_________ practice tends to be seen as a creative industry, which includes advertising, distribution and selling.

a. Product naming
b. Marketing
c. Customer acquisition management
d. Marketing myopia

5. The _________ is a marketing term and refers to all of the forces outside of marketing that affect marketing management's ability to build and maintain successful relationships with target customers. The _________ consists of both the macroenvironment and the microenvironment.

The microenvironment refers to the forces that are close to the company and affect its ability to serve its customers.

a. Psychographic
b. Customer franchise
c. Market environment
d. Business-to-consumer

6. _________ is difficult to define. For example, in 1952, Alfred Kroeber and Clyde Kluckhohn compiled a list of 164 definitions of '_________' in _________: A Critical Review of Concepts and Definitions. However, the word '_________' is most commonly used in three basic senses:

- excellence of taste in the fine arts and humanities
- an integrated pattern of human knowledge, belief, and behavior that depends upon the capacity for symbolic thought and social learning
- the set of shared attitudes, values, goals, and practices that characterizes an institution, organization or group.

When the concept first emerged in eighteenth- and nineteenth-century Europe, it connoted a process of cultivation or improvement, as in agriculture or horticulture. In the nineteenth century, it came to refer first to the betterment or refinement of the individual, especially through education, and then to the fulfillment of national aspirations or ideals.

a. Culture
b. Albert Einstein
c. AStore
d. African Americans

7. _________ in organizations and public policy is both the organizational process of creating and maintaining a plan; and the psychological process of thinking about the activities required to create a desired goal on some scale. As such, it is a fundamental property of intelligent behavior. This thought process is essential to the creation and refinement of a plan, or integration of it with other plans, that is, it combines forecasting of developments with the preparation of scenarios of how to react to them.

a. Planning
b. 6-3-5 Brainwriting
c. 180SearchAssistant
d. Power III

8. In marketing, _________ has come to mean the process by which marketers try to create an image or identity in the minds of their target market for its product, brand, or organization. It is the 'relative competitive comparison' their product occupies in a given market as perceived by the target market.

Re-_________ involves changing the identity of a product, relative to the identity of competing products, in the collective minds of the target market.

a. Moratorium
b. Containerization
c. GE matrix
d. Positioning

9. A _________ is a retail establishment which specializes in selling a wide range of products without a single predominant merchandise line. _________s usually sell products including apparel, furniture, appliances, electronics, and additionally select other lines of products such as paint, hardware, toiletries, cosmetics, photographic equipment, jewelery, toys, and sporting goods. Certain _________s are further classified as discount _________s.

a. 180SearchAssistant
b. Power III
c. Department store
d. 6-3-5 Brainwriting

10. The _________ is generally accepted as the use and specification of the four p's describing the strategic position of a product in the marketplace. One version of the origins of the _________ starts in 1948 when James Culliton said that a marketing decision should be a result of something similar to a recipe. This version continued in 1953 when Neil Borden, in his American Marketing Association presidential address, took the recipe idea one step further and coined the term 'Marketing-Mix'.

a. Power III
b. 6-3-5 Brainwriting
c. Marketing mix
d. 180SearchAssistant

11. A _________ is a commercial building for storage of goods. _________s are used by manufacturers, importers, exporters, wholesalers, transport businesses, customs, etc. They are usually large plain buildings in industrial areas of cities and towns.

a. Power III
b. Warehouse
c. 6-3-5 Brainwriting
d. 180SearchAssistant

12. _________ is a term used in marketing and strategic management to describe a product, service, brand, or company that has such a distinct sustainable competitive advantage that competing firms find it almost impossible to operate profitably in that industry. The existence of a _________ will eliminate almost all market entities, whether real or virtual. Many existing firms will leave the industry, thereby increasing the industry's concentration ratio.

a. Power III
b. 180SearchAssistant
c. 6-3-5 Brainwriting
d. Category killer

13. In commerce, a _________ is a superstore which combines a supermarket and a department store. The result is a very large retail facility which carries an enormous range of products under one roof, including full lines of groceries and general merchandise. In theory, _________s allow customers to satisfy all their routine weekly shopping needs in one trip.

a. Hypermarket
b. 6-3-5 Brainwriting
c. Power III
d. 180SearchAssistant

14. A _________ is a retail store, usually selling a wide variety of merchandise, in which customers pay annual membership fees in order to shop. The clubs are able to keep prices low due to the no-frills format of the stores. In addition, customers are required to buy large, wholesale quantities of the store's products, which makes these clubs attractive to both bargain hunters and small business owners.

a. Self service
b. Power centre
c. Consignment
d. Warehouse club

15. _________ is anything that is intended to save time, energy or frustration. A _________ store at a petrol station, for example, sells items that have nothing to do with gasoline/petrol, but it saves the consumer from having to go to a grocery store. '_________' is a very relative term and its meaning tends to change over time.

a. MaxDiff
b. Convenience
c. Demographic profile
d. Marketing buzz

16. A _________ is a small store or shop that sells candy, ice-cream, soft drinks, lottery tickets, newspapers and magazines, along with a small selection of food and grocery supplies. Stores that are part of gas stations may also sell motor oil, windshield washer fluid, radiator fluid, and maps. Often toiletries and other hygiene products are stocked, and some of these stores also offer money orders and wire transfer services or liquor products.

a. Convenience store
b. 6-3-5 Brainwriting
c. Power III
d. 180SearchAssistant

17. _________ is a sales technique in which a salesperson walks from one door of a house to another trying to sell a product or service to the general public. A variant of this involves cold calling first, when another sales representative attempts to gain agreement that a salesperson should visit. _________ selling is usually conducted in the afternoon hours, when the majority of people are at home.

a. Marketing management
b. Performance-based advertising
c. Fast moving consumer goods
d. Door-to-door

18. _________ commonly refers to the electronic retailing / _________ channels industry, which includes such billion dollar companies as Home shoppingN, QVC, eBay, ShopNBC, Buy.com, and Amazon.com. _________ allows consumers to shop for goods while in the privacy of their own home, as opposed to traditional shopping, which requires you to visit brick and mortar stores and shopping malls.

The _________ / electronic retailing industry was created in 1977 when small market radio talk show host Bob Circosta was asked to sell avocado-green-colored can openers live on the air by station owner Bud Paxson when an advertiser traded 112 units of product instead of paying his advertising bill.

a. Home shopping
b. 180SearchAssistant
c. Power III
d. 6-3-5 Brainwriting

19. _________ is a method of direct marketing in which a salesperson solicits to prospective customers to buy products or services, either over the phone or through a subsequent face to face or Web conferencing appointment scheduled during the call.

_________ can also include recorded sales pitches programmed to be played over the phone via automatic dialing. _________ has come under fire in recent years, being viewed as an annoyance by many.

a. Joe job
b. Phishing
c. Directory Harvest Attack
d. Telemarketing

20. _________ is a form of communication that typically attempts to persuade potential customers to purchase or to consume more of a particular brand of product or service. 'While now central to the contemporary global economy and the reproduction of global production networks, it is only quite recently that _________ has been more than a marginal influence on patterns of sales and production. The formation of modern _________ was intimately bound up with the emergence of new forms of monopoly capitalism around the end of the 19th and beginning of the 20th century as one element in corporate strategies to create, organize and where possible control markets, especially for mass produced consumer goods.

a. Advertising
b. ACNielsen
c. ADTECH
d. AMAX

21. _________ is the examining of goods or services from retailers with the intent to purchase at that time. _________ is an activity of selection and/or purchase. In some contexts it is considered a leisure activity as well as an economic one.

a. Khodebshchik
b. Discount store
c. Hawkers
d. Shopping

22. In economics, business, retail, and accounting, a _________ is the value of money that has been used up to produce something, and hence is not available for use anymore. In economics, a _________ is an alternative that is given up as a result of a decision. In business, the _________ may be one of acquisition, in which case the amount of money expended to acquire it is counted as _________.

a. Variable cost
b. Fixed costs
c. Transaction cost
d. Cost

23. Electronic commerce, commonly known as _________ or eCommerce, consists of the buying and selling of products or services over electronic systems such as the Internet and other computer networks. The amount of trade conducted electronically has grown extraordinarily with wide-spread Internet usage. A wide variety of commerce is conducted in this way, spurring and drawing on innovations in electronic funds transfer, supply chain management, Internet marketing, online transaction processing, electronic data interchange (EDI), inventory management systems, and automated data collection systems.

a. ACNielsen
b. AMAX
c. E-commerce
d. ADTECH

24. _________ is one of the four elements of marketing mix. An organization or set of organizations (go-betweens) involved in the process of making a product or service available for use or consumption by a consumer or business user.

The other three parts of the marketing mix are product, pricing, and promotion.

a. Japan Advertising Photographers' Association
b. Distribution
c. Comparison-Shopping agent
d. Better Living Through Chemistry

25. _________ is the management of the flow of goods, information and other resources, including energy and people, between the point of origin and the point of consumption in order to meet the requirements of consumers (frequently, and originally, military organizations.) _________ involves the integration of information, transportation, inventory, warehousing, material-handling, and packaging. _________ is a channel of the supply chain which adds the value of time and place utility.

a. Power III
b. 6-3-5 Brainwriting
c. 180SearchAssistant
d. Logistics

26. _________ can be defined as the idea generation, concept development, testing and manufacturing or implementation of a physical object or service. _________ers conceptualize and evaluate ideas, making them tangible through products in a more systematic approach. The role of a _________er encompasses many characteristics of the marketing manager, product manager, industrial designer and design engineer.

a. Product design
b. African Americans
c. AStore
d. Albert Einstein

27. A _________ is a plan of action designed to achieve a particular goal.

_________ is different from tactics. In military terms, tactics is concerned with the conduct of an engagement while _________ is concerned with how different engagements are linked.

a. Power III
b. 6-3-5 Brainwriting
c. 180SearchAssistant
d. Strategy

28. _________ refers to the methods, practices and operations conducted to promote and sustain certain categories of commercial activity. The term is understood to have different specific meanings depending on the context. Merchandise is a sale goods at a store

In marketing, one of the definitions of _________ is the practice in which the brand or image from one product or service is used to sell another.

a. Word of mouth
b. New Media Strategies
c. Merchandising
d. Marketing communication

29. _________, in microeconomics, are the cost advantages that a business obtains due to expansion. They are factors that cause a producer's average cost per unit to fall as output rises. Diseconomies of scale are the opposite.

a. ACNielsen
b. AMAX
c. ADTECH
d. Economies of scale

30. The break-even point for a product is the point where total revenue received equals the total costs associated with the sale of the product (TR=TC.) A break-even point is typically calculated in order for businesses to determine if it would be profitable to sell a proposed product, as opposed to attempting to modify an existing product instead so it can be made lucrative. _________ can also be used to analyse the potential profitability of an expenditure in a sales-based business.

In _________, margin of safety is how much output or sales level can fall before a business reaches its break-even point (BEP).

a. Contribution margin-based pricing
b. Pay Per Sale
c. Price skimming
d. Break even analysis

31. A _________ is defined by the International Co-operative Alliance's Statement on the Co-operative Identity as an autonomous association of persons united voluntarily to meet their common economic, social, and cultural needs and aspirations through a jointly-owned and democratically-controlled enterprise. It is a business organization owned and operated by a group of individuals for their mutual benefit. A _________ may also be defined as a business owned and controlled equally by the people who use its services or who work at it.

a. 180SearchAssistant
b. Cooperative
c. Power III
d. 6-3-5 Brainwriting

32. In economics, _________ describes demand that is not very sensitive to a change in price.

a. ACNielsen
b. ADTECH
c. AMAX
d. Inelastic

33. In economics, _________ is the desire to own something and the ability to pay for it. The term _________ signifies the ability or the willingness to buy a particular commodity at a given point of time .

a. Market dominance
b. Discretionary spending
c. Demand
d. Market system

34. _________ is either an activity of a living being (such as a human), consisting of receiving knowledge of the outside world through the senses, or the recording of data using scientific instruments. The term may also refer to any datum collected during this activity.

The scientific method requires _________s of nature to formulate and test hypotheses.

a. ADTECH
b. AMAX
c. Observation
d. ACNielsen

35. An _________ is a special-purpose computer system designed to perform one or a few dedicated functions, often with real-time computing constraints. It is usually embedded as part of a complete device including hardware and mechanical parts. In contrast, a general-purpose computer, such as a personal computer, can do many different tasks depending on programming.

a. AMAX
b. Embedded system
c. ADTECH
d. ACNielsen

36. The _________ is an independent agency of the United States government, established in 1914 by the _________ Act. Its principal mission is the promotion of 'consumer protection' and the elimination and prevention of what regulators perceive to be harmfully 'anti-competitive' business practices, such as coercive monopoly.

The _________ Act was one of President Wilson's major acts against trusts.

a. Power III
b. 6-3-5 Brainwriting
c. 180SearchAssistant
d. Federal Trade Commission

37. A personal and cultural _________ is a relative ethic _________, an assumption upon which implementation can be extrapolated. A _________ system is a set of consistent _________s and measures that is soo not true. A principle _________ is a foundation upon which other _________s and measures of integrity are based.

a. Perceptual maps
b. Supreme Court of the United States
c. Package-on-Package
d. Value

38. _________ refers to the additional value of a commodity over the cost of commodities used to produce it from the previous stage of production. An example is the price of gasoline at the pump over the price of the oil in it. In national accounts used in macroeconomics, it refers to the contribution of the factors of production, i.e., land, labor, and capital goods, to raising the value of a product and corresponds to the incomes received by the owners of these factors. The factors of production provide 'services' which raise the unit price of a product (X) relative to the cost per unit of intermediate goods used up in the production of X. _________ is shared between the factors of production (capital, labor, also human capital), giving rise to issues of distribution.

a. Consumer spending
b. Power III
c. Deregulation
d. Value added

39. A _________ is an explicit set of requirements to be satisfied by a material, product, or service.

In engineering, manufacturing, and business, it is vital for suppliers, purchasers, and users of materials, products, or services to understand and agree upon all requirements. A _________ is a type of a standard which is often referenced by a contract or procurement document.

a. Product development
b. New product development
c. Product optimization
d. Specification

40. _________ is the realization of an application idea, model, design, specification, standard, algorithm an _________ is a realization of a technical specification or algorithm as a program, software component, or other computer system. Many _________s may exist for a given specification or standard.

a. Implementation
b. ADTECH
c. AMAX
d. ACNielsen

41. A _________ is a written document that details the necessary actions to achieve one or more marketing objectives. It can be for a product or service, a brand, or a product line. _________s cover between one and five years.

a. Marketing plan
b. Prosumer
c. Disruptive technology
d. Marketing strategy

42. _________s function as professionals who deal with trade, dealing in commodities that they do not produce themselves, in order to produce profit.

_________s can be of two types:

1. A wholesale _________ operates in the chain between producer and retail _________. Some wholesale _________s only organize the movement of goods rather than move the goods themselves.
2. A retail _________ or retailer, sells commodities to consumers (including businesses.) A shop owner is a retail _________.

A _________ class characterizes many pre-modern societies. Its status can range from high (even achieving titles like that of _________ prince or nabob) to low, such as in Chinese culture, due to the soiling capabilities of profiting from 'mere' trade, rather than from the labor of others reflected in agricultural produce, craftsmanship, and tribute.

In the United States, '_________' is defined (under the Uniform Commercial Code) as any person while engaged in a business or profession or a seller who deals regularly in the type of goods sold.

a. Retail loss prevention
b. Trade credit
c. RFM
d. Merchant

43. _________ is an advertisement in which a particular product specifically mentions a competitor by name for the express purpose of showing why the competitor is inferior to the product naming it.

This should not be confused with parody advertisements, where a fictional product is being advertised for the purpose of poking fun at the particular advertisement, nor should it be confused with the use of a coined brand name for the purpose of comparing the product without actually naming an actual competitor. ('Wikipedia tastes better and is less filling than the Encyclopedia Galactica.')

In the 1980s, during what has been referred to as the cola wars, soft-drink manufacturer Pepsi ran a series of advertisements where people, caught on hidden camera, in a blind taste test, chose Pepsi over rival Coca-Cola.

a. Cost per conversion
b. Heavy-up
c. GL-70
d. Comparative advertising

44. Merchandising refers to the methods, practices and operations conducted to promote and sustain certain categories of commercial activity. The term is understood to have different specific meanings depending on the context. _________ is a sale goods at a store

In marketing, one of the definitions of merchandising is the practice in which the brand or image from one product or service is used to sell another.

a. Merchandise
b. Merchandising
c. Sales promotion
d. New Media Strategies

45. _________ wholesale represents a type of operation within the wholesale sector. Its main features are summarized best by the following definitions:

- _________ is a form of trade in which goods are sold from a wholesale warehouse operated either on a self-service basis, or on the basis of samples (with the customer selecting from specimen articles using a manual or computerized ordering system but not serving himself) or a combination of the two. Customers (retailers, professional users, caterers, institutional buyers, etc.) settle the invoice on the spot and in cash, and carry the goods away themselves.

- Though wholesalers buy primarily from manufacturers and sell mostly to retailers, industrial users and other wholesalers, they also perform many value added functions. The wholesaler, an intermediary, is used based on principles of specialisation and division of labour as well as contractual efficiency. (OECD -Organisation for Economic Cooperation and Development.)

a. Containerization
b. Cash and carry
c. Self branding
d. Davie Brown Index

46. A _________ is a party that mediates between a buyer and a seller. A _________ who also acts as a seller or as a buyer becomes a principal party to the deal. Distinguish agent: one who acts on behalf of a principal.

a. 180SearchAssistant
b. Spokesperson
c. Broker
d. Power III

47. In economics, an _________ is any good or commodity, transported from one country to another country in a legitimate fashion, typically for use in trade. _________ goods or services are provided to foreign consumers by domestic producers. _________ is an important part of international trade.

a. AMAX
b. ADTECH
c. ACNielsen
d. Export

1. In economics, _________ is the desire to own something and the ability to pay for it. The term _________ signifies the ability or the willingness to buy a particular commodity at a given point of time .

.

a. Market system
b. Discretionary spending
c. Demand
d. Market dominance

2. _________ is a term in economics, where demand for one good or service occurs as a result of demand for another. This may occur as the former is a part of production of the second. For example, demand for coal leads to _________ for mining, as coal must be mined for coal to be consumed.

a. Derived demand
b. Power III
c. 6-3-5 Brainwriting
d. 180SearchAssistant

3. _________ is a form of communication that typically attempts to persuade potential customers to purchase or to consume more of a particular brand of product or service. 'While now central to the contemporary global economy and the reproduction of global production networks, it is only quite recently that _________ has been more than a marginal influence on patterns of sales and production. The formation of modern _________ was intimately bound up with the emergence of new forms of monopoly capitalism around the end of the 19th and beginning of the 20th century as one element in corporate strategies to create, organize and where possible control markets, especially for mass produced consumer goods.

a. ADTECH
b. AMAX
c. ACNielsen
d. Advertising

4. _________ is a market coverage strategy in which a firm decides to ignore market segment differences and go after the whole market with one offer.it is type of marketing (or attempting to sell through persuasion) of a product to a wide audience. The idea is to broadcast a message that will reach the largest number of people possible. Traditionally _________ has focused on radio, television and newspapers as the medium used to reach this broad audience.

a. Business-to-consumer
b. Cyberdoc
c. Marketspace
d. Mass marketing

5. _________ involves disseminating information about a product, product line, brand, or company. It is one of the four key aspects of the marketing mix. (The other three elements are product marketing, pricing, and distribution). P>_________ is generally sub-divided into two parts:

- Above the line _________: Promotion in the media (e.g. TV, radio, newspapers, Internet and Mobile Phones) in which the advertiser pays an advertising agency to place the ad
- Below the line _________: All other _________. Much of this is intended to be subtle enough for the consumer to be unaware that _________ is taking place. E.g. sponsorship, product placement, endorsements, sales _________, merchandising, direct mail, personal selling, public relations, trade shows

a. Promotion
b. Davie Brown Index
c. Cashmere Agency
d. Bottling lines

6. _________ is the deliberate attempt to manage the public's perception of a subject. The subjects of _________ include people (for example, politicians and performing artists), goods and services, organizations of all kinds, and works of art or entertainment.

From a marketing perspective, _________ is one component of promotion.

a. Publicity
b. Little value placed on potential benefits
c. Pearson's chi-square
d. Brando

7. _________ is one of the four aspects of promotional mix. (The other three parts of the promotional mix are advertising, personal selling, and publicity/public relations.) Media and non-media marketing communication are employed for a pre-determined, limited time to increase consumer demand, stimulate market demand or improve product availability.

a. Marketing communication
b. New Media Strategies
c. Merchandise
d. Sales promotion

8. In economics, business, retail, and accounting, a _________ is the value of money that has been used up to produce something, and hence is not available for use anymore. In economics, a _________ is an alternative that is given up as a result of a decision. In business, the _________ may be one of acquisition, in which case the amount of money expended to acquire it is counted as _________.

a. Transaction cost
b. Variable cost
c. Fixed costs
d. Cost

9. _________, according to The American Marketing Association, is 'a planning process designed to assure that all brand contacts received by a customer or prospect for a product, service, or organization are relevant to that person and consistent over time.' (Marketing Power Dictionary)

_________ is a term used to describe a holistic approach to marketing. It aims to ensure consistency of message and the complementary use of media. The concept includes online and offline marketing channels.

a. ADTECH
b. ACNielsen
c. AMAX
d. Integrated marketing communications

10. _________ is defined by the American _________ Association as the activity, set of institutions, and processes for creating, communicating, delivering, and exchanging offerings that have value for customers, clients, partners, and society at large. The term developed from the original meaning which referred literally to going to market, as in shopping, or going to a market to sell goods or services.

_________ practice tends to be seen as a creative industry, which includes advertising, distribution and selling.

a. Product naming
b. Customer acquisition management
c. Marketing
d. Marketing myopia

11. _________ is a business discipline which is focused on the practical application of marketing techniques and the management of a firm's marketing resources and activities. Marketing managers are often responsible for influencing the level, timing, and composition of customer demand accepted definition of the term. In part, this is because the role of a marketing manager can vary significantly based on a business' size, corporate culture, and industry context.

a. Performance-based advertising
b. Door-to-door
c. Business structure
d. Marketing management

12. _________ is the practice of managing the flow of information between an organization and its publics. _________ - often referred to as _________ - gains an organization or individual exposure to their audiences using topics of public interest and news items that do not require direct payment. Because _________ places exposure in credible third-party outlets, it offers a third-party legitimacy that advertising does not have.

a. Public relations
b. Power III
c. Graphic communication
d. Symbolic analysis

13. _________ refers to messages and related media used to communicate with a market. Those who practice advertising, branding, direct marketing, graphic design, marketing, packaging, promotion, publicity, sponsorship, public relations, sales, sales promotion and online marketing are termed marketing communicators, _________ managers, or more briefly as marcom managers.

a. Merchandising
b. Sales promotion
c. Merchandise
d. Marketing communication

14. _________ is a business term meaning the market segment to which a particular good or service is marketed. It is mainly defined by age, gender, geography, socio-economic grouping, technographic, or any other combination of demographics. It is generally studied and mapped by an organization through lists and reports containing demographic information that may have an effect on the marketing of key products or services.

a. Market specialization
b. Category Development Index
c. Brando
d. Distribution

15. _________ is the reverse of encoding, which is the process of transforming information from one format into another. Information about _________ can be found in the following:

- Digital-to-analog converter, the use of analog circuit for _________ operations
- Code, a rule for converting a piece of information into another form or representation
- Code (cryptography), a method used to transform a message into an obscured form
- _________
- _________ methods, methods in communication theory for _________ codewords sent over a noisy channel
- Digital signal processing, the study of signals in a digital representation and the processing methods of these signals
- Word _________, the use of phonics to decipher print patterns and translate them into the sounds of language
- deCODE genetics

.

a. 6-3-5 Brainwriting
b. 180SearchAssistant
c. Power III
d. Decoding

16. _________ is the process of transforming information from one format into another. The opposite operation is called decoding.

There are a number of more specific meanings that apply in certain contexts:

- _________ is a basic perceptual process of interpreting incoming stimuli; technically speaking, it is a complex, multi-stage process of converting relatively objective sensory input (e.g., light, sound) into subjectively meaningful experience.
- A content format is a specific _________ format for converting a specific type of data to information.
- Character _________ is a code that pairs a set of natural language characters (such as an alphabet or syllabary) with a set of something else, such as numbers or electrical pulses.
- Text _________ uses a markup language to tag the structure and other features of a text to facilitate processing by computers.
- Semantics _________ of formal language A in formal language B is a method of representing all terms (e.g. programs or descriptions) of language A using language B.
- Electronic _________ transforms a signal into a code optimized for transmission or storage, generally done with a codec.
- Neural _________ is the way in which information is represented in neurons.
- Memory _________ is the process of converting sensations into memories.
- Encryption transforms information for secrecy.

.

a. AMAX
b. ACNielsen
c. ADTECH
d. Encoding

17. _________ in economics and business is the result of an exchange and from that trade we assign a numerical monetary value to a good, service or asset. If I trade 4 apples for an orange, the _________ of an orange is 4 - apples. Inversely, the _________ of an apple is 1/4 oranges.

a. Price
b. Discounts and allowances
c. Contribution margin-based pricing
d. Pricing

18. _________ is a term used in business to indicate a state of intense competitive rivalry accompanied by a multi-lateral series of price reduction. One competitor will lower its price, then others will lower their prices to match. If one of them reduces their price again, a new round of reductions starts.

a. Resale price maintenance
b. Competitor indexing
c. Pricing objectives
d. Price war

19. _________ is difficult to define. For example, in 1952, Alfred Kroeber and Clyde Kluckhohn compiled a list of 164 definitions of '_________' in _________: A Critical Review of Concepts and Definitions. However, the word '_________' is most commonly used in three basic senses:

- excellence of taste in the fine arts and humanities
- an integrated pattern of human knowledge, belief, and behavior that depends upon the capacity for symbolic thought and social learning
- the set of shared attitudes, values, goals, and practices that characterizes an institution, organization or group.

When the concept first emerged in eighteenth- and nineteenth-century Europe, it connoted a process of cultivation or improvement, as in agriculture or horticulture. In the nineteenth century, it came to refer first to the betterment or refinement of the individual, especially through education, and then to the fulfillment of national aspirations or ideals.

a. Albert Einstein
b. AStore
c. African Americans
d. Culture

20. _________ is a branch of philosophy which seeks to address questions about morality, such as how a moral outcome can be achieved in a specific situation (applied _________), how moral values should be determined (normative _________), what moral values people actually abide by (descriptive _________), what the fundamental semantic, ontological, and epistemic nature of _________ or morality is (meta-_________), and how moral capacity or moral agency develops and what its nature is (moral psychology.)

Socrates was one of the first Greek philosophers to encourage both scholars and the common citizen to turn their attention from the outside world to the condition of man. In this view, Knowledge having a bearing on human life was placed highest, all other knowledge being secondary.

a. Ethics
b. ADTECH
c. ACNielsen
d. AMAX

21. An _________ is the manufacturing of a good or service within a category. Although _________ is a broad term for any kind of economic production, in economics and urban planning _________ is a synonym for the secondary sector, which is a type of economic activity involved in the manufacturing of raw materials into goods and products.

There are four key industrial economic sectors: the primary sector, largely raw material extraction industries such as mining and farming; the secondary sector, involving refining, construction, and manufacturing; the tertiary sector, which deals with services (such as law and medicine) and distribution of manufactured goods; and the quaternary sector, a relatively new type of knowledge _________ focusing on technological research, design and development such as computer programming, and biochemistry.

a. AMAX
b. ADTECH
c. Industry
d. ACNielsen

22. _________ is a broad label that refers to any individuals or households that use goods and services generated within the economy. The concept of a _________ is used in different contexts, so that the usage and significance of the term may vary.

A _________ is a person who uses any product or service.

a. 180SearchAssistant
b. Power III
c. Consumer
d. 6-3-5 Brainwriting

23. _________ is the study of when, why, how, where and what people do or do not buy products. It blends elements from psychology, sociology,social psychology, anthropology and economics. It attempts to understand the buyer decision making process, both individually and in groups. It studies characteristics of individual consumers such as demographics and behavioural variables in an attempt to understand people's wants. It also tries to assess influences on the consumer from groups such as family, friends, reference groups, and society in general.

a. Consumer confidence
b. Multidimensional scaling
c. Consumer behavior
d. Communal marketing

24. _________ consists of the processes a company uses to track and organize its contacts with its current and prospective customers. _________ software is used to support these processes; information about customers and customer interactions can be entered, stored and accessed by employees in different company departments. Typical _________ goals are to improve services provided to customers, and to use customer contact information for targeted marketing.

a. Demand generation
b. Product bundling
c. Commercialization
d. Customer relationship management

25. Customer _________ consists of the processes a company uses to track and organize its contacts with its current and prospective customers. CRelationship management software is used to support these processes; information about customers and customer interactions can be entered, stored and accessed by employees in different company departments. Typical CRelationship management goals are to improve services provided to customers, and to use customer contact information for targeted marketing.

a. Marketing
b. Relationship management
c. Green marketing
d. Product bundling

26. _________ is the realization of an application idea, model, design, specification, standard, algorithm an _________ is a realization of a technical specification or algorithm as a program, software component, or other computer system. Many _________s may exist for a given specification or standard.

a. ADTECH
b. ACNielsen
c. AMAX
d. Implementation

27. _________ is one of the four elements of marketing mix. An organization or set of organizations (go-betweens) involved in the process of making a product or service available for use or consumption by a consumer or business user.

The other three parts of the marketing mix are product, pricing, and promotion.

a. Japan Advertising Photographers' Association
b. Comparison-Shopping agent
c. Better Living Through Chemistry
d. Distribution

28. _________ is an ongoing process that occurs strictly within a company or organization whereby the functional process aligns, motivates and empowers employees at all management levels to consistently deliver a satisfying customer experience. According to Burkitt and Zealley, 'the challenge for _________ is not only to get the right messages across, but to embed them in such a way that they both change and reinforce employee behaviour'.

a. Internal marketing
b. ADTECH
c. ACNielsen
d. AMAX

29. _________ is a concept that arose out of the theory of two-step flow of communication propounded by Paul Lazarsfeld and Elihu Katz. This theory is one of several models that try to explain the diffusion of innovations, ideas, or commercial products.

The opinion leader is the agent who is an active media user and who interprets the meaning of media messages or content for lower-end media users.

a. ACNielsen
b. Opinion leadership
c. Elasticity
d. Intellectual property

30. A _________ is a type of website, usually maintained by an individual with regular entries of commentary, descriptions of events, or other material such as graphics or video. Entries are commonly displayed in reverse-chronological order. '_________' can also be used as a verb, meaning to maintain or add content to a _________.

a. Power III
b. 180SearchAssistant
c. Blog
d. 6-3-5 Brainwriting

31. _________ is one of the four Ps of the marketing mix. The other three aspects are product, promotion, and place. It is also a key variable in microeconomic price allocation theory.

a. Relationship based pricing
b. Competitor indexing
c. Price
d. Pricing

32. _________ generally refers to a list of all planned expenses and revenues. It is a plan for saving and spending. A _________ is an important concept in microeconomics, which uses a _________ line to illustrate the trade-offs between two or more goods.

a. Power III
b. 180SearchAssistant
c. 6-3-5 Brainwriting
d. Budget

33. _________ Management is the succession of strategies used by management as a product goes through its _________. The conditions in which a product is sold changes over time and must be managed as it moves through its succession of stages.

The _________ goes through many phases, involves many professional disciplines, and requires many skills, tools and processes.

a. Chain stores
b. Supplier diversity
c. Product life cycle
d. Customer satisfaction

34. _________, in microeconomics, are the cost advantages that a business obtains due to expansion. They are factors that cause a producer's average cost per unit to fall as output rises. Diseconomies of scale are the opposite.

a. ADTECH
b. AMAX
c. ACNielsen
d. Economies of scale

1. _________ is difficult to define. For example, in 1952, Alfred Kroeber and Clyde Kluckhohn compiled a list of 164 definitions of '_________' in _________: A Critical Review of Concepts and Definitions. However, the word '_________' is most commonly used in three basic senses:

- excellence of taste in the fine arts and humanities
- an integrated pattern of human knowledge, belief, and behavior that depends upon the capacity for symbolic thought and social learning
- the set of shared attitudes, values, goals, and practices that characterizes an institution, organization or group.

When the concept first emerged in eighteenth- and nineteenth-century Europe, it connoted a process of cultivation or improvement, as in agriculture or horticulture. In the nineteenth century, it came to refer first to the betterment or refinement of the individual, especially through education, and then to the fulfillment of national aspirations or ideals.

a. African Americans
b. AStore
c. Albert Einstein
d. Culture

2. _________ is a broad label that refers to any individuals or households that use goods and services generated within the economy. The concept of a _________ is used in different contexts, so that the usage and significance of the term may vary.

A _________ is a person who uses any product or service.

a. Power III
b. 6-3-5 Brainwriting
c. 180SearchAssistant
d. Consumer

3. _________ is the study of when, why, how, where and what people do or do not buy products. It blends elements from psychology, sociology,social psychology, anthropology and economics. It attempts to understand the buyer decision making process, both individually and in groups. It studies characteristics of individual consumers such as demographics and behavioural variables in an attempt to understand people's wants. It also tries to assess influences on the consumer from groups such as family, friends, reference groups, and society in general.

a. Communal marketing
b. Consumer confidence
c. Multidimensional scaling
d. Consumer behavior

4. _________ in economics and business is the result of an exchange and from that trade we assign a numerical monetary value to a good, service or asset. If I trade 4 apples for an orange, the _________ of an orange is 4 - apples. Inversely, the _________ of an apple is 1/4 oranges.

a. Contribution margin-based pricing
b. Price
c. Pricing
d. Discounts and allowances

5. _________ occurs when cartels are illegal or overt collusion is absent. Put another way, two firms agree to play a certain strategy without explicitly saying so. This is also known as price leadership, as firms may stay within the law but still tacitly collude by monitoring each other's prices and keeping them the same. Usually, this occurs when a firm emerges to set the general industry price and other firms follow suit. Oligopolists usually try not to engage in price cutting, excessive advertising or other forms of competition.

a. Tacit collusion
b. Teaser rate
c. Chief privacy officer
d. Shop fitting

6. _________ is a form of communication that typically attempts to persuade potential customers to purchase or to consume more of a particular brand of product or service. 'While now central to the contemporary global economy and the reproduction of global production networks, it is only quite recently that _________ has been more than a marginal influence on patterns of sales and production. The formation of modern _________ was intimately bound up with the emergence of new forms of monopoly capitalism around the end of the 19th and beginning of the 20th century as one element in corporate strategies to create, organize and where possible control markets, especially for mass produced consumer goods.

a. AMAX
b. ADTECH
c. Advertising
d. ACNielsen

7. _________ are infrequent, technical, or unique functions performed by independent contractors or consultants whose occupation is the rendering of such services. Examples of _________ contracts include: accountants, actuaries, appraisers, archaeologists, architects, attorneys, brokerage firms, business consultants, business development managers, copywriters, engineers, law firms, physicians, public relations professionals, recruiters, researchers, real estate brokers, translators, software engineers and web designers. While not limited to licentiates (individuals holding professional licenses), the services are considered 'professional' and the contract may run to partnerships, firms, or corporations as well as to individuals.

a. 180SearchAssistant
b. Spokesperson
c. Power III
d. Professional services

8. _________ is the use of an object (typically referred to as an RFID tag) applied to or incorporated into a product, animal, or person for the purpose of identification and tracking using radio waves. Some tags can be read from several meters away and beyond the line of sight of the reader.

Most RFID tags contain at least two parts.

a. 180SearchAssistant
b. Power III
c. 6-3-5 Brainwriting
d. Radio-frequency identification

9. _________ is an advertisement in which a particular product specifically mentions a competitor by name for the express purpose of showing why the competitor is inferior to the product naming it.

This should not be confused with parody advertisements, where a fictional product is being advertised for the purpose of poking fun at the particular advertisement, nor should it be confused with the use of a coined brand name for the purpose of comparing the product without actually naming an actual competitor. ('Wikipedia tastes better and is less filling than the Encyclopedia Galactica.')

In the 1980s, during what has been referred to as the cola wars, soft-drink manufacturer Pepsi ran a series of advertisements where people, caught on hidden camera, in a blind taste test, chose Pepsi over rival Coca-Cola.

a. Cost per conversion
b. GL-70
c. Heavy-up
d. Comparative advertising

10. _________ consists of the processes a company uses to track and organize its contacts with its current and prospective customers. _________ software is used to support these processes; information about customers and customer interactions can be entered, stored and accessed by employees in different company departments. Typical _________ goals are to improve services provided to customers, and to use customer contact information for targeted marketing.

a. Customer relationship management
b. Demand generation
c. Product bundling
d. Commercialization

11. Customer _________ consists of the processes a company uses to track and organize its contacts with its current and prospective customers. CRelationship management software is used to support these processes; information about customers and customer interactions can be entered, stored and accessed by employees in different company departments. Typical CRelationship management goals are to improve services provided to customers, and to use customer contact information for targeted marketing.

a. Marketing
b. Green marketing
c. Relationship management
d. Product bundling

12. _________ is the provision of service to customers before, during and after a purchase.

According to Turban et al., '_________ is a series of activities designed to enhance the level of customer satisfaction - that is, the feeling that a product or service has met the customer expectation.'

Its importance varies by product, industry and customer.

a. COPC Inc.
b. Facing
c. Customer experience
d. Customer service

13. _________ is the set of reasons that determines one to engage in a particular behavior. The term is generally used for human _________ but, theoretically, it can be used to describe the causes for animal behavior as well

a. 180SearchAssistant
b. Power III
c. Role playing
d. Motivation

14. _________ involves disseminating information about a product, product line, brand, or company. It is one of the four key aspects of the marketing mix. (The other three elements are product marketing, pricing, and distribution). P>_________ is generally sub-divided into two parts:

- Above the line _________: Promotion in the media (e.g. TV, radio, newspapers, Internet and Mobile Phones) in which the advertiser pays an advertising agency to place the ad
- Below the line _________: All other _________. Much of this is intended to be subtle enough for the consumer to be unaware that _________ is taking place. E.g. sponsorship, product placement, endorsements, sales _________, merchandising, direct mail, personal selling, public relations, trade shows

a. Cashmere Agency
b. Bottling lines
c. Davie Brown Index
d. Promotion

15. _________ is one of the four aspects of promotional mix. (The other three parts of the promotional mix are advertising, personal selling, and publicity/public relations.) Media and non-media marketing communication are employed for a pre-determined, limited time to increase consumer demand, stimulate market demand or improve product availability.

a. New Media Strategies
b. Merchandise
c. Marketing communication
d. Sales promotion

16. _________ is the practice of individuals including commercial businesses, governments and institutions, facilitating the sale of their products or services to other companies or organizations that in turn resell them, use them as components in products or services they offer _________ is also called business-to-_________ for short. (Note that while marketing to government entities shares some of the same dynamics of organizational marketing, B2G Marketing is meaningfully different.)

a. Disruptive technology
b. Law of disruption
c. Business marketing
d. Mass marketing

17. _________ is a method of direct marketing in which a salesperson solicits to prospective customers to buy products or services, either over the phone or through a subsequent face to face or Web conferencing appointment scheduled during the call.

_________ can also include recorded sales pitches programmed to be played over the phone via automatic dialing. _________ has come under fire in recent years, being viewed as an annoyance by many.

a. Phishing
b. Joe job
c. Directory Harvest Attack
d. Telemarketing

18. _________ is the study of the Earth and its lands, features, inhabitants, and phenomena. A literal translation would be 'to describe or write about the Earth'. The first person to use the word '_________' was Eratosthenes .

a. Power III
b. 6-3-5 Brainwriting
c. Geography
d. 180SearchAssistant

19. _________ is defined by the American _________ Association as the activity, set of institutions, and processes for creating, communicating, delivering, and exchanging offerings that have value for customers, clients, partners, and society at large. The term developed from the original meaning which referred literally to going to market, as in shopping, or going to a market to sell goods or services.

_________ practice tends to be seen as a creative industry, which includes advertising, distribution and selling.

a. Product naming
b. Marketing
c. Customer acquisition management
d. Marketing myopia

20. In artificial intelligence, an _________ is an autonomous entity which observes and acts upon an environment (i.e. it is an agent) and directs its activity towards achieving goals (i.e. it is rational.) _________s may also learn or use knowledge to achieve their goals. They may be very simple or very complex: a reflex machine such as a thermostat is an _________, as is a human being, as is a community of human beings working together towards a goal.

a. ADTECH
b. AMAX
c. Intelligent agent
d. ACNielsen

21. A _________ is a structured collection of records or data that is stored in a computer system. The structure is achieved by organizing the data according to a _________ model. The model in most common use today is the relational model.

a. 6-3-5 Brainwriting
b. Database
c. Power III
d. 180SearchAssistant

22. An _________ or ad agency is a service business dedicated to creating, planning and handling advertising (and sometimes other forms of promotion) for its clients. An ad agency is independent from the client and provides an outside point of view to the effort of selling the client's products or services. An agency can also handle overall marketing and branding strategies and sales promotions for its clients.

a. Onsert
b. Advertising research
c. Advertising agency
d. Openad

23. A _________ is a relatively new executive level position at a corporation, company, organization typically reporting directly to the CEO or board of directors. The _________ is responsible for a brand's image, experience, and promise, and propagating it throughout all aspects of the company. The brand officer oversees marketing, advertising, design, public relations and customer service departments.

a. Chief executive officer
b. Financial analyst
c. Power III
d. Chief brand officer

24. Competitiveness is a comparative concept of the ability and performance of a firm, sub-sector or country to sell and supply goods and/or services in a given market. Although widely used in economics and business management, the usefulness of the concept, particularly in the context of national competitiveness, is vigorously disputed by economists, such as Paul Krugman .

The term may also be applied to markets, where it is used to refer to the extent to which the market structure may be regarded as perfectly _________.

a. Customs union
b. Geographical pricing
c. Free trade zone
d. Competitive

25. A _________ is a list of the general tasks and responsibilities of a position. Typically, it also includes to whom the position reports, specifications such as the qualifications needed by the person in the job, salary range for the position, etc. A _________ is usually developed by conducting a job analysis, which includes examining the tasks and sequences of tasks necessary to perform the job.

a. 6-3-5 Brainwriting
b. 180SearchAssistant
c. Power III
d. Job description

26. In economics, business, retail, and accounting, a _________ is the value of money that has been used up to produce something, and hence is not available for use anymore. In economics, a _________ is an alternative that is given up as a result of a decision. In business, the _________ may be one of acquisition, in which case the amount of money expended to acquire it is counted as _________.

a. Transaction cost
b. Fixed costs
c. Cost
d. Variable cost

27. _________ refer to a collection of facts usually collected as the result of experience, observation or experiment or a set of premises. This may consist of numbers, words particularly as measurements or observations of a set of variables. _________ are often viewed as a lowest level of abstraction from which information and knowledge are derived.

a. Pearson product-moment correlation coefficient
b. Mean
c. Sample size
d. Data

28. _________ is the physical search for minerals, fossils, precious metals or mineral specimens, and is also known as fossicking.

_________ is synonymous in some ways with mineral exploration which is an organised, large scale and at least semi-scientific effort undertaken by mineral resource companies to find commercially viable ore deposits. To actually be considered a prospector you must become registered as a professional prospector.

a. 6-3-5 Brainwriting
b. 180SearchAssistant
c. Power III
d. Prospecting

29. The term _________ was first coined by New York Times best selling author, Linda Richardson. _________ emphasizes customer needs and meeting those needs with solutions combining products and/or services. A consultative salesperson typically provides detailed instruction or advice on which solution best meets these needs.

a. Request for proposal
b. Sales management
c. Lead generation
d. Consultative selling

1. _________ is the term given to food that can be prepared and served very quickly. While any meal with low preparation time can be considered to be _________, typically the term refers to food sold in a restaurant or store with low quality preparation and served to the customer in a packaged form for take-out/take-away. The term '_________' was recognized in a dictionary by Merriam-Webster in 1951.

a. Fast food
b. 180SearchAssistant
c. Power III
d. 6-3-5 Brainwriting

2. _________ involves disseminating information about a product, product line, brand, or company. It is one of the four key aspects of the marketing mix. (The other three elements are product marketing, pricing, and distribution). P>_________ is generally sub-divided into two parts:

- Above the line _________: Promotion in the media (e.g. TV, radio, newspapers, Internet and Mobile Phones) in which the advertiser pays an advertising agency to place the ad
- Below the line _________: All other _________. Much of this is intended to be subtle enough for the consumer to be unaware that _________ is taking place. E.g. sponsorship, product placement, endorsements, sales _________, merchandising, direct mail, personal selling, public relations, trade shows

a. Promotion
b. Davie Brown Index
c. Cashmere Agency
d. Bottling lines

3. _________ refers to 'controlling human or societal behaviour by rules or restrictions.' _________ can take many forms: legal restrictions promulgated by a government authority, self-_________, social _________, co-_________ and market _________. One can consider _________ as actions of conduct imposing sanctions (such as a fine.) This action of administrative law, or implementing regulatory law, may be contrasted with statutory or case law.

a. Non-conventional trademark
b. CAN-SPAM
c. Rule of four
d. Regulation

4. _________ is a form of communication that typically attempts to persuade potential customers to purchase or to consume more of a particular brand of product or service. 'While now central to the contemporary global economy and the reproduction of global production networks, it is only quite recently that _________ has been more than a marginal influence on patterns of sales and production. The formation of modern _________ was intimately bound up with the emergence of new forms of monopoly capitalism around the end of the 19th and beginning of the 20th century as one element in corporate strategies to create, organize and where possible control markets, especially for mass produced consumer goods.

a. AMAX
b. Advertising
c. ACNielsen
d. ADTECH

5. _________ refers to the laws and rules defining the ways in which products can be advertised in a particular region. Rules can define a wide number of different aspects, such as placement, timing, and content. In the United States, false advertising and health-related ads are regulated the most.

a. ACNielsen
b. Advertising regulation
c. AMAX
d. ADTECH

6. _________ is one of the four aspects of promotional mix. (The other three parts of the promotional mix are advertising, personal selling, and publicity/public relations.) Media and non-media marketing communication are employed for a pre-determined, limited time to increase consumer demand, stimulate market demand or improve product availability.

a. New Media Strategies
b. Marketing communication
c. Merchandise
d. Sales promotion

7. Competitiveness is a comparative concept of the ability and performance of a firm, sub-sector or country to sell and supply goods and/or services in a given market. Although widely used in economics and business management, the usefulness of the concept, particularly in the context of national competitiveness, is vigorously disputed by economists, such as Paul Krugman .

The term may also be applied to markets, where it is used to refer to the extent to which the market structure may be regarded as perfectly _________.

a. Customs union
b. Free trade zone
c. Geographical pricing
d. Competitive

8. _________ is a broad label that refers to any individuals or households that use goods and services generated within the economy. The concept of a _________ is used in different contexts, so that the usage and significance of the term may vary.

A _________ is a person who uses any product or service.

a. Power III
b. 180SearchAssistant
c. 6-3-5 Brainwriting
d. Consumer

9. In economics, business, retail, and accounting, a _________ is the value of money that has been used up to produce something, and hence is not available for use anymore. In economics, a _________ is an alternative that is given up as a result of a decision. In business, the _________ may be one of acquisition, in which case the amount of money expended to acquire it is counted as _________.

a. Cost
b. Variable cost
c. Transaction cost
d. Fixed costs

10. _________ is a contract between two parties, one being the employer and the other being the employee. An employee may be defined as: 'A person in the service of another under any contract of hire, express or implied, oral or written, where the employer has the power or right to control and direct the employee in the material details of how the work is to be performed.' Black's Law Dictionary page 471 (5th ed. 1979.)

a. AMAX
b. ADTECH
c. ACNielsen
d. Employment

11. A _________ is a plan of action designed to achieve a particular goal.

_________ is different from tactics. In military terms, tactics is concerned with the conduct of an engagement while _________ is concerned with how different engagements are linked.

a. Power III
b. 180SearchAssistant
c. 6-3-5 Brainwriting
d. Strategy

12. In grammar, the _________ is the form of an adjective or adverb which denotes the degree or grade by which a person, thing and is used in this context with a subordinating conjunction, such as than, as...as, etc.

The structure of a _________ in English consists normally of the positive form of the adjective or adverb, plus the suffix -er e.g. 'he is taller than his father is', or 'the village is less picturesque than the town nearby'.

a. 6-3-5 Brainwriting
b. Comparative
c. Power III
d. 180SearchAssistant

13. _________ is an advertisement in which a particular product specifically mentions a competitor by name for the express purpose of showing why the competitor is inferior to the product naming it.

This should not be confused with parody advertisements, where a fictional product is being advertised for the purpose of poking fun at the particular advertisement, nor should it be confused with the use of a coined brand name for the purpose of comparing the product without actually naming an actual competitor. ('Wikipedia tastes better and is less filling than the Encyclopedia Galactica.')

In the 1980s, during what has been referred to as the cola wars, soft-drink manufacturer Pepsi ran a series of advertisements where people, caught on hidden camera, in a blind taste test, chose Pepsi over rival Coca-Cola.

a. Heavy-up
b. GL-70
c. Cost per conversion
d. Comparative advertising

14. The _________ is an independent agency of the United States government, established in 1914 by the _________ Act. Its principal mission is the promotion of 'consumer protection' and the elimination and prevention of what regulators perceive to be harmfully 'anti-competitive' business practices, such as coercive monopoly.

The _________ Act was one of President Wilson's major acts against trusts.

a. Federal Trade Commission
b. Power III
c. 6-3-5 Brainwriting
d. 180SearchAssistant

15. A _________ is an explicit set of requirements to be satisfied by a material, product, or service.

In engineering, manufacturing, and business, it is vital for suppliers, purchasers, and users of materials, products, or services to understand and agree upon all requirements. A _________ is a type of a standard which is often referenced by a contract or procurement document.

a. Product development
b. New product development
c. Product optimization
d. Specification

16. _________ is the pursuit of influencing outcomes -- including public-policy and resource allocation decisions within political, economic, and social systems and institutions -- that directly affect people's current lives. (Cohen, 2001)

Therefore, _________ can be seen as a deliberate process of speaking out on issues of concern in order to exert some influence on behalf of ideas or persons. Based on this definition, Cohen (2001) states that 'ideologues of all persuasions advocate' to bring a change in people's lives.

a. ACNielsen
b. ADTECH
c. AMAX
d. Advocacy

17. A _________ is defined by the International Co-operative Alliance's Statement on the Co-operative Identity as an autonomous association of persons united voluntarily to meet their common economic, social, and cultural needs and aspirations through a jointly-owned and democratically-controlled enterprise. It is a business organization owned and operated by a group of individuals for their mutual benefit. A _________ may also be defined as a business owned and controlled equally by the people who use its services or who work at it.

a. 6-3-5 Brainwriting
b. 180SearchAssistant
c. Cooperative
d. Power III

18. _________ is a branch of philosophy which seeks to address questions about morality, such as how a moral outcome can be achieved in a specific situation (applied _________), how moral values should be determined (normative _________), what moral values people actually abide by (descriptive _________), what the fundamental semantic, ontological, and epistemic nature of _________ or morality is (meta-_________), and how moral capacity or moral agency develops and what its nature is (moral psychology.)

Socrates was one of the first Greek philosophers to encourage both scholars and the common citizen to turn their attention from the outside world to the condition of man. In this view, Knowledge having a bearing on human life was placed highest, all other knowledge being secondary.

a. AMAX
b. ACNielsen
c. Ethics
d. ADTECH

19. _________ is defined by the American _________ Association as the activity, set of institutions, and processes for creating, communicating, delivering, and exchanging offerings that have value for customers, clients, partners, and society at large. The term developed from the original meaning which referred literally to going to market, as in shopping, or going to a market to sell goods or services.

_________ practice tends to be seen as a creative industry, which includes advertising, distribution and selling.

a. Marketing
b. Customer acquisition management
c. Product naming
d. Marketing myopia

20. In the mathematical discipline of graph theory a _________ or edge-independent set in a graph is a set of edges without common vertices. It may also be an entire graph consisting of edges without common vertices.

Given a graph G = (V,E), a _________ M in G is a set of pairwise non-adjacent edges; that is, no two edges share a common vertex.

a. 180SearchAssistant
b. 6-3-5 Brainwriting
c. Power III
d. Matching

21. _________ consists of the processes a company uses to track and organize its contacts with its current and prospective customers. _________ software is used to support these processes; information about customers and customer interactions can be entered, stored and accessed by employees in different company departments. Typical _________ goals are to improve services provided to customers, and to use customer contact information for targeted marketing.

a. Demand generation
b. Commercialization
c. Product bundling
d. Customer relationship management

22. _________ refer to a collection of facts usually collected as the result of experience, observation or experiment or a set of premises. This may consist of numbers, words particularly as measurements or observations of a set of variables. _________ are often viewed as a lowest level of abstraction from which information and knowledge are derived.

a. Sample size
b. Mean
c. Pearson product-moment correlation coefficient
d. Data

23. Electronic commerce, commonly known as _________ or eCommerce, consists of the buying and selling of products or services over electronic systems such as the Internet and other computer networks. The amount of trade conducted electronically has grown extraordinarily with wide-spread Internet usage. A wide variety of commerce is conducted in this way, spurring and drawing on innovations in electronic funds transfer, supply chain management, Internet marketing, online transaction processing, electronic data interchange (EDI), inventory management systems, and automated data collection systems.

a. ACNielsen
b. ADTECH
c. AMAX
d. E-commerce

24. _________ are long-format television commercials, typically five minutes or longer.. _________ are also known as paid programming (or teleshopping in Europe.) Originally, they were a phenomenon that started in the United States where they were typically shown overnight (usually 2:00 a.m. to 6:00 a.m.)

a. Infomercials
b. AMAX
c. ACNielsen
d. ADTECH

25. Customer _________ consists of the processes a company uses to track and organize its contacts with its current and prospective customers. CRelationship management software is used to support these processes; information about customers and customer interactions can be entered, stored and accessed by employees in different company departments. Typical CRelationship management goals are to improve services provided to customers, and to use customer contact information for targeted marketing.

a. Marketing
b. Product bundling
c. Green marketing
d. Relationship management

26. _________ is a form of advertisement, where branded goods or services are placed in a context usually devoid of ads, such as movies, the story line of television shows Broadcasting ' Cable reported, 'Two thirds of advertisers employ 'branded entertainment'--_________--with the vast majority of that (80%) in commercial TV programming.' The story, based on a survey by the Association of National Advertisers, added, 'Reasons for using in-show plugs varied from 'stronger emotional connection' to better dovetailing with relevant content, to targetting a specific group.'

_________ became common in the 1980s, but can be traced back to the nineteenth century in publishing.

a. Power III
b. 6-3-5 Brainwriting
c. 180SearchAssistant
d. Product placement

27. A _________ or banner ad is a form of advertising on the World Wide Web. This form of online advertising entails embedding an advertisement into a web page. It is intended to attract traffic to a website by linking to the website of the advertiser.

a. Web banner
b. Spamvertising
c. Consumer privacy
d. Disintermediation

28. _________ are a form of online advertising on the World Wide Web intended to attract web traffic or capture email addresses. It works when certain web sites open a new web browser window to display advertisements. The pop-up window containing an advertisement is usually generated by JavaScript, but can be generated by other means as well.

a. Customer intelligence
b. Pop-up ads
c. Power III
d. Project Portfolio Management

29. In environmental modeling and especially in hydrology, a _________ model means a model that is acceptably consistent with observed natural processes, i.e. that simulates well, for example, observed river discharge. It is a key concept of the so-called Generalized Likelihood Uncertainty Estimation (GLUE) methodology to quantify how uncertain environmental predictions are.

a. 180SearchAssistant
b. 6-3-5 Brainwriting
c. Power III
d. Behavioral

30. _________ or behavioural targeting is a technique used by online publishers and advertisers to increase the effectiveness of their campaigns.

_________ uses information collected on an individual's web-browsing behavior, such as the pages they have visited or the searches they have made, to select which advertisements to display to that individual. Practitioners believe this helps them deliver their online advertisements to the users who are most likely to be influenced by them.

a. Search engine image protection
b. Behavioral targeting
c. Contextual advertising
d. Hit inflation attack

31. In online marketing a _________, sometimes known as a lead capture page, is the page that appears when a potential customer clicks on an advertisement or a search-engine result link. The page will usually display content that is a logical extension of the advertisement or link, and that is optimized to feature specific keywords or phrases for indexing by search engines.

In pay per click (PPC) campaigns, the _________ will also be customized to measure the effectiveness of different advertisements.

a. Landing page
b. Hit inflation attack
c. Conversion optimization
d. VoloMedia

32. _________ in organizations and public policy is both the organizational process of creating and maintaining a plan; and the psychological process of thinking about the activities required to create a desired goal on some scale. As such, it is a fundamental property of intelligent behavior. This thought process is essential to the creation and refinement of a plan, or integration of it with other plans, that is, it combines forecasting of developments with the preparation of scenarios of how to react to them.

a. Planning
b. 6-3-5 Brainwriting
c. Power III
d. 180SearchAssistant

33. _________ is a fee paid on borrowed assets. It is the price paid for the use of borrowed money , or, money earned by deposited funds . Assets that are sometimes lent with _________ include money, shares, consumer goods through hire purchase, major assets such as aircraft, and even entire factories in finance lease arrangements.

a. ACNielsen
b. ADTECH
c. AMAX
d. Interest

34. The _________ is a marketing concept that was first proposed as a theory to explain a pattern among successful advertising campaigns of the early 1940s. It states that such campaigns made unique propositions to the customer and that this convinced them to switch brands. The term was invented by Rosser Reeves of Ted Bates ' Company.

a. ACNielsen
b. Unique selling proposition
c. AMAX
d. ADTECH

35. An _________ or ad agency is a service business dedicated to creating, planning and handling advertising (and sometimes other forms of promotion) for its clients. An ad agency is independent from the client and provides an outside point of view to the effort of selling the client's products or services. An agency can also handle overall marketing and branding strategies and sales promotions for its clients.

a. Openad
b. Advertising agency
c. Onsert
d. Advertising research

36. A _________ is a relatively new executive level position at a corporation, company, organization typically reporting directly to the CEO or board of directors. The _________ is responsible for a brand's image, experience, and promise, and propagating it throughout all aspects of the company. The brand officer oversees marketing, advertising, design, public relations and customer service departments.

a. Power III
b. Chief executive officer
c. Financial analyst
d. Chief brand officer

37. A _________ attribute is one that exists in a range of magnitudes, and can therefore be measured. Measurements of any particular _________ property are expressed as a specific quantity, referred to as a unit, multiplied by a number. Examples of physical quantities are distance, mass, and time.

a. Dolly Dimples
b. Lifestyle city
c. BeyondROI
d. Quantitative

38. False advertising or _________ is the use of false or misleading statements in advertising. As advertising has the potential to persuade people into commercial transactions that they might otherwise avoid, many governments around the world use regulations to control false, deceptive or misleading advertising. Truth in labeling refers to essentially the same concept, that customers have the right to know what they are buying, and that all necessary information should be on the label.

a. Misleading advertising
b. Power III
c. Fine print
d. Deceptive advertising

39. A personal and cultural _________ is a relative ethic _________, an assumption upon which implementation can be extrapolated. A _________ system is a set of consistent _________s and measures that is soo not true. A principle _________ is a foundation upon which other _________s and measures of integrity are based.

a. Package-on-Package
b. Perceptual maps
c. Value
d. Supreme Court of the United States

40. _________ or promotional products refers to articles of merchandise that are used in marketing and communication programs. These items are usually imprinted with a company's name, logo or slogan, and given away at trade shows, conferences, and as part of guerrilla marketing campaigns.

Almost anything can be branded with a company's name or logo and used for promotion.

a. Promotional products
b. Testimonial
c. Roll-in
d. Promotional items

41. _________ is one of the four elements of marketing mix. An organization or set of organizations (go-betweens) involved in the process of making a product or service available for use or consumption by a consumer or business user.

The other three parts of the marketing mix are product, pricing, and promotion.

a. Distribution
b. Better Living Through Chemistry
c. Comparison-Shopping agent
d. Japan Advertising Photographers' Association

1. _________ is defined by the American _________ Association as the activity, set of institutions, and processes for creating, communicating, delivering, and exchanging offerings that have value for customers, clients, partners, and society at large. The term developed from the original meaning which referred literally to going to market, as in shopping, or going to a market to sell goods or services.

_________ practice tends to be seen as a creative industry, which includes advertising, distribution and selling.

a. Marketing
b. Marketing myopia
c. Customer acquisition management
d. Product naming

2. _________ is one of the four Ps of the marketing mix. The other three aspects are product, promotion, and place. It is also a key variable in microeconomic price allocation theory.

a. Competitor indexing
b. Price
c. Pricing
d. Relationship based pricing

3. A personal and cultural _________ is a relative ethic _________, an assumption upon which implementation can be extrapolated. A _________ system is a set of consistent _________s and measures that is soo not true. A principle _________ is a foundation upon which other _________s and measures of integrity are based.

a. Value
b. Perceptual maps
c. Package-on-Package
d. Supreme Court of the United States

4. _________ is one of the four elements of marketing mix. An organization or set of organizations (go-betweens) involved in the process of making a product or service available for use or consumption by a consumer or business user.

The other three parts of the marketing mix are product, pricing, and promotion.

a. Better Living Through Chemistry
b. Japan Advertising Photographers' Association
c. Distribution
d. Comparison-Shopping agent

5. The break-even point for a product is the point where total revenue received equals the total costs associated with the sale of the product (TR=TC.) A break-even point is typically calculated in order for businesses to determine if it would be profitable to sell a proposed product, as opposed to attempting to modify an existing product instead so it can be made lucrative. _________ can also be used to analyse the potential profitability of an expenditure in a sales-based business.

In _________, margin of safety is how much output or sales level can fall before a business reaches its break-even point (BEP).

a. Break even analysis
b. Price skimming
c. Contribution margin-based pricing
d. Pay Per Sale

6. _________, in strategic management and marketing, is the percentage or proportion of the total available market or market segment that is being serviced by a company. It can be expressed as a company's sales revenue (from that market) divided by the total sales revenue available in that market. It can also be expressed as a company's unit sales volume (in a market) divided by the total volume of units sold in that market.

a. Cyberdoc
b. Demand generation
c. Customer relationship management
d. Market share

7. In economics, _________ is the process by which a firm determines the price and output level that returns the greatest profit. There are several approaches to this problem. The total revenue--total cost method relies on the fact that profit equals revenue minus cost, and the marginal revenue--marginal cost method is based on the fact that total profit in a perfectly competitive market reaches its maximum point where marginal revenue equals marginal cost.

a. 180SearchAssistant
b. Profit maximization
c. Power III
d. Profit margin

8. _________ is the practice of individuals including commercial businesses, governments and institutions, facilitating the sale of their products or services to other companies or organizations that in turn resell them, use them as components in products or services they offer _________ is also called business-to-_________ for short. (Note that while marketing to government entities shares some of the same dynamics of organizational marketing, B2G Marketing is meaningfully different.)

a. Law of disruption
b. Mass marketing
c. Disruptive technology
d. Business marketing

9. _________ or goals give direction to the whole pricing process. Determining what your objectives are is the first step in pricing. When deciding on _________ you must consider: 1) the overall financial, marketing, and strategic objectives of the company; 2) the objectives of your product or brand; 3) consumer price elasticity and price points; and 4) the resources you have available.

a. Transfer pricing
b. Competitor indexing
c. Discounts and allowances
d. Pricing objectives

10. _________ is an advertisement in which a particular product specifically mentions a competitor by name for the express purpose of showing why the competitor is inferior to the product naming it.

This should not be confused with parody advertisements, where a fictional product is being advertised for the purpose of poking fun at the particular advertisement, nor should it be confused with the use of a coined brand name for the purpose of comparing the product without actually naming an actual competitor. ('Wikipedia tastes better and is less filling than the Encyclopedia Galactica.')

In the 1980s, during what has been referred to as the cola wars, soft-drink manufacturer Pepsi ran a series of advertisements where people, caught on hidden camera, in a blind taste test, chose Pepsi over rival Coca-Cola.

a. Cost per conversion
b. Comparative advertising
c. GL-70
d. Heavy-up

11. _________ is a marketing strategy 'in which one firm tries to distinguish its product or service from competing products on the basis of attributes like design and workmanship' (McConnell-Brue, 2002, p. 437-438.) The firm can also distinguish its product offering through quality of service, extensive distribution, customer focus, or any other sustainable competitive advantage other than price.

a. Price fixing
b. Non-price competition
c. Price competition
d. Direct competition

12. _________ is a rivalry between individuals, groups, nations for territory, a niche, or allocation of resources. It arises whenever two or more parties strive for a goal which cannot be shared. _________ occurs naturally between living organisms which co-exist in the same environment.

a. Price competition
b. Non-price competition
c. Price fixing
d. Competition

13. _________ in economics and business is the result of an exchange and from that trade we assign a numerical monetary value to a good, service or asset. If I trade 4 apples for an orange, the _________ of an orange is 4 - apples. Inversely, the _________ of an apple is 1/4 oranges.

a. Discounts and allowances
b. Pricing
c. Price
d. Contribution margin-based pricing

14. _________ Management is the succession of strategies used by management as a product goes through its _________. The conditions in which a product is sold changes over time and must be managed as it moves through its succession of stages.

The _________ goes through many phases, involves many professional disciplines, and requires many skills, tools and processes.

a. Customer satisfaction
b. Supplier diversity
c. Product life cycle
d. Chain stores

15. _________ is the pricing technique of setting a relatively low initial entry price, often lower than the eventual market price, to attract new customers. The strategy works on the expectation that customers will switch to the new brand because of the lower price. _________ is most commonly associated with a marketing objective of increasing market share or sales volume, rather than to make profit in the short term.

a. Fee
b. Penetration pricing
c. Price war
d. Competitor indexing

16. In finance, the _________s between two currencies specifies how much one currency is worth in terms of the other. It is the value of a foreign nation's currency in terms of the home nation's currency. For example an _________ of 102 Japanese yen to the United States dollar means that JPY 102 is worth the same as USD 1.

a. ACNielsen
b. ADTECH
c. AMAX
d. Exchange rate

17. The (manufacturer's) suggested retail price (MSRP or SRP), _________ or recommended retail price (RRP) of a product is the price the manufacturer recommends that the retailer sell it for. The intention was to help to standardize prices among locations. While some stores always sell at, or below, the suggested retail price, others do so only when items are on sale or closeout.

a. Power III
b. Predatory pricing
c. 180SearchAssistant
d. List price

18. _________ is a form of communication that typically attempts to persuade potential customers to purchase or to consume more of a particular brand of product or service. 'While now central to the contemporary global economy and the reproduction of global production networks, it is only quite recently that _________ has been more than a marginal influence on patterns of sales and production. The formation of modern _________ was intimately bound up with the emergence of new forms of monopoly capitalism around the end of the 19th and beginning of the 20th century as one element in corporate strategies to create, organize and where possible control markets, especially for mass produced consumer goods.

a. ADTECH
b. AMAX
c. ACNielsen
d. Advertising

19. The _________ is an independent agency of the United States government, established in 1914 by the _________ Act. Its principal mission is the promotion of 'consumer protection' and the elimination and prevention of what regulators perceive to be harmfully 'anti-competitive' business practices, such as coercive monopoly.

The _________ Act was one of President Wilson's major acts against trusts.

a. 6-3-5 Brainwriting
b. 180SearchAssistant
c. Power III
d. Federal Trade Commission

20. _________ are reductions to a basic price of goods or services. They can occur anywhere in the distribution channel, modifying either the manufacturer's list price (determined by the manufacturer and often printed on the package), the retail price (set by the retailer and often attached to the product with a sticker), or the list price (which is quoted to a potential buyer, usually in written form.) The market price (also called effective price) is the amount actually paid.

a. Price points
b. Price shading
c. Price
d. Discounts and allowances

21. _________ is the set of reasons that determines one to engage in a particular behavior. The term is generally used for human _________ but, theoretically, it can be used to describe the causes for animal behavior as well

a. Role playing
b. Power III
c. Motivation
d. 180SearchAssistant

22. A _________ is an explicit set of requirements to be satisfied by a material, product, or service.

In engineering, manufacturing, and business, it is vital for suppliers, purchasers, and users of materials, products, or services to understand and agree upon all requirements. A _________ is a type of a standard which is often referenced by a contract or procurement document.

a. Product optimization
b. New product development
c. Specification
d. Product development

23. In marketing a _________ is a ticket or document that can be exchanged for a financial discount or rebate when purchasing a product. Customarily, _________s are issued by manufacturers of consumer packaged goods or by retailers, to be used in retail stores as a part of sales promotions. They are often widely distributed through mail, magazines, newspapers, the Internet, and mobile devices such as cell phones.

a. Marketing communication
b. Coupon
c. Merchandise
d. Merchandising

24. The business terms _________ and pull originated in the logistic and supply chain management, but are also widely used in marketing.

A _________-pull-system in business describes the move of a product or information between two subjects. On markets the consumers usually 'pulls' the goods or information they demand for their needs, while the offerers or suppliers '_________es' them toward the consumers.

a. Completely randomized designs
b. Gold Key Matching Service
c. Push
d. Manufacturers' representatives

25. _________ is anything that is generally accepted as payment for goods and services and repayment of debts. The main uses of _________ are as a medium of exchange, a unit of account, and a store of value. Some authors explicitly require _________ to be a standard of deferred payment.

a. Law of supply
b. Microeconomics
c. Leading indicator
d. Money

26. A _________ is an amount paid by way of reduction, return, or refund on what has already been paid or contributed. It is a type of sales promotion marketers use primarily as incentives or supplements to product sales. The mail-in _________ is the most common.

a. Personalization
b. Lifestyle city
c. Rebate
d. Strand

27. _________ is the study of the Earth and its lands, features, inhabitants, and phenomena. A literal translation would be 'to describe or write about the Earth'. The first person to use the word '_________' was Eratosthenes .

a. 6-3-5 Brainwriting
b. Power III
c. 180SearchAssistant
d. Geography

28. _________s are used in open sentences. For instance, in the formula x + 1 = 5, x is a _________ which represents an 'unknown' number. _________s are often represented by letters of the Roman alphabet, or those of other alphabets, such as Greek, and use other special symbols.

a. Quantitative
b. Personalization
c. Book of business
d. Variable

29. _________ refers to the additional value of a commodity over the cost of commodities used to produce it from the previous stage of production. An example is the price of gasoline at the pump over the price of the oil in it. In national accounts used in macroeconomics, it refers to the contribution of the factors of production, i.e., land, labor, and capital goods, to raising the value of a product and corresponds to the incomes received by the owners of these factors. The factors of production provide 'services' which raise the unit price of a product (X) relative to the cost per unit of intermediate goods used up in the production of X. _________ is shared between the factors of production (capital, labor, also human capital), giving rise to issues of distribution.

a. Power III
b. Value added
c. Deregulation
d. Consumer spending

30. _________ is a common market form. Many markets can be considered monopolistically competitive, often including the markets for restaurants, cereal, clothing, shoes and service industries in large cities. Short-run equilibrium of the firm under _________

Monopolistically competitive markets have the following characteristics:

- There are many producers and many consumers in a given market, and no business has total control over the market price.
- Consumers perceive that there are non-price differences among the competitors' products.
- There are few barriers to entry and exit.
- Producers have a degree of control over price.

Long-run equilibrium of the firm under _________

The characteristics of a monopolistically competitive market are almost the same as in perfect competition, with the exception of heterogeneous products, and that _________ involves a great deal of non-price competition (based on subtle product differentiation.) A firm making profits in the short run will break even in the long run because demand will decrease and average total cost will increase.

a. Recession
b. Monopolistic competition
c. Gross domestic product
d. Macroeconomics

31. In the mathematical discipline of graph theory a _________ or edge-independent set in a graph is a set of edges without common vertices. It may also be an entire graph consisting of edges without common vertices.

Given a graph G = (V,E), a _________ M in G is a set of pairwise non-adjacent edges; that is, no two edges share a common vertex.

a. Matching
b. 6-3-5 Brainwriting
c. Power III
d. 180SearchAssistant

32. An _________ or ad agency is a service business dedicated to creating, planning and handling advertising (and sometimes other forms of promotion) for its clients. An ad agency is independent from the client and provides an outside point of view to the effort of selling the client's products or services. An agency can also handle overall marketing and branding strategies and sales promotions for its clients.

a. Onsert
b. Openad
c. Advertising research
d. Advertising agency

33. A _________ is a relatively new executive level position at a corporation, company, organization typically reporting directly to the CEO or board of directors. The _________ is responsible for a brand's image, experience, and promise, and propagating it throughout all aspects of the company. The brand officer oversees marketing, advertising, design, public relations and customer service departments.

a. Financial analyst
b. Chief executive officer
c. Chief brand officer
d. Power III

34. _________ refers to 'controlling human or societal behaviour by rules or restrictions.' _________ can take many forms: legal restrictions promulgated by a government authority, self-_________, social _________, co-_________ and market _________. One can consider _________ as actions of conduct imposing sanctions (such as a fine.) This action of administrative law, or implementing regulatory law, may be contrasted with statutory or case law.

a. Regulation
b. Non-conventional trademark
c. CAN-SPAM
d. Rule of four

35. _________ refers to the laws and rules defining the ways in which products can be advertised in a particular region. Rules can define a wide number of different aspects, such as placement, timing, and content. In the United States, false advertising and health-related ads are regulated the most.

a. Advertising regulation
b. ACNielsen
c. AMAX
d. ADTECH

36. In economics, business, retail, and accounting, a _________ is the value of money that has been used up to produce something, and hence is not available for use anymore. In economics, a _________ is an alternative that is given up as a result of a decision. In business, the _________ may be one of acquisition, in which case the amount of money expended to acquire it is counted as _________.

a. Variable cost
b. Transaction cost
c. Cost
d. Fixed costs

37. In economics, '_________' can refer to any kind of predatory pricing. However, the word is now generally used only in the context of international trade law, where _________ is defined as the act of a manufacturer in one country exporting a product to another country at a price which is either below the price it charges in its home market or is below its costs of production. The term has a negative connotation, but advocates of free markets see '_________' as beneficial for consumers and believe that protectionism to prevent it would have net negative consequences.

a. Gold Key Matching Service
b. Sample sales
c. Hawkers
d. Dumping

38. An _________ is an unplanned or otherwise spontaneous purchase. One who tends to make such purchases is referred to as an impulse purchaser or impulse buyer.

Marketers and retailers tend to exploit these impulses which are tied to the basic want for instant gratification.

a. ACNielsen
b. ADTECH
c. AMAX
d. Impulse purchase

39. A _________ is a tax imposed on goods when they are moved across a political boundary. They are usually associated with protectionism, the economic policy of restraining trade between nations. For political reasons, _________s are usually imposed on imported goods, although they may also be imposed on exported goods.

a. Fiscal policy
b. Power III
c. Tariff
d. Monetary policy

40. _________ exists when sales of identical goods or services are transacted at different prices from the same provider. In a theoretical market with perfect information, no transaction costs or prohibition on secondary exchange (or re-selling) to prevent arbitrage, _________ can only be a feature of monopoly and oligopoly markets, where market power can be exercised. Otherwise, the moment the seller tries to sell the same good at different prices, the buyer at the lower price can arbitrage by selling to the consumer buying at the higher price but with a tiny discount.

a. Penetration pricing
b. Price
c. Resale price maintenance
d. Price discrimination

41. _________ is an agreement between business competitors to sell the same product or service at the same price. In general, it is an agreement intended to ultimately push the price of a product as high as possible, leading to profits for all the sellers. _________ can also involve any agreement to fix, peg, discount or stabilize prices.

a. Price competition
b. Direct competition
c. Non-price competition
d. Price fixing

42. The _________ of 1936 (or Anti-Price Discrimination Act, 15 U.S.C. Â§ 13) is a United States federal law that prohibits what were considered, at the time of passage, to be anticompetitive practices by producers, specifically price discrimination. It grew out of practices in which chain stores were allowed to purchase goods at lower prices than other retailers.

a. Registered trademark symbol
b. Robinson-Patman Act
c. Fair Debt Collection Practices Act
d. Trademark infringement

43. _________ in organizations and public policy is both the organizational process of creating and maintaining a plan; and the psychological process of thinking about the activities required to create a desired goal on some scale. As such, it is a fundamental property of intelligent behavior. This thought process is essential to the creation and refinement of a plan, or integration of it with other plans, that is, it combines forecasting of developments with the preparation of scenarios of how to react to them.

a. 180SearchAssistant
b. Power III
c. 6-3-5 Brainwriting
d. Planning

44. A _________ is a plan of action designed to achieve a particular goal.

_________ is different from tactics. In military terms, tactics is concerned with the conduct of an engagement while _________ is concerned with how different engagements are linked.

a. 180SearchAssistant
b. Power III
c. 6-3-5 Brainwriting
d. Strategy

1. _________ is the use of an object (typically referred to as an RFID tag) applied to or incorporated into a product, animal, or person for the purpose of identification and tracking using radio waves. Some tags can be read from several meters away and beyond the line of sight of the reader.

Most RFID tags contain at least two parts.

a. Power III
b. 180SearchAssistant
c. 6-3-5 Brainwriting
d. Radio-frequency identification

2. _________ is one of the four Ps of the marketing mix. The other three aspects are product, promotion, and place. It is also a key variable in microeconomic price allocation theory.

a. Relationship based pricing
b. Competitor indexing
c. Price
d. Pricing

3. A personal and cultural _________ is a relative ethic _________, an assumption upon which implementation can be extrapolated. A _________ system is a set of consistent _________s and measures that is soo not true. A principle _________ is a foundation upon which other _________s and measures of integrity are based.

a. Perceptual maps
b. Value
c. Supreme Court of the United States
d. Package-on-Package

4. _________, Gross profit margin or Gross Profit Rate can be defined as the amount of contribution to the business enterprise, after paying for direct-fixed and direct-variable unit costs, required to cover overheads (fixed commitments) and provide a buffer for unknown items. It expresses the relationship between gross profit and sales revenue.

It can be expressed in absolute terms:

Gross Profit = Revenue − Cost of Goods Sold

or as the ratio of gross profit to sales revenue, usually in the form of a percentage:

_________ Percentage = (Revenue-Cost of Goods Sold)/Revenue

Cost of goods sold includes variable costs and fixed costs directly linked to the product, such as material and labor.

a. Power III
b. Profit maximization
c. 180SearchAssistant
d. Gross margin

5. The break-even point for a product is the point where total revenue received equals the total costs associated with the sale of the product (TR=TC.) A break-even point is typically calculated in order for businesses to determine if it would be profitable to sell a proposed product, as opposed to attempting to modify an existing product instead so it can be made lucrative. _________ can also be used to analyse the potential profitability of an expenditure in a sales-based business.

In _________, margin of safety is how much output or sales level can fall before a business reaches its break-even point (BEP).

a. Price skimming
b. Pay Per Sale
c. Contribution margin-based pricing
d. Break even analysis

6. A _________ is a collection of symbols, experiences and associations connected with a product, a service, a person or any other artifact or entity.

_________s have become increasingly important components of culture and the economy, now being described as 'cultural accessories and personal philosophies'.

Some people distinguish the psychological aspect of a _________ from the experiential aspect.

a. Store brand
b. Brandable software
c. Brand equity
d. Brand

7. In economics, business, retail, and accounting, a _________ is the value of money that has been used up to produce something, and hence is not available for use anymore. In economics, a _________ is an alternative that is given up as a result of a decision. In business, the _________ may be one of acquisition, in which case the amount of money expended to acquire it is counted as _________.

a. Variable cost
b. Fixed costs
c. Transaction cost
d. Cost

8. In economics, _________ are business expenses that are not dependent on the activities of the business They tend to be time-related, such as salaries or rents being paid per month. This is in contrast to variable costs, which are volume-related (and are paid per quantity.)

In management accounting, _________ are defined as expenses that do not change in proportion to the activity of a business, within the relevant period or scale of production.

a. Variable cost
b. Marginal cost
c. Transaction cost
d. Fixed costs

9. _________ is a branch of philosophy which seeks to address questions about morality, such as how a moral outcome can be achieved in a specific situation (applied _________), how moral values should be determined (normative _________), what moral values people actually abide by (descriptive _________), what the fundamental semantic, ontological, and epistemic nature of _________ or morality is (meta-_________), and how moral capacity or moral agency develops and what its nature is (moral psychology.)

Socrates was one of the first Greek philosophers to encourage both scholars and the common citizen to turn their attention from the outside world to the condition of man. In this view, Knowledge having a bearing on human life was placed highest, all other knowledge being secondary.

a. Ethics
b. AMAX
c. ACNielsen
d. ADTECH

10. _________s are used in open sentences. For instance, in the formula x + 1 = 5, x is a _________ which represents an 'unknown' number. _________s are often represented by letters of the Roman alphabet, or those of other alphabets, such as Greek, and use other special symbols.

a. Book of business
b. Quantitative
c. Personalization
d. Variable

11. _________s are expenses that change in proportion to the activity of a business. In other words, _________ is the sum of marginal costs. It can also be considered normal costs.

a. Transaction cost
b. Marginal cost
c. Fixed costs
d. Variable cost

12. In mathematics, an _________, or central tendency of a data set refers to a measure of the 'middle' or 'expected' value of the data set. There are many different descriptive statistics that can be chosen as a measurement of the central tendency of the data items.

An _________ is a single value that is meant to typify a list of values.

a. ACNielsen
b. AMAX
c. ADTECH
d. Average

13. In economics, _________ is equal to total cost divided by the number of goods produced (the output quantity, Q.) It is also equal to the sum of average variable costs (total variable costs divided by Q) plus average fixed costs (total fixed costs divided by Q.) _________s may be dependent on the time period considered (increasing production may be expensive or impossible in the short term, for example.)

a. ACNielsen
b. ADTECH
c. Average variable cost
d. Average cost

14. _________ is an economics term used to describe the total fixed costs (TFC) divided by the quantity (Q) of units produced.

_________ is a per-unit measure of fixed costs. As the total number of goods produced increases, the _________ decreases because the same amount of fixed costs are being spread over a larger number of units.

a. ACNielsen
b. Average variable cost
c. ADTECH
d. Average fixed cost

15. _________ is an economics term to describe a firms variable costs (labor, electricity, etc.) divided by the quantity (Q) of total units of output.

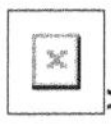

Where:

- TVC = Total Variable Cost
- _________ = Average variable cost
- Q = Quantity of Units Produced

_________ plus average fixed cost equals average total cost:

_________ + AFC = ATC.

.

a. ACNielsen
b. Average fixed cost
c. ADTECH
d. Average variable cost

16. In economics, and cost accounting, _________ describes the total economic cost of production and is made up of variable costs, which vary according to the quantity of a good produced and include inputs such as labor and raw materials, plus fixed costs, which are independent of the quantity of a good produced and include inputs (capital) that cannot be varied in the short term, such as buildings and machinery. _________ in economics includes the total opportunity cost of each factor of production in addition to fixed and variable costs.

The rate at which _________ changes as the amount produced changes is called marginal cost.

a. Product proliferation
b. Household production function
c. Hoarding
d. Total cost

17. In economics, _________ is the desire to own something and the ability to pay for it. The term _________ signifies the ability or the willingness to buy a particular commodity at a given point of time .

.

a. Market system
b. Discretionary spending
c. Market dominance
d. Demand

18. In economics, the _________ can be defined as the graph depicting the relationship between the price of a certain commodity, and the amount of it that consumers are willing and able to purchase at that given price. It is a graphic representation of a demand schedule The _________ for all consumers together follows from the _________ of every individual consumer: the individual demands at each price are added together.

_________s are used to estimate behaviors in competitive markets, and are often combined with supply curves to estimate the equilibrium price (the price at which sellers together are willing to sell the same amount as buyers together are willing to buy, also known as market clearing price) and the equilibrium quantity (the amount of that good or service that will be produced and bought without surplus/excess supply or shortage/excess demand) of that market.

a. Power III
b. Demand curve
c. 6-3-5 Brainwriting
d. 180SearchAssistant

19. In economic models, the _________ time frame assumes no fixed factors of production. Firms can enter or leave the marketplace, and the cost (and availability) of land, labor, raw materials, and capital goods can be assumed to vary. In contrast, in the short-run time frame, certain factors are assumed to be fixed, because there is not sufficient time for them to change.
a. 180SearchAssistant
b. Power III
c. 6-3-5 Brainwriting
d. Long-run

20. _________ is the use of marginal concepts within economics. (Marginal concepts are associated with a specific change in the quantity used of a good or of a service, as opposed to some notion of the over-all significance of that class of good or service, or of some total quantity thereof.) The central concept of _________ proper is that of marginal utility, but marginalists following the lead of Alfred Marshall were further heavily dependent upon the concept of marginal physical productivity in their explanation of cost; and the neoclassical tradition that emerged from British _________ generally abandoned the concept of utility and gave marginal rates of substitution a more fundamental rôle in analysis.
a. 180SearchAssistant
b. Power III
c. Marginalism
d. 6-3-5 Brainwriting

21. In economics and finance, _________ is the change in total cost that arises when the quantity produced changes by one unit. It is the cost of producing one more unit of a good. Mathematically, the _________ function is expressed as the first derivative of the total cost (TC) function with respect to quantity (Q.)
a. Marginal cost
b. Fixed costs
c. Variable cost
d. Transaction cost

22. In microeconomics, _________ is the extra revenue that an additional unit of product will bring. It is the additional income from selling one more unit of a good; sometimes equal to price. It can also be described as the change in total revenue/change in number of units sold.
a. Total cost
b. Hoarding
c. Product proliferation
d. Marginal revenue

23. In microeconomics, _________ is the total number of dollars received by a firm from the sale of a product.
a. Total revenue
b. 180SearchAssistant
c. Power III
d. Nonmarket

24. _________ in economics and business is the result of an exchange and from that trade we assign a numerical monetary value to a good, service or asset. If I trade 4 apples for an orange, the _________ of an orange is 4 - apples. Inversely, the _________ of an apple is 1/4 oranges.
a. Pricing
b. Discounts and allowances
c. Contribution margin-based pricing
d. Price

25. _________ occurs when cartels are illegal or overt collusion is absent. Put another way, two firms agree to play a certain strategy without explicitly saying so. This is also known as price leadership, as firms may stay within the law but still tacitly collude by monitoring each other's prices and keeping them the same. Usually, this occurs when a firm emerges to set the general industry price and other firms follow suit. Oligopolists usually try not to engage in price cutting, excessive advertising or other forms of competition.

a. Chief privacy officer
b. Shop fitting
c. Teaser rate
d. Tacit collusion

26. _________ is a term used in business to indicate a state of intense competitive rivalry accompanied by a multi-lateral series of price reduction. One competitor will lower its price, then others will lower their prices to match. If one of them reduces their price again, a new round of reductions starts.

a. Pricing objectives
b. Competitor indexing
c. Resale price maintenance
d. Price war

27. Switching barriers or _________s are terms used in microeconomics, strategic management, and marketing to describe any impediment to a customer's changing of suppliers.

In many markets, consumers are forced to incur costs when switching from one supplier to another. These costs are called _________s and can come in many different shapes.

a. Strategic group
b. Chaotics
c. Strategic business unit
d. Switching cost

28. _________ refers to the additional value of a commodity over the cost of commodities used to produce it from the previous stage of production. An example is the price of gasoline at the pump over the price of the oil in it. In national accounts used in macroeconomics, it refers to the contribution of the factors of production, i.e., land, labor, and capital goods, to raising the value of a product and corresponds to the incomes received by the owners of these factors. The factors of production provide 'services' which raise the unit price of a product (X) relative to the cost per unit of intermediate goods used up in the production of X. _________ is shared between the factors of production (capital, labor, also human capital), giving rise to issues of distribution.

a. Consumer spending
b. Deregulation
c. Power III
d. Value added

29. Electronic commerce, commonly known as _________ or eCommerce, consists of the buying and selling of products or services over electronic systems such as the Internet and other computer networks. The amount of trade conducted electronically has grown extraordinarily with wide-spread Internet usage. A wide variety of commerce is conducted in this way, spurring and drawing on innovations in electronic funds transfer, supply chain management, Internet marketing, online transaction processing, electronic data interchange (EDI), inventory management systems, and automated data collection systems.

a. AMAX
b. ADTECH
c. ACNielsen
d. E-commerce

30. In retail sales, a _________ is a form of fraud in which the party putting forth the fraud lures in customers by advertising a product or service at an unprofitably low price, then reveals to potential customers that the advertised good is not available but that a substitute is.

The goal of the bait-and-switch is to convince some buyers to purchase the substitute good as a means of avoiding disappointment over not getting the bait, or as a way to recover sunk costs expended to try to obtain the bait. It suggests that the seller will not show the original product or product advertised but instead will demonstrate a more expensive product.

a. Transpromotional
b. Bait and switch
c. Promotional products
d. Roll-in

31. The _________ is an independent agency of the United States government, established in 1914 by the _________ Act. Its principal mission is the promotion of 'consumer protection' and the elimination and prevention of what regulators perceive to be harmfully 'anti-competitive' business practices, such as coercive monopoly.

The _________ Act was one of President Wilson's major acts against trusts.

a. Federal Trade Commission
b. Power III
c. 6-3-5 Brainwriting
d. 180SearchAssistant

32. _________ or price ending is a marketing practice based on the theory that certain prices have a psychological impact. The retail prices are often expressed as 'odd prices': a little less than a round number, e.g. $19.99 or Â£6.95 (but not necessarily mathematically odd, it could also be 2.98.) The theory is this drives demand greater than would be expected if consumers were perfectly rational.

a. Chain stores
b. Supplier diversity
c. Psychological pricing
d. First-mover advantage

33. _________ is a form of communication that typically attempts to persuade potential customers to purchase or to consume more of a particular brand of product or service. 'While now central to the contemporary global economy and the reproduction of global production networks, it is only quite recently that _________ has been more than a marginal influence on patterns of sales and production. The formation of modern _________ was intimately bound up with the emergence of new forms of monopoly capitalism around the end of the 19th and beginning of the 20th century as one element in corporate strategies to create, organize and where possible control markets, especially for mass produced consumer goods.

a. ADTECH
b. ACNielsen
c. AMAX
d. Advertising

34. _________ refers to the laws and rules defining the ways in which products can be advertised in a particular region. Rules can define a wide number of different aspects, such as placement, timing, and content. In the United States, false advertising and health-related ads are regulated the most.

a. ACNielsen
b. ADTECH
c. AMAX
d. Advertising regulation

35. _________ refers to 'controlling human or societal behaviour by rules or restrictions.' _________ can take many forms: legal restrictions promulgated by a government authority, self-_________, social _________, co-_________ and market _________. One can consider _________ as actions of conduct imposing sanctions (such as a fine.) This action of administrative law, or implementing regulatory law, may be contrasted with statutory or case law.

a. Regulation
b. CAN-SPAM
c. Non-conventional trademark
d. Rule of four

36. A _________ is an explicit set of requirements to be satisfied by a material, product, or service.

In engineering, manufacturing, and business, it is vital for suppliers, purchasers, and users of materials, products, or services to understand and agree upon all requirements. A _________ is a type of a standard which is often referenced by a contract or procurement document.

a. Product development
b. New product development
c. Product optimization
d. Specification

1. _________ is the realization of an application idea, model, design, specification, standard, algorithm an _________ is a realization of a technical specification or algorithm as a program, software component, or other computer system. Many _________s may exist for a given specification or standard.

a. ADTECH
b. AMAX
c. Implementation
d. ACNielsen

2. _________ is defined by the American _________ Association as the activity, set of institutions, and processes for creating, communicating, delivering, and exchanging offerings that have value for customers, clients, partners, and society at large. The term developed from the original meaning which referred literally to going to market, as in shopping, or going to a market to sell goods or services.

_________ practice tends to be seen as a creative industry, which includes advertising, distribution and selling.

a. Product naming
b. Marketing myopia
c. Customer acquisition management
d. Marketing

3. _________ is a business discipline which is focused on the practical application of marketing techniques and the management of a firm's marketing resources and activities. Marketing managers are often responsible for influencing the level, timing, and composition of customer demand accepted definition of the term. In part, this is because the role of a marketing manager can vary significantly based on a business' size, corporate culture, and industry context.

a. Business structure
b. Performance-based advertising
c. Door-to-door
d. Marketing management

4. _________ refer to a collection of facts usually collected as the result of experience, observation or experiment or a set of premises. This may consist of numbers, words particularly as measurements or observations of a set of variables. _________ are often viewed as a lowest level of abstraction from which information and knowledge are derived.

a. Mean
b. Sample size
c. Pearson product-moment correlation coefficient
d. Data

5. _________ describes the situation when output from (or information about the result of) an event or phenomenon in the past will influence the same event/phenomenon in the present or future. When an event is part of a chain of cause-and-effect that forms a circuit or loop, then the event is said to 'feed back' into itself.

_________ is also a synonym for:

- _________ Signal; the information about the initial event that is the basis for subsequent modification of the event.
- _________ Loop; the causal path that leads from the initial generation of the _________ signal to the subsequent modification of the event.

_________ is a mechanism, process or signal that is looped back to control a system within itself. Such a loop is called a _________ loop.

a. Power III
b. 6-3-5 Brainwriting
c. 180SearchAssistant
d. Feedback

6. _________ is a fee paid on borrowed assets. It is the price paid for the use of borrowed money , or, money earned by deposited funds . Assets that are sometimes lent with _________ include money, shares, consumer goods through hire purchase, major assets such as aircraft, and even entire factories in finance lease arrangements.

a. ACNielsen
b. ADTECH
c. Interest
d. AMAX

7. _________ is a market coverage strategy in which a firm decides to ignore market segment differences and go after the whole market with one offer.it is type of marketing (or attempting to sell through persuasion) of a product to a wide audience. The idea is to broadcast a message that will reach the largest number of people possible. Traditionally _________ has focused on radio, television and newspapers as the medium used to reach this broad audience.

a. Marketspace
b. Cyberdoc
c. Business-to-consumer
d. Mass marketing

8. _________, in marketing, manufacturing, and management, is the use of flexible computer-aided manufacturing systems to produce custom output. Those systems combine the low unit costs of mass production processes with the flexibility of individual customization.

'_________' is the new frontier in business competition for both manufacturing and service industries.

a. Vertical integration
b. Flanking marketing warfare strategies
c. Power III
d. Mass customization

9. On an intranet or B2E Enterprise Web portals, personalization is often based on user attributes such as department, functional area, or role. The term _________ in this context refers to the ability of users to modify the page layout or specify what content should be displayed.

There are two categories of personalizations:

1. Rule-based
2. Content-based

Web personalization models include rules-based filtering, based on 'if this, then that' rules processing, and collaborative filtering, which serves relevant material to customers by combining their own personal preferences with the preferences of like-minded others. Collaborative filtering works well for books, music, video, etc.

a. Movin'
b. Self branding
c. Cashmere Agency
d. Customization

10. In accounting, _________ has a very specific meaning. It is an outflow of cash or other valuable assets from a person or company to another person or company. This outflow of cash is generally one side of a trade for products or services that have equal or better current or future value to the buyer than to the seller.

a. ACNielsen
b. Expense
c. AMAX
d. ADTECH

11. _________ often refers to either primary or secondary research. Secondary research involves a company using information compiled from various sources, which is about a new or existing product. The advantages of secondary research are that it is relatively cheap and easily accessible.

a. Market research
b. Mystery shoppers
c. Mystery shopping
d. Questionnaire

12. The _________ is generally accepted as the use and specification of the four p's describing the strategic position of a product in the marketplace. One version of the origins of the _________ starts in 1948 when James Culliton said that a marketing decision should be a result of something similar to a recipe. This version continued in 1953 when Neil Borden, in his American Marketing Association presidential address, took the recipe idea one step further and coined the term 'Marketing-Mix'.

a. Power III
b. 180SearchAssistant
c. 6-3-5 Brainwriting
d. Marketing mix

13. _________ is a business management strategy aimed at embedding awareness of quality in all organizational processes. _________ has been widely used in manufacturing, education, call centers, government, and service industries, as well as NASA space and science programs.

When used together as a phrase, the three words in this expression have the following meanings:

- Total: Involving the entire organization, supply chain, and/or product life cycle
- Quality: With its usual definitions, with all its complexities
- Management: The system of managing with steps like Plan, Organize, Control, Lead, Staff, provisioning and organizing.

As defined by the International Organization for Standardization (ISO):

> '_________ is a management approach for an organization, centered on quality, based on the participation of all its members and aiming at long-term success through customer satisfaction, and benefits to all members of the organization and to society.' ISO 8402:1994

One major aim is to reduce variation from every process so that greater consistency of effort is obtained. (Royse, D., Thyer, B., Padgett D., ' Logan T., 2006)

In Japan, _________ comprises four process steps, namely:

1. Kaizen - Focuses on 'Continuous Process Improvement', to make processes visible, repeatable and measurable.
2. Atarimae Hinshitsu - The idea that 'things will work as they are supposed to' .
3. Kansei - Examining the way the user applies the product leads to improvement in the product itself.
4. Miryokuteki Hinshitsu - The idea that 'things should have an aesthetic quality' (for example, a pen will write in a way that is pleasing to the writer.)

_________ requires that the company maintain this quality standard in all aspects of its business. This requires ensuring that things are done right the first time and that defects and waste are eliminated from operations.

a. 180SearchAssistant
b. Power III
c. 6-3-5 Brainwriting
d. Total quality management

14. In economics, business, retail, and accounting, a _________ is the value of money that has been used up to produce something, and hence is not available for use anymore. In economics, a _________ is an alternative that is given up as a result of a decision. In business, the _________ may be one of acquisition, in which case the amount of money expended to acquire it is counted as _________.

a. Transaction cost
b. Fixed costs
c. Variable cost
d. Cost

15. _________ is an advertisement in which a particular product specifically mentions a competitor by name for the express purpose of showing why the competitor is inferior to the product naming it.

This should not be confused with parody advertisements, where a fictional product is being advertised for the purpose of poking fun at the particular advertisement, nor should it be confused with the use of a coined brand name for the purpose of comparing the product without actually naming an actual competitor. ('Wikipedia tastes better and is less filling than the Encyclopedia Galactica.')

In the 1980s, during what has been referred to as the cola wars, soft-drink manufacturer Pepsi ran a series of advertisements where people, caught on hidden camera, in a blind taste test, chose Pepsi over rival Coca-Cola.

a. Comparative advertising
b. Heavy-up
c. Cost per conversion
d. GL-70

16. A _________ is a collection of symbols, experiences and associations connected with a product, a service, a person or any other artifact or entity.

_________s have become increasingly important components of culture and the economy, now being described as 'cultural accessories and personal philosophies'.

Some people distinguish the psychological aspect of a _________ from the experiential aspect.

a. Brand equity
b. Brand
c. Brandable software
d. Store brand

17. _________ is a contract between two parties, one being the employer and the other being the employee. An employee may be defined as: 'A person in the service of another under any contract of hire, express or implied, oral or written, where the employer has the power or right to control and direct the employee in the material details of how the work is to be performed.' Black's Law Dictionary page 471 (5th ed. 1979.)

a. AMAX
b. ACNielsen
c. ADTECH
d. Employment

18. _________ is the process of comparing the cost, cycle time, productivity, or quality of a specific process or method to another that is widely considered to be an industry standard or best practice. The result is often a business case for making changes in order to make improvements. The term _________ was first used by cobblers to measure ones feet for shoes.

a. Benchmarking
b. Strategic group
c. Switching cost
d. Business strategy

19. _________ is a broad label that refers to any individuals or households that use goods and services generated within the economy. The concept of a _________ is used in different contexts, so that the usage and significance of the term may vary.

A _________ is a person who uses any product or service.

a. Power III
b. 6-3-5 Brainwriting
c. Consumer
d. 180SearchAssistant

20. _________ is the study of when, why, how, where and what people do or do not buy products. It blends elements from psychology, sociology,social psychology, anthropology and economics. It attempts to understand the buyer decision making process, both individually and in groups. It studies characteristics of individual consumers such as demographics and behavioural variables in an attempt to understand people's wants. It also tries to assess influences on the consumer from groups such as family, friends, reference groups, and society in general.

a. Multidimensional scaling
b. Communal marketing
c. Consumer behavior
d. Consumer confidence

21. _________, a business term, is a measure of how products and services supplied by a company meet or surpass customer expectation. It is seen as a key performance indicator within business and is part of the four perspectives of a Balanced Scorecard.

In a competitive marketplace where businesses compete for customers, _________ is seen as a key differentiator and increasingly has become a key element of business strategy.

a. Customer base
b. Supplier diversity
c. Psychological pricing
d. Customer satisfaction

22. A _________ is an explicit set of requirements to be satisfied by a material, product, or service.

In engineering, manufacturing, and business, it is vital for suppliers, purchasers, and users of materials, products, or services to understand and agree upon all requirements. A _________ is a type of a standard which is often referenced by a contract or procurement document.

a. Product development
b. New product development
c. Product optimization
d. Specification

23. _________ consists of the processes a company uses to track and organize its contacts with its current and prospective customers. _________ software is used to support these processes; information about customers and customer interactions can be entered, stored and accessed by employees in different company departments. Typical _________ goals are to improve services provided to customers, and to use customer contact information for targeted marketing.

a. Commercialization
b. Customer relationship management
c. Demand generation
d. Product bundling

24. Customer _________ consists of the processes a company uses to track and organize its contacts with its current and prospective customers. CRelationship management software is used to support these processes; information about customers and customer interactions can be entered, stored and accessed by employees in different company departments. Typical CRelationship management goals are to improve services provided to customers, and to use customer contact information for targeted marketing.

a. Product bundling
b. Marketing
c. Green marketing
d. Relationship management

25. The general definition of an _________ is an evaluation of a person, organization, system, process, project or product. _________s are performed to ascertain the validity and reliability of information; also to provide an assessment of a system's internal control. The goal of an _________ is to express an opinion on the person/organization/system (etc) in question, under evaluation based on work done on a test basis.

a. ACNielsen
b. Audit
c. AMAX
d. ADTECH

1. In economics, business, retail, and accounting, a _________ is the value of money that has been used up to produce something, and hence is not available for use anymore. In economics, a _________ is an alternative that is given up as a result of a decision. In business, the _________ may be one of acquisition, in which case the amount of money expended to acquire it is counted as _________.

a. Fixed costs
b. Cost
c. Variable cost
d. Transaction cost

2. _________ is one of the four Ps of the marketing mix. The other three aspects are product, promotion, and place. It is also a key variable in microeconomic price allocation theory.

a. Relationship based pricing
b. Price
c. Competitor indexing
d. Pricing

3. A _________ is a plan of action designed to achieve a particular goal.

_________ is different from tactics. In military terms, tactics is concerned with the conduct of an engagement while _________ is concerned with how different engagements are linked.

a. Power III
b. 6-3-5 Brainwriting
c. 180SearchAssistant
d. Strategy

4. _________ generally refers to a list of all planned expenses and revenues. It is a plan for saving and spending. A _________ is an important concept in microeconomics, which uses a _________ line to illustrate the trade-offs between two or more goods.

a. 180SearchAssistant
b. Power III
c. 6-3-5 Brainwriting
d. Budget

5. _________ is a market coverage strategy in which a firm decides to ignore market segment differences and go after the whole market with one offer.it is type of marketing (or attempting to sell through persuasion) of a product to a wide audience. The idea is to broadcast a message that will reach the largest number of people possible. Traditionally _________ has focused on radio, television and newspapers as the medium used to reach this broad audience.

a. Cyberdoc
b. Business-to-consumer
c. Marketspace
d. Mass marketing

6. In economics, an externality or spillover of an economic transaction is an impact on a party that is not directly involved in the transaction. In such a case, prices do not reflect the full costs or benefits in production or consumption of a product or service. A positive impact is called an _________ benefit, while a negative impact is called an _________ cost.

a. External
b. AMAX
c. ADTECH
d. ACNielsen

7. The break-even point for a product is the point where total revenue received equals the total costs associated with the sale of the product (TR=TC.) A break-even point is typically calculated in order for businesses to determine if it would be profitable to sell a proposed product, as opposed to attempting to modify an existing product instead so it can be made lucrative. _________ can also be used to analyse the potential profitability of an expenditure in a sales-based business.

In _________, margin of safety is how much output or sales level can fall before a business reaches its break-even point (BEP).

a. Break even analysis
b. Contribution margin-based pricing
c. Price skimming
d. Pay Per Sale

8. _________ is defined by the American _________ Association as the activity, set of institutions, and processes for creating, communicating, delivering, and exchanging offerings that have value for customers, clients, partners, and society at large. The term developed from the original meaning which referred literally to going to market, as in shopping, or going to a market to sell goods or services.

_________ practice tends to be seen as a creative industry, which includes advertising, distribution and selling.

a. Customer acquisition management
b. Marketing myopia
c. Product naming
d. Marketing

9. _________ is a fee paid on borrowed assets. It is the price paid for the use of borrowed money , or, money earned by deposited funds . Assets that are sometimes lent with _________ include money, shares, consumer goods through hire purchase, major assets such as aircraft, and even entire factories in finance lease arrangements.

a. Interest
b. ACNielsen
c. AMAX
d. ADTECH

10. Consumer market research is a form of applied sociology that concentrates on understanding the behaviours, whims and preferences, of consumers in a market-based economy, and aims to understand the effects and comparative success of marketing campaigns. The field of consumer _________ as a statistical science was pioneered by Arthur Nielsen with the founding of the ACNielsen Company in 1923 .

Thus _________ is the systematic and objective identification, collection, analysis, and dissemination of information for the purpose of assisting management in decision making related to the identification and solution of problems and opportunities in marketing.

a. Logit analysis
b. Marketing research process
c. Focus group
d. Marketing research

11. In accounting, _________ has a very specific meaning. It is an outflow of cash or other valuable assets from a person or company to another person or company. This outflow of cash is generally one side of a trade for products or services that have equal or better current or future value to the buyer than to the seller.

a. AMAX
b. ADTECH
c. ACNielsen
d. Expense

12. _________ is the realization of an application idea, model, design, specification, standard, algorithm an _________ is a realization of a technical specification or algorithm as a program, software component, or other computer system. Many _________s may exist for a given specification or standard.

a. AMAX
b. ADTECH
c. Implementation
d. ACNielsen

13. The _________ is generally accepted as the use and specification of the four p's describing the strategic position of a product in the marketplace. One version of the origins of the _________ starts in 1948 when James Culliton said that a marketing decision should be a result of something similar to a recipe. This version continued in 1953 when Neil Borden, in his American Marketing Association presidential address, took the recipe idea one step further and coined the term 'Marketing-Mix'.

a. Power III
b. 180SearchAssistant
c. 6-3-5 Brainwriting
d. Marketing mix

14. A _________ is a written document that details the necessary actions to achieve one or more marketing objectives. It can be for a product or service, a brand, or a product line. _________s cover between one and five years.

a. Prosumer
b. Marketing strategy
c. Disruptive technology
d. Marketing plan

15. _________s function as professionals who deal with trade, dealing in commodities that they do not produce themselves, in order to produce profit.

_________s can be of two types:

1. A wholesale _________ operates in the chain between producer and retail _________. Some wholesale _________s only organize the movement of goods rather than move the goods themselves.
2. A retail _________ or retailer, sells commodities to consumers (including businesses.) A shop owner is a retail _________.

A _________ class characterizes many pre-modern societies. Its status can range from high (even achieving titles like that of _________ prince or nabob) to low, such as in Chinese culture, due to the soiling capabilities of profiting from 'mere' trade, rather than from the labor of others reflected in agricultural produce, craftsmanship, and tribute.

In the United States, '_________' is defined (under the Uniform Commercial Code) as any person while engaged in a business or profession or a seller who deals regularly in the type of goods sold.

a. Retail loss prevention
b. Merchant
c. RFM
d. Trade credit

16. A _________ is an amount paid by way of reduction, return, or refund on what has already been paid or contributed. It is a type of sales promotion marketers use primarily as incentives or supplements to product sales. The mail-in _________ is the most common.

a. Strand
b. Rebate
c. Personalization
d. Lifestyle city

17. A _________ is a type of wholesale merchant business that buys goods and bulk products from importers, other wholesalers and then sells to retailers. _________s can deal in any commodity destined for the retail market. Typical categories are food, lumber, hardware, fuel, and textiles.

a. Refusal to deal
b. Tacit collusion
c. Chief privacy officer
d. Jobbing house

18. The phrase _________, according to the Organization for Economic Co-operation and Development, refers to 'creative work undertaken on a systematic basis in order to increase the stock of knowledge, including knowledge of man, culture and society, and the use of this stock of knowledge to devise new applications [sic]' Though it is questionable that an organization is needed for this definition, as it is quite obvious that _________ refers to the _________ of something.

New product design and development is more often than not a crucial factor in the survival of a company. In an industry that is fast changing, firms must continually revise their design and range of products.

a. 180SearchAssistant
b. Power III
c. 6-3-5 Brainwriting
d. Research and development

19. _________ is subcontracting a process, such as product design or manufacturing, to a third-party company. The decision to outsource is often made in the interest of lowering cost or making better use of time and energy costs, redirecting or conserving energy directed at the competencies of a particular business, or to make more efficient use of land, labor, capital, (information) technology and resources. _________ became part of the business lexicon during the 1980s.

a. ACNielsen
b. Intangible assets
c. In-house
d. Outsourcing

20. _________ is an advertisement in which a particular product specifically mentions a competitor by name for the express purpose of showing why the competitor is inferior to the product naming it.

This should not be confused with parody advertisements, where a fictional product is being advertised for the purpose of poking fun at the particular advertisement, nor should it be confused with the use of a coined brand name for the purpose of comparing the product without actually naming an actual competitor. ('Wikipedia tastes better and is less filling than the Encyclopedia Galactica.')

In the 1980s, during what has been referred to as the cola wars, soft-drink manufacturer Pepsi ran a series of advertisements where people, caught on hidden camera, in a blind taste test, chose Pepsi over rival Coca-Cola.

a. Cost per conversion
b. GL-70
c. Heavy-up
d. Comparative advertising

21. A _________ is a collection of symbols, experiences and associations connected with a product, a service, a person or any other artifact or entity.

_________s have become increasingly important components of culture and the economy, now being described as 'cultural accessories and personal philosophies'.

Some people distinguish the psychological aspect of a _________ from the experiential aspect.

a. Store brand
b. Brandable software
c. Brand equity
d. Brand

22. _________ is a modern day comedy of cross-cultural conflict and romance, directed by John Jeffcoat, released in 2006.

Todd Anderson (Josh Hamilton) spends his days managing a customer call center for Western Novelty, an American novelty product company, in Seattle, until he and his entire department are _________ to India. Adding insult to injury, Todd is sent to India to train his replacement.

a. ACNielsen
b. Outsourced
c. AMAX
d. ADTECH

23. _________ is a technique used in propaganda and advertising. Also known as association, this is a technique of projecting positive or negative qualities (praise or blame) of a person, entity, object, or value (an individual, group, organization, nation, patriotism, etc.) to another in order to make the second more acceptable or to discredit it.

a. Supplier
b. Micro ads
c. Sexism,
d. Transfer

24. _________, in marketing, manufacturing, and management, is the use of flexible computer-aided manufacturing systems to produce custom output. Those systems combine the low unit costs of mass production processes with the flexibility of individual customization.

'_________' is the new frontier in business competition for both manufacturing and service industries.

a. Power III
b. Vertical integration
c. Flanking marketing warfare strategies
d. Mass customization

25. On an intranet or B2E Enterprise Web portals, personalization is often based on user attributes such as department, functional area, or role. The term _________ in this context refers to the ability of users to modify the page layout or specify what content should be displayed.

There are two categories of personalizations:

1. Rule-based
2. Content-based

Web personalization models include rules-based filtering, based on 'if this, then that' rules processing, and collaborative filtering, which serves relevant material to customers by combining their own personal preferences with the preferences of like-minded others. Collaborative filtering works well for books, music, video, etc.

a. Movin'
b. Cashmere Agency
c. Self branding
d. Customization

26. _________ consists of the processes a company uses to track and organize its contacts with its current and prospective customers. _________ software is used to support these processes; information about customers and customer interactions can be entered, stored and accessed by employees in different company departments. Typical _________ goals are to improve services provided to customers, and to use customer contact information for targeted marketing.

a. Product bundling
b. Commercialization
c. Demand generation
d. Customer relationship management

27. Customer _________ consists of the processes a company uses to track and organize its contacts with its current and prospective customers. CRelationship management software is used to support these processes; information about customers and customer interactions can be entered, stored and accessed by employees in different company departments. Typical CRelationship management goals are to improve services provided to customers, and to use customer contact information for targeted marketing.

a. Relationship management
b. Product bundling
c. Green marketing
d. Marketing

28. _________ refer to a collection of facts usually collected as the result of experience, observation or experiment or a set of premises. This may consist of numbers, words particularly as measurements or observations of a set of variables. _________ are often viewed as a lowest level of abstraction from which information and knowledge are derived.

a. Pearson product-moment correlation coefficient
b. Sample size
c. Mean
d. Data

29. A _________ is a process that can allow an organization to concentrate its limited resources on the greatest opportunities to increase sales and achieve a sustainable competitive advantage. A _________ should be centered around the key concept that customer satisfaction is the main goal.

A _________ is most effective when it is an integral component of corporate strategy, defining how the organization will successfully engage customers, prospects, and competitors in the market arena.

a. Psychographic
b. Societal marketing
c. Cyberdoc
d. Marketing strategy

30. Human beings are also considered to be _________ because they have the ability to change raw materials into valuable _________. The term Human _________ can also be defined as the skills, energies, talents, abilities and knowledge that are used for the production of goods or the rendering of services. While taking into account human beings as _________, the following things have to be kept in mind:

- The size of the population
- The capabilities of the individuals in that population

Many _________ cannot be consumed in their original form. They have to be processed in order to change them into more usable commodities.

a. 180SearchAssistant
b. Power III
c. 6-3-5 Brainwriting
d. Resources

31. _________ is a contract between two parties, one being the employer and the other being the employee. An employee may be defined as: 'A person in the service of another under any contract of hire, express or implied, oral or written, where the employer has the power or right to control and direct the employee in the material details of how the work is to be performed.' Black's Law Dictionary page 471 (5th ed. 1979.)

a. AMAX
b. ACNielsen
c. ADTECH
d. Employment

1. A _________ is an amount paid by way of reduction, return, or refund on what has already been paid or contributed. It is a type of sales promotion marketers use primarily as incentives or supplements to product sales. The mail-in _________ is the most common.

a. Strand
b. Rebate
c. Lifestyle city
d. Personalization

2. _________ is defined by the American _________ Association as the activity, set of institutions, and processes for creating, communicating, delivering, and exchanging offerings that have value for customers, clients, partners, and society at large. The term developed from the original meaning which referred literally to going to market, as in shopping, or going to a market to sell goods or services.

_________ practice tends to be seen as a creative industry, which includes advertising, distribution and selling.

a. Customer acquisition management
b. Marketing myopia
c. Product naming
d. Marketing

3. The _________ is a marketing term and refers to all of the forces outside of marketing that affect marketing management's ability to build and maintain successful relationships with target customers. The _________ consists of both the macroenvironment and the microenvironment.

The microenvironment refers to the forces that are close to the company and affect its ability to serve its customers.

a. Market environment
b. Customer franchise
c. Psychographic
d. Business-to-consumer

4. A _________ is a written document that details the necessary actions to achieve one or more marketing objectives. It can be for a product or service, a brand, or a product line. _________s cover between one and five years.

a. Prosumer
b. Disruptive technology
c. Marketing strategy
d. Marketing Plan

5. A _________ is an explicit set of requirements to be satisfied by a material, product, or service.

In engineering, manufacturing, and business, it is vital for suppliers, purchasers, and users of materials, products, or services to understand and agree upon all requirements. A _________ is a type of a standard which is often referenced by a contract or procurement document.

a. New product development
b. Product development
c. Product optimization
d. Specification

6. _________ is a form of communication that typically attempts to persuade potential customers to purchase or to consume more of a particular brand of product or service. 'While now central to the contemporary global economy and the reproduction of global production networks, it is only quite recently that _________ has been more than a marginal influence on patterns of sales and production. The formation of modern _________ was intimately bound up with the emergence of new forms of monopoly capitalism around the end of the 19th and beginning of the 20th century as one element in corporate strategies to create, organize and where possible control markets, especially for mass produced consumer goods.

a. AMAX
b. Advertising
c. ADTECH
d. ACNielsen

7. _________ is a broad label that refers to any individuals or households that use goods and services generated within the economy. The concept of a _________ is used in different contexts, so that the usage and significance of the term may vary.

A _________ is a person who uses any product or service.

a. Power III
b. Consumer
c. 6-3-5 Brainwriting
d. 180SearchAssistant

8. In the mathematical discipline of graph theory a _________ or edge-independent set in a graph is a set of edges without common vertices. It may also be an entire graph consisting of edges without common vertices.

Given a graph G = (V,E), a _________ M in G is a set of pairwise non-adjacent edges; that is, no two edges share a common vertex.

a. Power III
b. Matching
c. 180SearchAssistant
d. 6-3-5 Brainwriting

9. _________ is a business term meaning the market segment to which a particular good or service is marketed. It is mainly defined by age, gender, geography, socio-economic grouping, technographic, or any other combination of demographics. It is generally studied and mapped by an organization through lists and reports containing demographic information that may have an effect on the marketing of key products or services.

a. Distribution
b. Market specialization
c. Category Development Index
d. Brando

10. _________ is one of the four elements of marketing mix. An organization or set of organizations (go-betweens) involved in the process of making a product or service available for use or consumption by a consumer or business user.

The other three parts of the marketing mix are product, pricing, and promotion.

a. Comparison-Shopping agent
b. Japan Advertising Photographers' Association
c. Better Living Through Chemistry
d. Distribution

11. The _________ is generally accepted as the use and specification of the four p's describing the strategic position of a product in the marketplace. One version of the origins of the _________ starts in 1948 when James Culliton said that a marketing decision should be a result of something similar to a recipe. This version continued in 1953 when Neil Borden, in his American Marketing Association presidential address, took the recipe idea one step further and coined the term 'Marketing-Mix'.

a. Power III
b. 6-3-5 Brainwriting
c. 180SearchAssistant
d. Marketing mix

12. _________ is a business discipline which is focused on the practical application of marketing techniques and the management of a firm's marketing resources and activities. Marketing managers are often responsible for influencing the level, timing, and composition of customer demand accepted definition of the term. In part, this is because the role of a marketing manager can vary significantly based on a business' size, corporate culture, and industry context.

a. Marketing management
b. Door-to-door
c. Performance-based advertising
d. Business structure

13. An _________ is the manufacturing of a good or service within a category. Although _________ is a broad term for any kind of economic production, in economics and urban planning _________ is a synonym for the secondary sector, which is a type of economic activity involved in the manufacturing of raw materials into goods and products.

There are four key industrial economic sectors: the primary sector, largely raw material extraction industries such as mining and farming; the secondary sector, involving refining, construction, and manufacturing; the tertiary sector, which deals with services (such as law and medicine) and distribution of manufactured goods; and the quaternary sector, a relatively new type of knowledge _________ focusing on technological research, design and development such as computer programming, and biochemistry.

a. ADTECH
b. ACNielsen
c. AMAX
d. Industry

14. _________ is the process of estimation in unknown situations. Prediction is a similar, but more general term. Both can refer to estimation of time series, cross-sectional or longitudinal data.

a. Forecasting
b. 180SearchAssistant
c. 6-3-5 Brainwriting
d. Power III

15. The _________ or _________ is used by business and government to classify and measure economic activity in Canada, Mexico and the United States. It has largely replaced the older Standard Industrial Classification system; however, certain government departments and agencies, such as the U.S. Securities and Exchange Commission (SEC), still use the SIC codes.

The _________ numbering system is a six-digit code.

a. North American Industry Classification System
b. 6-3-5 Brainwriting
c. Power III
d. 180SearchAssistant

16. In economics, business, retail, and accounting, a _________ is the value of money that has been used up to produce something, and hence is not available for use anymore. In economics, a _________ is an alternative that is given up as a result of a decision. In business, the _________ may be one of acquisition, in which case the amount of money expended to acquire it is counted as _________.

a. Cost
b. Variable cost
c. Transaction cost
d. Fixed costs

17. _________ is a market coverage strategy in which a firm decides to ignore market segment differences and go after the whole market with one offer.it is type of marketing (or attempting to sell through persuasion) of a product to a wide audience. The idea is to broadcast a message that will reach the largest number of people possible. Traditionally _________ has focused on radio, television and newspapers as the medium used to reach this broad audience.

a. Business-to-consumer
b. Marketspace
c. Cyberdoc
d. Mass marketing

18. _________ a research method involving the use of questionnaires and/or statistical surveys to gather data about people and their thoughts and behaviours.

a. Z-test
b. T-test
c. Survey research
d. Control chart

19. The break-even point for a product is the point where total revenue received equals the total costs associated with the sale of the product (TR=TC.) A break-even point is typically calculated in order for businesses to determine if it would be profitable to sell a proposed product, as opposed to attempting to modify an existing product instead so it can be made lucrative. _________ can also be used to analyse the potential profitability of an expenditure in a sales-based business.

In _________, margin of safety is how much output or sales level can fall before a business reaches its break-even point (BEP).

a. Pay Per Sale
b. Price skimming
c. Contribution margin-based pricing
d. Break even analysis

20. _________ generally refers to a list of all planned expenses and revenues. It is a plan for saving and spending. A _________ is an important concept in microeconomics, which uses a _________ line to illustrate the trade-offs between two or more goods.

a. Power III
b. 6-3-5 Brainwriting
c. Budget
d. 180SearchAssistant

21. _________ consists of the processes a company uses to track and organize its contacts with its current and prospective customers. _________ software is used to support these processes; information about customers and customer interactions can be entered, stored and accessed by employees in different company departments. Typical _________ goals are to improve services provided to customers, and to use customer contact information for targeted marketing.

a. Product bundling
b. Commercialization
c. Customer relationship management
d. Demand generation

22. Customer _________ consists of the processes a company uses to track and organize its contacts with its current and prospective customers. CRelationship management software is used to support these processes; information about customers and customer interactions can be entered, stored and accessed by employees in different company departments. Typical CRelationship management goals are to improve services provided to customers, and to use customer contact information for targeted marketing.

a. Marketing
b. Product bundling
c. Relationship management
d. Green marketing

23. A _________ is a list of the general tasks and responsibilities of a position. Typically, it also includes to whom the position reports, specifications such as the qualifications needed by the person in the job, salary range for the position, etc. A _________ is usually developed by conducting a job analysis, which includes examining the tasks and sequences of tasks necessary to perform the job.

a. Job description
b. 6-3-5 Brainwriting
c. Power III
d. 180SearchAssistant

24. The Program (or Project) Evaluation and Review Technique, commonly abbreviated _________, is a model for project management designed to analyze and represent the tasks involved in completing a given project.

_________ is a method to analyze the involved tasks in completing a given project, especially the time needed to complete each task, and identifying the minimum time needed to complete the total project.

This model was invented by Booz Allen Hamilton, Inc.

a. PERT
b. Power III
c. 6-3-5 Brainwriting
d. 180SearchAssistant

25. In economics, an _________ is any good or commodity, transported from one country to another country in a legitimate fashion, typically for use in trade. _________ goods or services are provided to foreign consumers by domestic producers. _________ is an important part of international trade.

a. AMAX
b. ADTECH
c. ACNielsen
d. Export

26. _________ is exchange of capital, goods, and services across international borders or territories. In most countries, it represents a significant share of gross domestic product (GDP.) While _________ has been present throughout much of history , its economic, social, and political importance has been on the rise in recent centuries.

a. ACNielsen
b. ADTECH
c. International trade
d. Incoterms

27. A _________ is a collection of symbols, experiences and associations connected with a product, a service, a person or any other artifact or entity.

_________s have become increasingly important components of culture and the economy, now being described as 'cultural accessories and personal philosophies'.

Some people distinguish the psychological aspect of a _________ from the experiential aspect.

a. Store brand
b. Brandable software
c. Brand equity
d. Brand

28. _________ is the realization of an application idea, model, design, specification, standard, algorithm an _________ is a realization of a technical specification or algorithm as a program, software component, or other computer system. Many _________s may exist for a given specification or standard.

a. ADTECH
b. ACNielsen
c. AMAX
d. Implementation

29. A _________ is a firm that manufactures components or products for another 'hiring' firm. Many industries utilize this process, especially the aerospace, defense, computer, semiconductor, energy, medical, food manufacturing, personal care, and automotive fields. Some types of contract manufacturing include CNC machining, complex assembly, aluminum die casting, grinding, broaching, gears, and forging.

a. Power III
b. 180SearchAssistant
c. Productivity
d. Contract manufacturer

30. The verb _________ or grant _________ means to give permission. The noun _________ refers to that permission as well as to the document memorializing that permission. _________ may be granted by a party to another party as an element of an agreement between those parties.

a. 180SearchAssistant
b. 6-3-5 Brainwriting
c. Power III
d. License

31. A _________ or transnational corporation is a corporation or enterprise that manages production or delivers services in more than one country. It can also be referred to as an international corporation.

The first modern MNC is generally thought to be the British East India Company, established in 1600.

a. HD share
b. Multinational corporation
c. Checkoff
d. Hechsher

32. A _________, in business matters, is an entity that is controlled by a bigger and more powerful entity. The controlled entity is called a company, corporation, or limited liability company and in some cases can be a government or state-owned enterprise, and the controlling entity is called its parent (or the parent company.) The reason for this distinction is that a lone company cannot be a _________ of any organization; only an entity representing a legal fiction as a separate entity can be a _________.

a. 180SearchAssistant
b. 6-3-5 Brainwriting
c. Power III
d. Subsidiary

33. A _________ is an entity formed between two or more parties to undertake economic activity together. The parties agree to create a new entity by both contributing equity, and they then share in the revenues, expenses, and control of the enterprise. The venture can be for one specific project only, or a continuing business relationship such as the Fuji Xerox _________.

a. Consumer protection
b. Trademark attorney
c. Gripe site
d. Joint venture

1. The _________ is an independent agency of the United States government, established in 1914 by the _________ Act. Its principal mission is the promotion of 'consumer protection' and the elimination and prevention of what regulators perceive to be harmfully 'anti-competitive' business practices, such as coercive monopoly.

The _________ Act was one of President Wilson's major acts against trusts.

a. Federal Trade Commission
b. Power III
c. 180SearchAssistant
d. 6-3-5 Brainwriting

2. _________ is defined by the American _________ Association as the activity, set of institutions, and processes for creating, communicating, delivering, and exchanging offerings that have value for customers, clients, partners, and society at large. The term developed from the original meaning which referred literally to going to market, as in shopping, or going to a market to sell goods or services.

_________ practice tends to be seen as a creative industry, which includes advertising, distribution and selling.

a. Marketing myopia
b. Product naming
c. Customer acquisition management
d. Marketing

3. A _________ is an explicit set of requirements to be satisfied by a material, product, or service.

In engineering, manufacturing, and business, it is vital for suppliers, purchasers, and users of materials, products, or services to understand and agree upon all requirements. A _________ is a type of a standard which is often referenced by a contract or procurement document.

a. Specification
b. Product optimization
c. New product development
d. Product development

4. _________ is a form of communication that typically attempts to persuade potential customers to purchase or to consume more of a particular brand of product or service. 'While now central to the contemporary global economy and the reproduction of global production networks, it is only quite recently that _________ has been more than a marginal influence on patterns of sales and production. The formation of modern _________ was intimately bound up with the emergence of new forms of monopoly capitalism around the end of the 19th and beginning of the 20th century as one element in corporate strategies to create, organize and where possible control markets, especially for mass produced consumer goods.

a. AMAX
b. ADTECH
c. ACNielsen
d. Advertising

5. _________ refers to the laws and rules defining the ways in which products can be advertised in a particular region. Rules can define a wide number of different aspects, such as placement, timing, and content. In the United States, false advertising and health-related ads are regulated the most.

a. AMAX
b. ADTECH
c. ACNielsen
d. Advertising regulation

6. _________ refers to 'controlling human or societal behaviour by rules or restrictions.' _________ can take many forms: legal restrictions promulgated by a government authority, self-_________, social _________, co-_________ and market _________. One can consider _________ as actions of conduct imposing sanctions (such as a fine.) This action of administrative law, or implementing regulatory law, may be contrasted with statutory or case law.

a. Regulation
b. Non-conventional trademark
c. Rule of four
d. CAN-SPAM

7. The _________ is an economic indicator that measures the satisfaction of consumers across the U.S. economy. It is produced by the National Quality Research Center (NQRC) at the University of Michigan in Ann Arbor, Michigan.

The _________ interviews about 80,000 Americans annually and asks about their satisfaction with the goods and services they have consumed.

a. ADTECH
b. AMAX
c. American Customer Satisfaction Index
d. ACNielsen

8. _________ is a broad label that refers to any individuals or households that use goods and services generated within the economy. The concept of a _________ is used in different contexts, so that the usage and significance of the term may vary.

A _________ is a person who uses any product or service.

a. 180SearchAssistant
b. Power III
c. 6-3-5 Brainwriting
d. Consumer

9. _________ is the study of when, why, how, where and what people do or do not buy products. It blends elements from psychology, sociology,social psychology, anthropology and economics. It attempts to understand the buyer decision making process, both individually and in groups. It studies characteristics of individual consumers such as demographics and behavioural variables in an attempt to understand people's wants. It also tries to assess influences on the consumer from groups such as family, friends, reference groups, and society in general.

a. Multidimensional scaling
b. Consumer confidence
c. Communal marketing
d. Consumer behavior

10. _________, a business term, is a measure of how products and services supplied by a company meet or surpass customer expectation. It is seen as a key performance indicator within business and is part of the four perspectives of a Balanced Scorecard.

In a competitive marketplace where businesses compete for customers, _________ is seen as a key differentiator and increasingly has become a key element of business strategy.

a. Customer Satisfaction
b. Supplier diversity
c. Customer base
d. Psychological pricing

11. The break-even point for a product is the point where total revenue received equals the total costs associated with the sale of the product (TR=TC.) A break-even point is typically calculated in order for businesses to determine if it would be profitable to sell a proposed product, as opposed to attempting to modify an existing product instead so it can be made lucrative. _________ can also be used to analyse the potential profitability of an expenditure in a sales-based business.

In _________, margin of safety is how much output or sales level can fall before a business reaches its break-even point (BEP).

a. Contribution margin-based pricing
b. Price skimming
c. Pay Per Sale
d. Break even analysis

12. _________ is a business term meaning the market segment to which a particular good or service is marketed. It is mainly defined by age, gender, geography, socio-economic grouping, technographic, or any other combination of demographics. It is generally studied and mapped by an organization through lists and reports containing demographic information that may have an effect on the marketing of key products or services.

a. Brando
b. Category Development Index
c. Distribution
d. Market specialization

13. _________ is the process of using quantitative methods and qualitative methods to evaluate consumer response to a product idea prior to the introduction of a product to the market. It can also be used to generate communication designed to alter consumer attitudes toward existing products. These methods involve the evaluation by consumers of product concepts having certain rational benefits, such as 'a detergent that removes stains but is gentle on fabrics,' or non-rational benefits, such as 'a shampoo that lets you be yourself.' Such methods are commonly referred to as _________ and have been performed using field surveys, personal interviews and focus groups, in combination with various quantitative methods, to generate and evaluate product concepts.

a. Logit analysis
b. Market analysis
c. Cross tabulation
d. Concept testing

14. In economics, business, retail, and accounting, a _________ is the value of money that has been used up to produce something, and hence is not available for use anymore. In economics, a _________ is an alternative that is given up as a result of a decision. In business, the _________ may be one of acquisition, in which case the amount of money expended to acquire it is counted as _________.

a. Variable cost
b. Fixed costs
c. Cost
d. Transaction cost

15. _________ involves disseminating information about a product, product line, brand, or company. It is one of the four key aspects of the marketing mix. (The other three elements are product marketing, pricing, and distribution). P>_________ is generally sub-divided into two parts:

- Above the line _________: Promotion in the media (e.g. TV, radio, newspapers, Internet and Mobile Phones) in which the advertiser pays an advertising agency to place the ad
- Below the line _________: All other _________. Much of this is intended to be subtle enough for the consumer to be unaware that _________ is taking place. E.g. sponsorship, product placement, endorsements, sales _________, merchandising, direct mail, personal selling, public relations, trade shows

a. Davie Brown Index
b. Bottling lines
c. Cashmere Agency
d. Promotion

16. The philosophy of _________ holds that the only thing that exists is matter, and is considered a form of physicalism. Fundamentally, all things are composed of material and all phenomena (including consciousness) are the result of material interactions; therefore, matter is the only substance. As a theory, _________ belongs to the class of monist ontology.

a. 180SearchAssistant
b. 6-3-5 Brainwriting
c. Materialism
d. Power III

17. _________ is the use of sexual or erotic imagery in advertising to draw interest to a particular product, for purpose of sale. A feature of _________ is that the imagery used, such as that of a pretty woman, typically has no connection to the product being advertised. The purpose of the imagery is to attract attention of the potential customer or user.

a. Power III
b. 6-3-5 Brainwriting
c. Sex in advertising
d. 180SearchAssistant

18. A personal and cultural _________ is a relative ethic _________, an assumption upon which implementation can be extrapolated. A _________ system is a set of consistent _________s and measures that is soo not true. A principle _________ is a foundation upon which other _________s and measures of integrity are based.

a. Perceptual maps
b. Package-on-Package
c. Value
d. Supreme Court of the United States

19. Consumer market research is a form of applied sociology that concentrates on understanding the behaviours, whims and preferences, of consumers in a market-based economy, and aims to understand the effects and comparative success of marketing campaigns. The field of consumer _________ as a statistical science was pioneered by Arthur Nielsen with the founding of the ACNielsen Company in 1923 .

Thus _________ is the systematic and objective identification, collection, analysis, and dissemination of information for the purpose of assisting management in decision making related to the identification and solution of problems and opportunities in marketing.

a. Logit analysis
b. Marketing research
c. Marketing research process
d. Focus group

20. _________ is a set of six steps which defines the tasks to be accomplished in conducting a marketing research study. These include problem definition, developing an approach to problem, research design formulation, field work, data preparation and analysis, and report generation and presentation.

a. Market analysis
b. Marketing research process
c. Preference-rank translation
d. Simple random sampling

21. _________ in organizations and public policy is both the organizational process of creating and maintaining a plan; and the psychological process of thinking about the activities required to create a desired goal on some scale. As such, it is a fundamental property of intelligent behavior. This thought process is essential to the creation and refinement of a plan, or integration of it with other plans, that is, it combines forecasting of developments with the preparation of scenarios of how to react to them.

a. 6-3-5 Brainwriting
b. 180SearchAssistant
c. Power III
d. Planning

22. A _________ is a plan of action designed to achieve a particular goal.

_________ is different from tactics. In military terms, tactics is concerned with the conduct of an engagement while _________ is concerned with how different engagements are linked.

a. 6-3-5 Brainwriting
b. 180SearchAssistant
c. Power III
d. Strategy

23. Competitiveness is a comparative concept of the ability and performance of a firm, sub-sector or country to sell and supply goods and/or services in a given market. Although widely used in economics and business management, the usefulness of the concept, particularly in the context of national competitiveness, is vigorously disputed by economists, such as Paul Krugman .

The term may also be applied to markets, where it is used to refer to the extent to which the market structure may be regarded as perfectly _________.

a. Customs union
b. Geographical pricing
c. Free trade zone
d. Competitive

24. _________ is, in very basic words, a position a firm occupies against its competitors.

According to Michael Porter, the three methods for creating a sustainable _________ are through:

1. Cost leadership - Cost advantage occurs when a firm delivers the same services as its competitors but at a lower cost;

2.

a. Power III
b. Competitive advantage
c. 6-3-5 Brainwriting
d. 180SearchAssistant

25. _________ is the ability of an individual or group to seclude themselves or information about themselves and thereby reveal themselves selectively. The boundaries and content of what is considered private differ among cultures and individuals, but share basic common themes. _________ is sometimes related to anonymity, the wish to remain unnoticed or unidentified in the public realm.

a. 6-3-5 Brainwriting
b. Privacy
c. Power III
d. 180SearchAssistant

26. Electronic commerce, commonly known as _________ or eCommerce, consists of the buying and selling of products or services over electronic systems such as the Internet and other computer networks. The amount of trade conducted electronically has grown extraordinarily with wide-spread Internet usage. A wide variety of commerce is conducted in this way, spurring and drawing on innovations in electronic funds transfer, supply chain management, Internet marketing, online transaction processing, electronic data interchange (EDI), inventory management systems, and automated data collection systems.

a. E-commerce
b. ACNielsen
c. AMAX
d. ADTECH

27. _________ are long-format television commercials, typically five minutes or longer.. _________ are also known as paid programming (or teleshopping in Europe.) Originally, they were a phenomenon that started in the United States where they were typically shown overnight (usually 2:00 a.m. to 6:00 a.m.)

a. AMAX
b. ACNielsen
c. Infomercials
d. ADTECH

28. _________ is the equation of personal happiness with consumption and the purchase of material possessions.

The term is often associated with criticisms of consumption starting with Thorstein Veblen.

Veblen's subject of examination, the newly emergent middle class arising at the turn of the twentieth century, comes to full fruition by the end of the twentieth century through the process of globalization.

In economics, _________ refers to economic policies placing emphasis on consumption.

a. 180SearchAssistant
b. Power III
c. Consumerism
d. 6-3-5 Brainwriting

29. In economics, _________ is the desire to own something and the ability to pay for it. The term _________ signifies the ability or the willingness to buy a particular commodity at a given point of time .

.

a. Market system
b. Demand
c. Market dominance
d. Discretionary spending

30. The Program (or Project) Evaluation and Review Technique, commonly abbreviated _________, is a model for project management designed to analyze and represent the tasks involved in completing a given project.

_________ is a method to analyze the involved tasks in completing a given project, especially the time needed to complete each task, and identifying the minimum time needed to complete the total project.

This model was invented by Booz Allen Hamilton, Inc.

a. Power III
b. 6-3-5 Brainwriting
c. 180SearchAssistant
d. PERT

31. _________ is one of the four Ps of the marketing mix. The other three aspects are product, promotion, and place. It is also a key variable in microeconomic price allocation theory.

a. Pricing
b. Price
c. Relationship based pricing
d. Competitor indexing

32. In economics, the _________ can be defined as the graph depicting the relationship between the price of a certain commodity, and the amount of it that consumers are willing and able to purchase at that given price. It is a graphic representation of a demand schedule The _________ for all consumers together follows from the _________ of every individual consumer: the individual demands at each price are added together.

_________s are used to estimate behaviors in competitive markets, and are often combined with supply curves to estimate the equilibrium price (the price at which sellers together are willing to sell the same amount as buyers together are willing to buy, also known as market clearing price) and the equilibrium quantity (the amount of that good or service that will be produced and bought without surplus/excess supply or shortage/excess demand) of that market.

a. Demand curve
b. Power III
c. 6-3-5 Brainwriting
d. 180SearchAssistant

33. In economics, _________ is the ratio of the percent change in one variable to the percent change in another variable. It is a tool for measuring the responsiveness of a function to changes in parameters in a relative way. Commonly analyzed are _________ of substitution, price and wealth.
a. ACNielsen
b. Opinion leadership
c. Intellectual property
d. Elasticity

34. Price _________ is defined as the measure of responsiveness in the quantity demanded for a commodity as a result of change in price of the same commodity. It is a measure of how consumers react to a change in price. In other words, it is percentage change in quantity demanded as per the percentage change in price of the same commodity.
a. ADTECH
b. ACNielsen
c. AMAX
d. Elasticity of demand

35. In economics, _________ describes demand that is not very sensitive to a change in price.
a. ADTECH
b. Inelastic
c. ACNielsen
d. AMAX

36. In microeconomics, _________ is the total number of dollars received by a firm from the sale of a product.
a. 180SearchAssistant
b. Nonmarket
c. Total revenue
d. Power III

37. In descriptive statistics, the _________ is the length of the smallest interval which contains all the data. It is calculated by subtracting the smallest observation (sample minimum) from the greatest (sample maximum) and provides an indication of statistical dispersion.

It is measured in the same units as the data.

a. Just-In-Case
b. Personalization
c. Japan Advertising Photographers' Association
d. Range

38. _________ is an economic model based on price, utility and quantity in a market. It concludes that in a competitive market, price will function to equalize the quantity demanded by consumers, and the quantity supplied by producers, resulting in an economic equilibrium of price and quantity. Similarly, an increase in the number of workers tends to result in lower wages and vice-versa.
a. 180SearchAssistant
b. Power III
c. Supply and demand
d. 6-3-5 Brainwriting

39. In statistics, an _________ is a term in a statistical model added when the effect of two or more variables is not simply additive. Such a term reflects that the effect of one variable depends on the values of one or more other variables.

Thus, for a response Y and two variables x_1 and x_2 an additive model would be:

$$Y = ax_1 + bx_2 + \text{error}$$

In contrast to this,

$$Y = ax_1 + bx_2 + c(x_1 \times x_2) + \text{error},$$

is an example of a model with an _________ between variables x_1 and x_2 ('error' refers to the random variable whose value by which y differs from the expected value of y.)

a. Interaction
b. AMAX
c. ACNielsen
d. ADTECH

40. _________ is a rivalry between individuals, groups, nations for territory, a niche, or allocation of resources. It arises whenever two or more parties strive for a goal which cannot be shared. _________ occurs naturally between living organisms which co-exist in the same environment.

a. Competition
b. Non-price competition
c. Price competition
d. Price fixing

41. _________ is a common market form. Many markets can be considered monopolistically competitive, often including the markets for restaurants, cereal, clothing, shoes and service industries in large cities. Short-run equilibrium of the firm under

____

Monopolistically competitive markets have the following characteristics:

- There are many producers and many consumers in a given market, and no business has total control over the market price.
- Consumers perceive that there are non-price differences among the competitors' products.
- There are few barriers to entry and exit.
- Producers have a degree of control over price.

Long-run equilibrium of the firm under _________

The characteristics of a monopolistically competitive market are almost the same as in perfect competition, with the exception of heterogeneous products, and that _________ involves a great deal of non-price competition (based on subtle product differentiation.) A firm making profits in the short run will break even in the long run because demand will decrease and average total cost will increase.

a. Recession
b. Monopolistic competition
c. Macroeconomics
d. Gross domestic product

42. _________ in economics and business is the result of an exchange and from that trade we assign a numerical monetary value to a good, service or asset. If I trade 4 apples for an orange, the _________ of an orange is 4 - apples. Inversely, the _________ of an apple is 1/4 oranges.

a. Contribution margin-based pricing
b. Discounts and allowances
c. Pricing
d. Price

43. _________ is the set of reasons that determines one to engage in a particular behavior. The term is generally used for human _________ but, theoretically, it can be used to describe the causes for animal behavior as well

a. Power III
b. 180SearchAssistant
c. Role playing
d. Motivation

44. In accounting, _________ has a very specific meaning. It is an outflow of cash or other valuable assets from a person or company to another person or company. This outflow of cash is generally one side of a trade for products or services that have equal or better current or future value to the buyer than to the seller.

a. Expense
b. ACNielsen
c. AMAX
d. ADTECH

45. _________, Gross profit margin or Gross Profit Rate can be defined as the amount of contribution to the business enterprise, after paying for direct-fixed and direct-variable unit costs, required to cover overheads (fixed commitments) and provide a buffer for unknown items. It expresses the relationship between gross profit and sales revenue.

It can be expressed in absolute terms:

Gross Profit = Revenue − Cost of Goods Sold

or as the ratio of gross profit to sales revenue, usually in the form of a percentage:

_________ Percentage = (Revenue-Cost of Goods Sold)/Revenue

Cost of goods sold includes variable costs and fixed costs directly linked to the product, such as material and labor.

a. Power III
b. 180SearchAssistant
c. Profit maximization
d. Gross margin

46. _________ is the realization of an application idea, model, design, specification, standard, algorithm an _________ is a realization of a technical specification or algorithm as a program, software component, or other computer system. Many _________s may exist for a given specification or standard.

a. ADTECH
b. Implementation
c. AMAX
d. ACNielsen

47. A _________ is a type of wholesale merchant business that buys goods and bulk products from importers, other wholesalers and then sells to retailers. _________s can deal in any commodity destined for the retail market. Typical categories are food, lumber, hardware, fuel, and textiles.

a. Tacit collusion
b. Chief privacy officer
c. Jobbing house
d. Refusal to deal

48. A _________ is a written document that details the necessary actions to achieve one or more marketing objectives. It can be for a product or service, a brand, or a product line. _________s cover between one and five years.

a. Marketing strategy
b. Prosumer
c. Marketing plan
d. Disruptive technology

49. A _________ is a collection of symbols, experiences and associations connected with a product, a service, a person or any other artifact or entity.

_________s have become increasingly important components of culture and the economy, now being described as 'cultural accessories and personal philosophies'.

Some people distinguish the psychological aspect of a _________ from the experiential aspect.

a. Brandable software
b. Brand equity
c. Store brand
d. Brand

50. _________ is a lightweight markup language, originally created by John Gruber and Aaron Swartz to help maximum readability and 'publishability' of both its input and output forms. The language takes many cues from existing conventions for marking up plain text in email. _________ converts its marked-up text input to valid, well-formed XHTML and replaces left-pointing angle brackets ('<') and ampersands with their corresponding character entity references.

a. Power III
b. 180SearchAssistant
c. 6-3-5 Brainwriting
d. Markdown

51. The _________ is a marketing term and refers to all of the forces outside of marketing that affect marketing management's ability to build and maintain successful relationships with target customers. The _________ consists of both the macroenvironment and the microenvironment.

The microenvironment refers to the forces that are close to the company and affect its ability to serve its customers.

a. Customer franchise
b. Business-to-consumer
c. Psychographic
d. Market environment

52. _________ consists of the sale of goods or merchandise from a fixed location, such as a department store or kiosk in small or individual lots for direct consumption by the purchaser. _________ may include subordinated services, such as delivery. Purchasers may be individuals or businesses.

a. Warehouse store
b. Thrifting
c. Charity shop
d. Retailing

53. _________ is a fee paid on borrowed assets. It is the price paid for the use of borrowed money , or, money earned by deposited funds . Assets that are sometimes lent with _________ include money, shares, consumer goods through hire purchase, major assets such as aircraft, and even entire factories in finance lease arrangements.

a. Interest
b. ACNielsen
c. AMAX
d. ADTECH

54. The _________ is a professional association for marketers. As of 2008 it had approximately 40,000 members. There are collegiate chapters on 250 campuses.

a. AMAX
b. ACNielsen
c. ADTECH
d. American Marketing Association

55. _________ is the management of the flow of goods, information and other resources, including energy and people, between the point of origin and the point of consumption in order to meet the requirements of consumers (frequently, and originally, military organizations.) _________ involves the integration of information, transportation, inventory, warehousing, material-handling, and packaging. _________ is a channel of the supply chain which adds the value of time and place utility.

a. Power III
b. 180SearchAssistant
c. 6-3-5 Brainwriting
d. Logistics

56. the term _________ is that part of Supply Chain Management that plans, implements, and controls the efficient, effective, forward, and reverse flow and storage of goods, services, and related information between the point of origin and the point of consumption in order to meet customers' requirements.

Software is used for logistics automation which helps the supply chain industry in automating the work flow as well as management of the system. There are very few generalized software available in the new market in the said topology.

a. Corporate transparency
b. Digital strategy
c. Crisis management
d. Logistics Management

57. Human beings are also considered to be _________ because they have the ability to change raw materials into valuable _________. The term Human _________ can also be defined as the skills, energies, talents, abilities and knowledge that are used for the production of goods or the rendering of services. While taking into account human beings as _________, the following things have to be kept in mind:

- The size of the population
- The capabilities of the individuals in that population

Many _________ cannot be consumed in their original form. They have to be processed in order to change them into more usable commodities.

a. Power III
b. 6-3-5 Brainwriting
c. Resources
d. 180SearchAssistant

58. In economics, an externality or spillover of an economic transaction is an impact on a party that is not directly involved in the transaction. In such a case, prices do not reflect the full costs or benefits in production or consumption of a product or service. A positive impact is called an _________ benefit, while a negative impact is called an _________ cost.

a. ADTECH
b. ACNielsen
c. AMAX
d. External

59. A _________ is a list of the general tasks and responsibilities of a position. Typically, it also includes to whom the position reports, specifications such as the qualifications needed by the person in the job, salary range for the position, etc. A _________ is usually developed by conducting a job analysis, which includes examining the tasks and sequences of tasks necessary to perform the job.

a. 180SearchAssistant
b. Power III
c. Job description
d. 6-3-5 Brainwriting

60. _________ is one of the four growth strategies of the Product-Market Growth Matrix defined by Ansoff. _________ occurs when a company enters/penetrates a market with current products. The best way to achieve this is by gaining competitors' customers (part of their market share.)

a. Horizontal market
b. Pasar pagi
c. Marketization
d. Market penetration

61. _________ is a business discipline which is focused on the practical application of marketing techniques and the management of a firm's marketing resources and activities. Marketing managers are often responsible for influencing the level, timing, and composition of customer demand accepted definition of the term. In part, this is because the role of a marketing manager can vary significantly based on a business' size, corporate culture, and industry context.

a. Door-to-door
b. Performance-based advertising
c. Business structure
d. Marketing management

62. _________ refers to a business or organization attempting to acquire goods or services to accomplish the goals of the enterprise. Though there are several organizations that attempt to set standards in the _________ process, processes can vary greatly between organizations. Typically the word '_________' is not used interchangeably with the word 'procurement', since procurement typically includes Expediting, Supplier Quality, and Traffic and Logistics (T'L) in addition to _________.

a. Purchasing
b. Drop shipping
c. Supply chain
d. Supply network

63. _________ is one of the four elements of marketing mix. An organization or set of organizations (go-betweens) involved in the process of making a product or service available for use or consumption by a consumer or business user.

The other three parts of the marketing mix are product, pricing, and promotion.

a. Better Living Through Chemistry
b. Distribution
c. Japan Advertising Photographers' Association
d. Comparison-Shopping agent

64. A _________ researches, selects, develops, and places a company's products.

A _________ considers numerous factors such as target demographic, the products offered by the competition, and how well the product fits in with the company's business model. Generally, a _________ manages one or more tangible products.

a. Power III
b. Promotional mix
c. Pick and pack
d. Product manager

65. _________ is the provision of service to customers before, during and after a purchase.

According to Turban et al., '_________ is a series of activities designed to enhance the level of customer satisfaction - that is, the feeling that a product or service has met the customer expectation.'

Its importance varies by product, industry and customer.

a. Customer service
b. Customer experience
c. Facing
d. COPC Inc.

66. _________ is an advertisement in which a particular product specifically mentions a competitor by name for the express purpose of showing why the competitor is inferior to the product naming it.

This should not be confused with parody advertisements, where a fictional product is being advertised for the purpose of poking fun at the particular advertisement, nor should it be confused with the use of a coined brand name for the purpose of comparing the product without actually naming an actual competitor. ('Wikipedia tastes better and is less filling than the Encyclopedia Galactica.')

In the 1980s, during what has been referred to as the cola wars, soft-drink manufacturer Pepsi ran a series of advertisements where people, caught on hidden camera, in a blind taste test, chose Pepsi over rival Coca-Cola.

a. GL-70
b. Cost per conversion
c. Heavy-up
d. Comparative advertising

67. _________ is one of the four aspects of promotional mix. (The other three parts of the promotional mix are advertising, personal selling, and publicity/public relations.) Media and non-media marketing communication are employed for a pre-determined, limited time to increase consumer demand, stimulate market demand or improve product availability.

a. Merchandise
b. Sales promotion
c. New Media Strategies
d. Marketing communication

68. A _________ is a type of website, usually maintained by an individual with regular entries of commentary, descriptions of events, or other material such as graphics or video. Entries are commonly displayed in reverse-chronological order. '_________' can also be used as a verb, meaning to maintain or add content to a _________.

a. Power III
b. 180SearchAssistant
c. Blog
d. 6-3-5 Brainwriting

69. The _________, a unit of the United States Department of Labor, is the principal fact-finding agency for the U.S. government in the broad field of labor economics and statistics. The BLS is an independent national statistical agency that collects, processes, analyzes, and disseminates essential statistical data to the American public, the U.S. Congress, other Federal agencies, State and local governments, business, and labor representatives. The BLS also serves as a statistical resource to the Department of Labor.

a. Bureau of Labor Statistics
b. Power III
c. Gross national product
d. Consumer Expenditure Survey

70. In economic models, the _________ time frame assumes no fixed factors of production. Firms can enter or leave the marketplace, and the cost (and availability) of land, labor, raw materials, and capital goods can be assumed to vary. In contrast, in the short-run time frame, certain factors are assumed to be fixed, because there is not sufficient time for them to change.

a. 180SearchAssistant
b. Long-run
c. 6-3-5 Brainwriting
d. Power III

71. _________ is a mathematical science pertaining to the collection, analysis, interpretation or explanation, and presentation of data. It also provides tools for prediction and forecasting based on data. It is applicable to a wide variety of academic disciplines, from the natural and social sciences to the humanities, government and business.

a. Type I error
b. Null hypothesis
c. Median
d. Statistics

72. _________ is a measure of the strength of a brand, product, service relative to competitive offerings. There is often a geographic element to the competitive landscape. In defining _________, you must see to what extent a product, brand, or firm controls a product category in a given geographic area.

a. Market dominance
b. Productivity
c. Discretionary spending
d. Market system

Chapter 1

1. c	2. c	3. b	4. d	5. b	6. d	7. d	8. d	9. c	10. d
11. d	12. d	13. d	14. d	15. d	16. c	17. c	18. d	19. d	20. b
21. d	22. d	23. b	24. d	25. d	26. d	27. c	28. d	29. c	30. a
31. d	32. a	33. d	34. d	35. a	36. a	37. c	38. a	39. c	40. b
41. d	42. b	43. a	44. d	45. b	46. d				

Chapter 2

1. d	2. c	3. a	4. a	5. a	6. d	7. d	8. b	9. a	10. c
11. a	12. b	13. d	14. c	15. a	16. b	17. a	18. d	19. a	20. d
21. d	22. d	23. d	24. d	25. b	26. d	27. d	28. d	29. d	30. c
31. d	32. c	33. c	34. d	35. d	36. d	37. d	38. b	39. d	40. c
41. d	42. d	43. d	44. d						

Chapter 3

1. d	2. d	3. d	4. b	5. a	6. d	7. d	8. b	9. c	10. d
11. a	12. c	13. a	14. a	15. d	16. d	17. c	18. d	19. d	20. a
21. a	22. a	23. d	24. c	25. b	26. c	27. a	28. d	29. d	30. a

Chapter 4

1. d	2. b	3. b	4. c	5. c	6. d	7. a	8. d	9. c	10. c
11. d	12. b	13. d	14. c	15. d	16. a	17. b	18. d	19. b	20. b
21. d	22. a	23. b	24. a	25. b	26. d	27. d	28. d	29. d	30. a
31. a	32. c	33. c	34. d	35. d	36. d	37. d	38. c	39. a	40. d
41. b	42. d	43. a	44. d	45. c	46. a	47. d	48. d	49. d	50. d
51. d	52. c	53. a	54. b	55. d					

Chapter 5

1. a	2. a	3. c	4. b	5. d	6. c	7. d	8. d	9. b	10. c
11. a	12. d	13. b	14. c	15. c	16. d	17. c	18. d	19. d	20. c
21. b	22. b	23. d	24. d	25. a	26. a	27. d	28. d	29. d	30. a
31. a									

Chapter 6

1. a	2. a	3. d	4. c	5. b	6. d	7. a	8. a	9. d	10. c
11. c	12. b	13. c	14. c	15. a	16. d	17. d	18. d	19. c	20. b
21. d	22. d	23. a	24. d	25. d	26. a	27. d	28. c		

Chapter 7

1. d	2. a	3. b	4. d	5. a	6. a	7. d	8. d	9. c	10. a
11. a	12. b	13. b	14. d	15. c	16. c	17. c	18. b	19. d	20. c
21. c	22. a	23. d	24. a	25. d	26. b	27. d	28. a	29. d	30. d
31. c	32. d	33. c	34. a	35. a	36. b	37. d	38. d	39. c	40. c
41. d	42. d	43. c							

Chapter 8

1. c	2. d	3. c	4. b	5. d	6. d	7. d	8. d	9. a	10. b
11. d	12. d	13. c	14. d	15. b	16. c	17. d	18. d	19. a	20. a
21. b	22. b	23. c	24. d	25. c	26. d	27. a	28. d	29. d	30. d
31. d	32. b	33. d	34. d	35. d	36. d	37. d	38. c	39. d	40. a
41. a	42. c	43. d	44. d	45. d	46. d	47. d	48. b	49. d	50. c
51. d	52. d	53. d							

Chapter 9

1. d	2. a	3. d	4. c	5. d	6. c	7. d	8. d	9. d	10. d
11. b	12. a	13. d	14. d	15. a	16. d	17. c	18. c	19. b	20. d
21. b	22. d	23. d	24. a	25. d	26. d	27. d	28. d	29. d	30. d
31. c	32. d	33. a	34. d	35. a	36. d	37. d	38. d	39. a	40. a
41. d									

Chapter 10

1. d	2. b	3. b	4. b	5. b	6. d	7. d	8. b	9. d	10. b
11. d	12. c	13. c	14. b	15. b	16. b	17. d	18. b	19. d	20. d
21. a	22. a	23. d	24. d	25. b	26. d	27. b	28. b	29. d	30. a
31. d	32. d	33. c	34. d	35. d	36. b	37. a	38. c	39. d	40. d
41. d	42. a								

Chapter 11

1. d	2. d	3. d	4. a	5. c	6. d	7. b	8. a	9. d	10. d
11. d	12. c	13. d	14. d	15. b	16. c	17. b	18. d	19. c	20. a
21. d									

Chapter 12

1. b	2. d	3. d	4. a	5. d	6. c	7. d	8. d	9. d	10. c
11. c	12. d	13. c	14. d	15. d	16. d	17. b	18. a	19. d	20. c
21. d	22. c	23. d	24. a	25. c	26. d	27. d	28. b	29. d	30. b
31. d	32. d								

Chapter 13

1. c	2. c	3. d	4. b	5. c	6. a	7. a	8. d	9. c	10. c
11. b	12. d	13. a	14. d	15. b	16. a	17. d	18. a	19. d	20. a
21. d	22. d	23. c	24. b	25. d	26. a	27. d	28. c	29. d	30. d
31. b	32. d	33. c	34. c	35. b	36. d	37. d	38. d	39. d	40. a
41. a	42. d	43. d	44. a	45. b	46. c	47. d			

Chapter 14

1. c	2. a	3. d	4. d	5. a	6. a	7. d	8. d	9. d	10. c
11. d	12. a	13. d	14. a	15. d	16. d	17. a	18. d	19. d	20. a
21. c	22. c	23. c	24. d	25. b	26. d	27. d	28. a	29. b	30. c
31. d	32. d	33. c	34. d						

Chapter 15

1. d	2. d	3. d	4. b	5. a	6. c	7. d	8. d	9. d	10. a
11. c	12. d	13. d	14. d	15. d	16. c	17. d	18. c	19. b	20. c
21. b	22. c	23. d	24. d	25. d	26. c	27. d	28. d	29. d	

Chapter 16

1. a	2. a	3. d	4. b	5. b	6. d	7. d	8. d	9. a	10. d
11. d	12. b	13. d	14. a	15. d	16. d	17. c	18. c	19. a	20. d
21. d	22. d	23. d	24. a	25. d	26. d	27. a	28. b	29. d	30. b
31. a	32. a	33. d	34. b	35. b	36. d	37. d	38. d	39. c	40. d
41. a									

Chapter 17

1. a	2. c	3. a	4. c	5. a	6. d	7. b	8. d	9. d	10. b
11. b	12. d	13. c	14. c	15. b	16. d	17. d	18. d	19. d	20. d
21. c	22. c	23. b	24. c	25. d	26. c	27. d	28. d	29. b	30. b
31. a	32. d	33. c	34. a	35. a	36. c	37. d	38. d	39. c	40. d
41. d	42. b	43. d	44. d						

Chapter 18

1. d	2. d	3. b	4. d	5. d	6. d	7. d	8. d	9. a	10. d
11. d	12. d	13. d	14. d	15. d	16. d	17. d	18. b	19. d	20. c
21. a	22. d	23. a	24. d	25. d	26. d	27. d	28. d	29. d	30. b
31. a	32. c	33. d	34. d	35. a	36. d				

Chapter 19

1. c	2. d	3. d	4. d	5. d	6. c	7. d	8. d	9. d	10. b
11. a	12. d	13. d	14. d	15. a	16. b	17. d	18. a	19. c	20. c
21. d	22. d	23. b	24. d	25. b					

Chapter 20

1. b	2. d	3. d	4. d	5. d	6. a	7. a	8. d	9. a	10. d
11. d	12. c	13. d	14. d	15. b	16. b	17. d	18. d	19. d	20. d
21. d	22. b	23. d	24. d	25. d	26. d	27. a	28. d	29. d	30. d
31. d									

Chapter 21

1. b	2. d	3. a	4. d	5. d	6. b	7. b	8. b	9. b	10. d
11. d	12. a	13. d	14. a	15. a	16. a	17. d	18. c	19. d	20. c
21. c	22. c	23. a	24. a	25. d	26. c	27. d	28. d	29. d	30. d
31. b	32. d	33. d							

Chapter 22

1. a	2. d	3. a	4. d	5. d	6. a	7. c	8. d	9. d	10. a
11. d	12. d	13. d	14. c	15. d	16. c	17. c	18. c	19. b	20. b
21. d	22. d	23. d	24. b	25. b	26. a	27. c	28. c	29. b	30. d
31. a	32. a	33. d	34. d	35. b	36. c	37. d	38. c	39. a	40. a
41. b	42. d	43. d	44. a	45. d	46. b	47. c	48. c	49. d	50. d
51. d	52. d	53. a	54. d	55. d	56. d	57. c	58. d	59. c	60. d
61. d	62. a	63. b	64. d	65. a	66. d	67. b	68. c	69. a	70. b
71. d	72. a								

www.ingramcontent.com/pod-product-compliance
Lightning Source LLC
Chambersburg PA
CBHW082202230426
43672CB00015B/2870
* 9 7 8 1 4 2 8 8 7 1 3 3 5 *